A TALE OF A BUSINESS FAILURE

BY

JOHN D. DAVIS, CPA/ABV, CVA, CFE

Danbury Publishing Company, Ltd.

A Tale of a Business Failure
Copyright © 2009
Danbury Publishing Company, Ltd.

ALL RIGHTS RESERVED

No portion of this publication may be reproduced, stored in any electronic system, or transmitted in any form or by any means, electronic, mechanical, photocopy, recording, or otherwise without written permission from the author. Brief quotations may be used in literary reviews.

Limit of Liability and Disclaimer of Warranty: While the publisher and author have used their best efforts in preparing this book, they make no representations or warranties with respect to the accuracy or completeness of the contents of this book and specifically disclaim any implied warranties of merchantability or fitness for a particular purpose. The advice and strategies contained herein may not be suitable for your situation. Therefore, you should consult with a professional where appropriate. Neither the publisher nor the author shall be liable for any loss of profit or any other commercial damages, including but not limited to special, incidental, consequential or other damages.

Library of Congress Control Number: 2009906907

ISBN 978-0-9824217-0-3

Cover Design: Jim Gundlach, Signature Design, Inc.
Editor: Chuck Murr

For information contact:

John D. Davis, CPA/ABV, CVA, CFE
7205 Pearl Road
Middleburg Heights, Ohio 44130
440-887-9150

Please visit www.danburypublishing.com for online ordering.

Printed in the USA
By Morris Publishing
3212 East Highway 30
Kearney, NE 68847
800-650-7888

To Liz,

--For surviving the nightmare to live the dream…

Preface

Entrepreneur: One who organizes and directs a business undertaking, assuming the risk for the sake of the profit.

As I recall the events of this story, I realize that there are some important facts that need to be understood. First of all, this story is true, based on my recollection of events and facts. As I lived the story, I could tell that some day this would make a great book. Always wanting to write, I kept good notes regarding the events that transpired.

Second, this was a good company and the participants, including me, were capable managers with suitable skills, abilities and backgrounds. It is important to remember this as the story unfolds, because it's easy to think that we were just a bunch of stooges playing business. That is far from true.

Third, except for me, the names in the book are fictional.

Fourth, this story could be about any company in any industry, in any city with any number of shareholders and participants. Through the benefit of my consulting practice, I have witnessed this story elsewhere, with other facts and other participants. There is a common thread that binds, though. And it is likely that you may find a common thread to your business as well.

Fifth, this was a part-time venture for me. Although I was a shareholder, I was not involved in the daily operations of the business. My role was executive management, accounting and finance. However, I was deeply emotionally involved with the business. But with my somewhat outside perspective, I saw many of the situations differently, and sometimes more clearly, than the others involved.

Sixth, it is important to know that this business operated in an industry that was an oligopoly. An oligopoly is in an industry or market that is controlled and dominated by a small number of companies or suppliers. It is similar to a monopoly, but the oligopoly allows for the industry to fragment. In this instance, a few very large companies dominated the industry. The remaining companies were small, niche-based companies that could compete, but typically against smaller fragmented companies within the industry. Thousands of industries operate like this. Some are obvious, others not so obvious.

Remember that this story is being told as a lesson. The lesson that you will learn will be different than what others learn, and different from the lessons that I have learned. I would be surprised if you walk away from this story learning nothing. Trust me, there are lessons to be learned in this book. And remember, this story could happen to you. As entrepreneurs, we all have one foot on the banana peel and we are all just one slip away from disaster.

Chapter 1

There is only one road to true human greatness: Through the school of hard knocks.
--Albert Einstein

Driving today is not like driving any other day. It feels as if things are moving in slow motion. Maybe I am watching only as a ghost, and not actually living. Maybe I am a spectator about to bear witness from the sidelines and not a player in the game. Maybe this is not happening at all, but just another nightmare only to be interrupted by a barking dog next door.

As the traffic light changes to green and the car horns blare behind me, I realize this is not slumber and those are angry commuters. Yes, this is real and I am barely alive inside.

As I turn right to make my final approach, I notice the number of "For Lease" signs on the factory-lined street. I had made this trip hundreds of times and never paid attention. Maybe I was too afraid to notice.

These factories once bustled with activity, stamping, plating, coating, molding, and forging. If you can think of it, it was once made here. Or somewhere just like here. This is a manufacturing town, nothing more, nothing less.

This road was not unlike others. I suspect roads like this exist in every town. There's row after row of small brick buildings. Small offices to the front with dirty paned windows, a large box structure to the back, and loading docks on the side at the rear. They all look the same, function the same, and die the same. Even the nameless bar and grill is boarded up, speckled with graffiti and shame. The only identity it has is the "available" sign in the front. But it's just an illusion; no one wants that place. Who would come? There are no lunch breaks being had, no after work beers, or late-night burgers. That era ended long ago in a quiet exodus to far away places. First it was Mexico, then China, and soon to some place in Africa or Sri Lanka. This manufacturing hub slowly faded into ruin at a pace so subtle that it was hardly even noticed.

Up ahead on the right is the cemetery. I am getting close. "Rats," I think to myself, another red light. For what? I don't know. There isn't a car on the road.

The GM plant at the intersection hasn't operated for at least eight years. But what a structure it is -- a million feet or more under one roof. I can't really tell, but it just seems to go on forever. The rust-covered stacks tell it all. It is nothing more than a white elephant standing at the side of a road that has passed it by. Half of the rail lines that once serviced this grand factory have been stolen for scrap by crack-heads looking for one more fix. The power substation has been decommissioned for safety reasons, although the affixed ad says it can still function. Sure, but at what price to repair? It can be subleased for a song, but who would bother? Or, more importantly, who could use that much space?

The cemetery certainly looks lush. The dark green grass and finely trimmed hedges appear oddly out of place among the rusty old factories. My guess is that they were here first, unsuspecting of future industrial neighbors. Or maybe these were the early neighbors of the factories from an era before cars and easy access to work. In any event, it provides a calm serenity for the area, a reminder of life -- and of death.

As I get closer I am almost afraid to look. But there it is, as big as day, painted in bright red, and outlined in black. There is no confusion as to the message: "Auction Today".

The plant looks bigger today, massively dwarfing the tombstones next door. For years, mysterious rumors abounded that the plant was haunted. In fact, one prior business owner was so convinced of the creepiness, that he moved his office away from the facility and worked elsewhere. Maybe he was right. Maybe this is all the ghosts' doing.

The parking lot is congested, but not full as I expected. The only space left is next to the dumpster. Just great. Now I'll end up with a screw in my tire. I really expected more cars, though. I figured that I would be parked across the street or around the corner. Never did I think I would get a space in the lot. It is a bad space, though. And it's a worse sign.

I start to gather my things, and grab my briefcase. Wait a minute, what am I doing? I don't need to take anything with me. By the time I turn to the open the door, a man is standing outside, looking through the window. With the sun behind him and a cigarette in his hand, he looks unfamiliar. Then I recognized him. It is Joe Rundle, the banker assigned to me through the work out department at the bank.

"John, you made it," Joe says as he extends a guest-welcome handshake.

"Of course," I reply sheepishly.

"I must thank you, you just made me fifty bucks."

"Really, how in heavens did I do that?"

"Oh, the auctioneer and I had a bit of a wager. You see, he told me that the owners never come to the auction, since it is way too humiliating. I, on the other hand, knew different. I knew you would be here. He wasn't convinced, so alas the bet."

"That's great, Joe. Maybe you should apply it to our loan balance."

Now I am scared.

As we make our way to the building, I can hear my heart pound. I really shouldn't be here. The auctioneer was right. Who am I to change protocol? He knows what's best. He's done this before. He's a pro. I am afraid of the humiliation. I am afraid of who will be here. I am afraid that the equipment won't sell. I am simply afraid.

Suddenly, Joe stops, turns to me and quips, "Do you know that Lake Bank brought their legal counsel today? What's that about? You know as well as I do that they will get nothing from this auction. It just figures, John. Don't they realize that they are in a second position? Don't they realize that there will not be enough funds to even come close to covering our bank's loans, let alone their debt? They might as well be general creditors, John, don't you think?"

As Joe continues to ask questions, I continue to not answer. Then my heart skips two beats, and begins to race. I really don't feel well. I really don't want to be here. But it's way too late to turn back.

Before I can enter the building, Bill, our former plant manager approaches me. He greets me with a serious smile and shakes my hand. I am quickly introduced to his friend, Fred. I just keep thinking, not now, not today. This is not the day for introductions. I want to remain anonymous. As I try to stay with his conversation, my mind wanders. I catch the tail end of Bill's dialog "...So John, our intention is to get paid today for the work that was done."

"What?" I reply as I drift back from my fog.

"Didn't you hear me the first time, John? Fred is the guy that installed the lock-up fence inside the warehouse for us. He is my friend and runs a small business. He really needs the money and I told him that he would get paid. He needs the money, John. It's really unfair. I know that the equipment will sell. The machines, they're in good shape, and a lot of money will come in, so he should get some. He earned it. I told him he would get paid."

I gaze over at Fred. He looks like a good guy, and I know that he did a great job. I remember that we owe him about $1,200. I can't look him in the eye.

Sheepishly, I respond. "Fred, you did a great job on the fence, and we owe you the money. But this is not my auction. I turned over the assets to the bank. We owed them a lot of money when the plant shut down. The man I walked in with is the person in charge. But before you bother him, see the three men in the suits standing by the wall over there? They are from the second bank involved. Whatever money is left over, they get."

Fred retorts, "So which men will give me my money?"

"Fred, there won't be enough money to pay you. We owe over a million dollars to the two banks. The equipment may bring in $300,000 at the auction if that. There is only an $185,000 guarantee from the auctioneers. There won't be any extra money."

"Well, why don't you pay me?" replied Fred.

"I can't, Fred. I just can't. It's very complicated. There are others involved, too. It is very, very complicated."

Fred and Bill turned away angrily and marched straight up to Joe the banker. I could see Joe glare over his glasses at me as he listened to their plight. I look down. After a few minutes, they walk away unsatisfied and make their way to the door. They are not staying.

Joe makes his way to me and says, "Can you believe those guys? What nerve."

I don't respond.

The auctioneer sees me talking to Joe, and jumps down from his podium cart. He is much shorter than I expected. Auctioneers always look so big over the crowd from their perch. I was disappointed. I expected a taller man.

"So this is the guy that cost me fifty bucks. Well no thanks to you!" the auctioneer quips.

We exchange handshakes, and just like that, he leaps back to his podium. I guess that's how auctioneers are, all fast talk and no time to listen.

I take a moment to look around. The shop looks great. I have never seen it look this clean and empty. The fabricating equipment is still arranged in production order, and it looks really good. We always kept our equipment in top working condition. That won't matter now, though. It will still sell for a song.

I never realized how big the plant was. With the assembly areas crowded with parts, and sub-assemblies, the shipping area crowded with boxes, crates and pallets, and raw material lining the fab aisles, its no wonder the shop always looked small.

Not now though, it is an empty cavern.

All of the lights are on, something I have not seen for a while. As we were running out of capital, we kept turning off more of the lights to save costs. In fact, the only time we would turn them all on is if a customer came for a visit. But even with all of the light, as I scan the crowd, the faces appear as shadows and the figures as outlines. They're ghosts, and I don't want to recognize them. Maybe no one will recognize me.

Suddenly, a face emerges from the blur, with an outstretched open hand. It is a glad face that I surely recognize.

"John, what brings you here?"

"A better question Tom, is what are you doing here?"

"Oh, I represent Lake Bank in this matter. This auction is a bit of a mess. The company is really upside-down and a lot is at stake. I am here to ensure that Lake Bank's interests are fully acknowledged."

Tom then asks, "Are you here with a client, or looking for bargains for yourself for one of your deals?"

"Tom, I am one of the shareholders. This is one of my deals. I guess I helped make this mess."

He looks at me, astonished. And as if a light bulb went off in his head, he recalls me speaking of having difficulty with one of my investments. Strange that we should end up working together like this. This is a man of influence, with skill and contacts at one of the largest law firms in the city. It's a consultant's dream contact. Up until now, I would get referrals from his firm for business appraisals, forensic accounting and litigation support. Not likely anymore. Not after this embarrassment.

Before we can begin our conversation, his clients approach us. The moment of true dread. From the point of the company's initial struggle to the point of demise, I knew that they would lose. Their bank is the mezzanine lender with a secondary, subordinated position to our primary bank. And, they have no foreclosure rights. That is two strikes too many. For them, it must be like floating in a non-functioning space capsule with no way home. Their fate was sealed. They could only stand on the sidelines and hope for a foul. Maybe, if the primary lender failed to act with propriety, maybe they could recover something. It was pretty unlikely and I felt bad.

"John, it is nice to see you," said one gentleman.

"What?" I think to myself. "Are these guys out of their minds? I am the guy who blew it, caused the grief, and now will cause a large loss for the bank. Are they certain that they know who I am?"

I reply aloud, "Gentlemen, it is always a pleasure, I just wish it were on better circumstances."

Not much more was said, which was good.

Before the festivities could begin, I decided to tour the office one last time. As I made my way, I passed the engineering department. It was ransacked. The computers kept in there posed a big issue with the auction. I noticed that they were still set up at their workstations against my recommendation to the bank. They contained the drawings, prints and machine code to manufacture the patented parts. They had a separate intangible value aside from the equipment, and I had several potential buyers for the technology that we developed. The secrets needed to be preserved to protect the value. I was miffed.

As I hunted around for Joe the banker, I finally found him in the plant manager's office. He was relaxing, looking out the window and puffing on a cigarette.

"John, where have you been?" he said through the haze. "I have been looking for you."

At that moment he slowly approached me. Getting about halfway through the room, he stopped and ashed his butt. Suddenly, he began to fumble with his belt buckle. And just like that, he undid his pants, and they fell down halfway over his thighs. I am astonished.

"Joe, I was afraid that there was more to this chance meeting, but aren't you taking this to a whole new level?" I quipped. "I mean I knew that I would get screwed today, but this isn't what I really had in mind!"

He looks quizzically at me, furls his brow, and begins to carefully tuck his dress shirt into his slacks, and carefully redresses himself. As if a light went on, he begins to laugh out loud at my curious comments. "John, I want to go over the idea of selling the patents. Counsel has raised plenty of issues. I just want to get a meeting time set up."

"Whew. You had me pretty worried there for a moment Joe with the pants and all. Any morning next week, just let me know. But more importantly, what is going to happen to these computers? They can't be sold at this auction today."

"These computers will not be sold," he reassured. "They are not part of the auction."

As we turned and walked out the door, Joe paused and glanced back at the spot where he had fixed his pants and then looked back at me with a smile. As if on cue, we both started laughing together.

The auction was about ready to begin. I made one last pass through the plant to look at the inventory. We had vending machines at various levels of completion that were being auctioned. I wanted to buy one or two, so I needed a few minutes to identify the likely candidates.

As I made my way to the front, I still could not get over how empty the plant was. The component inventory was haphazardly arranged in rows. Finished parts, assemblies, and components were commingled -- providing no sense of order. I was confused as to how the auctioneer could sell these items since they were not identified or separated into any logical order.

As the auction began, I could see the heads of the participating shadows bow together to share a whisper. Then the heads would part and just stare in my direction. I knew that they were staring at me. I was humiliated. I could not remember a time in my life when I felt this ashamed.

The auction was sad. The two automated robotic turret presses that were anticipated to so gloriously produce through unattended days and nights, the equipment that we invested over one million dollars in -- was all sold for a paltry $180,000.

The parts inventory was sold in rows. Without any part identification, each row brought in hundreds of dollars, instead of the tens of thousands that it may have been worth. In fact, over 60 dollar-bill validators for which we paid $250 apiece were sold with the locking cabinet in which they were stored. The cabinet, all contents included, brought in $175 from only one bidder. Ironically, the bidder was a parts supply house. What a steal. No one else but the bidder understood the value of the inventory, so it went for pennies.

When we got to the finished inventory, no one would even bid. The auctioneer was getting edgy and recognized that he had covered his minimum and wanted to wrap up for the day. So, instead of selling the completed machines individually or in groups of two or three, he decided to sell entire rows of 30 or 40 vending machines. Each row brought in about $1,000. It was sad. All told, our inventory that was worth about $800,000 to $900,000 was sold for about $25,000.

The highest profit turned on any single inventory item was likely the three vending machines that I carved out for myself. The moment I started bidding on the machines, others took notice and started bidding too. As if these machines were lined with gold or secrets, the price just kept increasing. People who were not even bidding on machines entered the bidding until it became a frenzy. I ended up paying $1,500 for three machines whereas others were getting 30 machines for $1,000. I couldn't believe it. And the sad thing was that the only reason I wanted these specific machines was that they were the last ones completed off of the line and had a sentimental value to me.

The whole process didn't take long, maybe a few hours. Imagine, just a few hours to completely unwind and liquidate an entire business that took decades to build. It was like a tornado blew through and demolished the entire business just like that.

As the auction was wrapping up, I stood there lifeless, thinking of all of the things that went wrong, all of the things we tried, and all of the things that failed. If only one of the last-ditch efforts would have worked I would not be here right now. If only one less thing went wrong, the business could have been saved.

I then started thinking about how it all began -- and ended. I could not get out of my mind the first day I walked the plant floor, the day that we bought the company -- and the day we closed.

As we made our way into the plant, I just walked and stared forward as if in a trance at a funeral procession. I could not get out of my mind how this whole thing started. Suddenly, as if I was dead, witnessing my whole life in an instant, the story started over. I could see it all very clearly, even the ending, me standing next to the auctioneer. If I could have only seen this happening back then, I would not be here now. But it was too late.

Chapter 2

You don't just stumble into the future. You create your own future.

--Roger Smith

Sometime before industrialization, someone had a great idea to start a company providing a specific mechanical skill that would shape raw materials into a usable product that can then be marketed and sold, on a contract "as needed" basis. My guess is that blacksmiths may have been the earliest form of "job shop" and from that moment on, the concept of a job shop was formed.

The value that created the profit was skill. The skill necessary was based solely on the "conversion" necessary. If something was formed, it took a certain skill that was unlike the skill of molding. If something was welded, it took a skill beyond bolting. The primary skill of the craftsman is what drove the initial job shop. But as a job shop grows, the required skills change. It is no longer only required to be a craftsman, but also a businessman. And not every skilled craftsman is a good businessman.

When demand is high enough that shortages exist for a certain skilled craftsman, the lack of business skill can be overshadowed by demand. Essentially, the demand increases prices, which increases profits, which ultimately can masquerade operational inefficiency or mistakes.

In a demand-controlled industry, a job shop can get away with cost plus pricing. And, if a company is smart and learns to control costs, it can increase its profit over competitors. Nonetheless, the small job shop can easily exist with little business acumen in an industry that has high demand and short supply. The key to success for these businesses is to stay small and produce only to the level that allows prices to stay high.

I suspect that is how this business began. I was not around at the start of the company. And since I came in 12 or 13 years later as an investor, the true roots of the company were buried. Sure, I did due diligence to uncover the "story" of the history, but unless you lived it, it was not much more than a story. No one tells of the real beginning, it is too personal, too deep. Besides, most people wouldn't believe it anyway.

I have tried to explain to employees at my accounting and consulting practice the difficulty in starting the business. The sleepless nights overshadowed by the excitement. The peanut butter and jelly sandwiches for dinner in the late hours, doing clerical work that I could not afford to hire someone to do. The small office in an outdated building tastefully decorated with standard auction issue furniture. With money being so tight that the only way to gain any benefit was to buy a car in the business name so that I at least got something in return for my effort...an irrevocable payment every month.

They just looked at me like I'm nuts. But I can understand, since they are standing in a world that my business did not live in then. They only see the money and success now that years of effort brings, not the difficult beginnings. They will never understand. They can't understand because they did not live it.

So I believe that this operation has a similar story, one that I would likely not believe either -- mostly because the company has done so well.

Being involved in a manufacturing business was always a plan of mine. I think it was the thrill of something being made that was exciting to me. It was making something, from nothing, for a profit – an entrepreneur's dream. Instead of selling a service as I do so routinely in my accounting practice, I get to sell a product. Something tangible. Something that I can see on the street and say, "Hey, we made that!"

I was not a rookie when I bought into this company. Young, but not a rookie. As a seasoned CPA and consultant, I had intense training in diligence, details, and endurance. Ten years young was my current accounting practice at the time that I did this deal. My firm was born from the experience and training that I gained from a national firm, but which I localized and resized to fit the needs of the average family business. From the beginning, I offered consulting services. Although I believe that consulting is a service that is overstated these days.

For me, the breadth of consulting services that I have provided has meandered over the years. Initially, it was automating manual accounting systems to computer systems. Slowly, it switched to merger and acquisition services, based strongly on my love of business valuation. Then the business valuation needs shifted to estate and trust planning. After a while, business valuation for estates became mundane, so eventually I strayed into court as an expert witness. The timing was right, too, because enough of the hair that I had left turned gray to allow me to "look" like an expert. Now, almost exclusively, the area of my practice is centered on business valuation, forensic accounting and litigation support. But that's for now. Because of my eclectic nature, I cannot predict my career much beyond a few years. And I am excited for the future because I know that it will involve something new. Likely it will be a spin on what I already do, but it will be different enough to keep me interested and excited.

In addition to living vicariously through my clients and projects, I posted my first successful deal just prior to this one. It was a turn-around situation in the transportation and logistics industry. A friend and I decided that together we had the skills to fix a business that was probably not worth much more than a piece of chewed gum stuck to the heel of an old boot. The business needed to be revamped, but my friend had the skills, experience and foresight in the transportation industry. I added the business, finance and marketing side. With smart moves, hard work and a little luck we managed the turnaround, and we were making good money for our efforts.

Although I had a successful accounting business, I never really felt like an entrepreneur. Maybe it was too easy, the start-up, that is. (As long as the Financial Accounting Standards Board and the IRS are involved, accounting and taxation will never be an easy profession.) But the business start up wasn't too much of a challenge; it just took hard work, time and patience.

The trucking company deal went pretty well. It was a moderate risk with fantastic results. I was feeling confident because everything that I had learned about business and finance really worked. So the trucking company turnaround left me beaming with confidence. And why not? I beat the odds big time, and it was time to parlay the stack into a bigger stack. Isn't that what business is all about anyway? It was my time now.

Since I was active with my accounting clients consulting on their business acquisitions, I had a pretty good flow of deals coming across my desk. I also had good sources of information flowing from brokers, investment bankers and other consultants. But the source of this deal was different.

I learned of this new opportunity first hand from Paul, one of the owners. I had a long relationship with the company through the "consulting" aspect of my accounting practice. Years ago, I had been referred to the company by a software company that I represented as a reseller. They were having difficulty with an older version of software that was no longer supported by the manufacturer. I was one of the "old guys" in the business being over age 30, so I was summonsed to the case. A few times a year I was called in to fix problems that crept up.

The software problem was easily fixed, the software upgraded and the relationship cemented. I was their computer guy. It's a thought that somewhat appalls me today. It just seems so mundane compared to my innermost aspirations. As time wore on, I was called in on occasion to fix things, change things, and train people. It was a good relationship. Each time I visited, I paid special attention to the activities of the company. Call it intellectual curiosity. My motive was never anything beyond learning more. I love businesses, and I love how they work. I love the action. And I especially love new product ideas, which this company had. They were always tinkering around with something new, improving what they did; experimenting. I liked it. Visiting them was always a pleasure.

This happened for several years, and like nearly all of my clientele, I built up a good relationship with all of the office folks, and I especially built a good relationship with Paul.

I immediately liked Paul. He was salt from the earth. And I knew he had a concealed start-up story just like mine. Of course, we were both too embarrassed to ever reveal our deep secrets, the secrets of our start-up that we both ultimately knew.

Paul understood manufacturing and business, and he was a natural leader. His employees respected him; his customers and vendors liked him. His finance and accounting background was a bit crude, but not unlike other businesses with which I worked. The intricacies of accounting and finance are bestowed upon a few, and the rest of the world looks to those individuals for support. But Paul knew enough to be effective. He did not need to understand all of the details, but he had a firm grasp on the big picture.

When it came to sheet metal manufacturing, he was unmatched by his competitors. His attention to detail and quality made his company first class in the industry. In fact, his products were the benchmark of quality within the industries he serviced. A great deal of this success came because of his team building ability. He did not do it all. In fact, by the time I became involved, he did none of it. He managed his team as a leader. He built his team, treated his employees well, and they responded in a manner that made everyone better.

Then it happened. One day I was called to fix a rather mundane, almost pointless printing problem that could have been ignored. It was an excuse. The appointment, which took virtually only minutes, was conveniently scheduled at the end of the workday. I was quickly asked by Paul to have a drink after work, an offer I could not refuse.

Over cocktails, Paul quizzed me on how to value a company. It seemed to be an odd question for a guy they called to fix their computers. But Paul was an astute guy and he knew there was more to my experience than the services I provided. Because of his partners, though, he was never in a position to engage me in any other capacity. Their accountant was firmly in place, and I for one, respected that relationship.

Because of Paul's question, and because of my observation in the office, I sensed that the owners were having trouble getting along. Several years prior, the company fell on hard times at the loss of a big contract, and two new financial partners entered the business. Both new partners had products being manufactured at the plant so both had vested interest in the success of the company. They both bought in to secure their own survival. The real issue was the chemistry. Two investors and one entrepreneur can be a disaster. And that was becoming the case. Paul wanted out.

Paul knew he had restrictive buyout provisions in the close corporation agreement, but he needed me to help interpret these, as well as help value his interest. So I did.

The buyout provisions of the buy-sell arrangement were interesting. Any shareholder could put their shares up to be sold. The other shareholders then had to set the price that they were willing to pay. The offeree shareholder then had the option to either accept the buyout price, or instead, buy out the offeror shareholders shares at the price they set. This mechanism is very simple and very effective. In my world, this type of buy-sell agreement is known as an "I cut; you choose" contract. Named after the old trick mothers have played on children for years to avoid fighting over dividing a cake. Do you remember how that game worked? Mom would give the knife to the first child to cut the cake, and then would let the second child choose their piece. The cake cutter always seemed to get the pieces carved perfectly even so as to not end up with the smaller piece.

In this instance, though, it was two against one. So for Paul to option to buy meant he had to buy out both shareholders. The bigger problem was that the offer price tossed out by his partners was too low -- thus the company was undervalued. So Paul was getting screwed.

Paul was ticked off by this new information. Not only was he working with guys he didn't like, he was getting short changed in trying to get out. That's typical of a small company deal where the balance of power was unequal at the outset.

Then, I dropped the bomb.

"Paul, the company is undervalued, you should buy them out," I told him.

Paul didn't like that. His first instinct was to take the money and run. But after reading the non-compete clauses included in the close corporation agreement, staying in started to seem pretty smart. But how could he do it?

I put together projected financial statements and began the outline for a business plan. The goal: secure acquisition financing, and take out the other partners. It all seemed like a good idea and the plan was coming together. The company was profitable and undervalued. It had a strong product line. It had management and key employees in place for long periods of time. It was a banker's dream. And, the economy was robust. Banks were doling out money like neighbors passing out candy on Halloween. And the primary operator was one of the buyers. Everything was coming together. A deal was forming.

Then it hit. Paul's personal credit was a mess. When the business floundered financially a few years prior, he ran up credit card bills to keep the company and his household afloat. Then, under the wisdom of a credit counselor, he settled with most of the credit card companies for cents on the dollar. He might as well have filed for bankruptcy. His credit was cooked.

Through this whole process, months had passed. Nothing was happening too fast since so much was at stake. I liked Paul from the start, and through this process, I saw a whole new person. He was in charge, full of ideas and a good shop guy. He could build things, and run a business. That's a good combination for a factory. What he lacked was a background in finance. He lacked what I had to offer.

Paul recognized this before I did. But I remained focused on the task at hand. My responsibility in this engagement was to counsel Paul on the best courses of action to take, and to assist in obtaining the goals that were clearly laid out.

Then it happened, the statement that changed my life.

"John, why don't you buy the company with me?"

Paul's words will forever ring in my ears.

How could I resist? I mean, let's face it, an undervalued company that was really strong, that could be leveraged with 90% acquisition financing...it was just to good to be true.

Unfortunately, although the company was undervalued, it still had significant value. For me to be in, I was only willing to risk enough to buy 25% of the equity. That left me a minority shareholder and basically, out in the cold regarding company decisions.

Now, it was time to get a bank loan. I knew the most important aspect of my ownership was the bank requirement for personal guarantees. My strong credit, successful accounting practice, and good story made me a valuable shareholder. This would ultimately be the difference for Paul either buying or selling.

Paul and I agreed to go forward together. I would purchase 25% of the shares and Paul would get credit for his built-in equity. To even out the control issues, we agreed to strip the votes from our shares and transfer them to a voting trust. Paul and I would then be trustees that voted the shares. We each had one vote. To avoid deadlocks, we contrived a complicated tie-breaking mechanism that, once exhausted, ultimately ended with a coin-toss. In other words, if we could not agree on a course of action, nor could the disagreement be mediated by two of our pre-chosen advisors, fate would make the decision. It made sense to us, because fate based decision-making was probably better than creating a fight that ultimately could not be won. Sometimes the process of the decision becomes more fatal to the company by causing divide, than the actual impact of the decision. We recognized this and wanted to avoid the behavior problems. Besides, we entered into this with a great deal of respect for each other, plus we were friends.

As we worked together, Paul and I became even closer friends. The negotiation for the buyout, which seemed perfunctory based on the close corporation agreement, quickly became a mess.

The problem that faced us was time. The exiting shareholders were not entirely happy with their failed opportunity to low-ball Paul. Because of the buy-out provision, they were now selling their interests for less than full value. Although they negotiated hard for terms, they were essentially stuck with the initial price they offered Paul, so they ultimately short sold their own interest. Never once did they think that Paul would be able to buy them out. This turned out to be a very expensive miscalculation on their part.

Since there were two shareholders to be bought out, it required getting two people to agree to the terms, not just one. And like any other shareholders agreement, it goes out the window when it comes down to deal time. Now it was a negotiation. It was everyone vying for as much as they could get. Greed can be a real pain in the butt.

This entire process was new to Paul. In addition to the negotiation, that seemed to ebb and flow to the point of "deal" to "no deal" almost daily, I was parading bankers through the plant. Pitching the story was not hard. The deal really made sense. The salaries of the two exiting shareholders nearly covered the cash flow required for the new debt service. Nearly every banker I talked with wanted the deal. It ultimately came down to terms and amount. We were in the driver's seat.

So eventually, the letter of intent was pounded out and signed. However, there was a glitch for us that made this difficult. We had a timetable to close the deal and if we failed to make it, the other shareholders would buy Paul out at 10% less than the final offer to them. So there was a big incentive for them to have us fail in completing the deal. But at this point, there was nothing they could do but wait.

All we needed to do was finalize the bank notes, and get the final contract drafted. As the contracts were under construction, I narrowed the banker field down to two. The final meetings with both proved to me that we were making the right decision. Finally the decision was made, we married a bank and they ordered the documents.

Since the loan was an asset-based transaction, the bank deal took extra time to close. An asset-based loan is one where the financing amounts are based upon a formula or percentage of specific assets on hand. In our case, the assets were the accounts receivable, inventories and manufacturing equipment. The need for physical inventories, equipment appraisals, coupled with a new customer risk, caused delay in the process. Additionally, the attorneys involved needed to drag out the terms long enough to justify the amount that they wanted to bill for the project. It is hard to justify 200 billable hours in only three days. We were starting to bump into the deadline.

My first instinct was to call the sellers and negotiate for more time. I failed miserably. In fact, the sharks sensed blood and dropped a bomb -- moving the timetable up to 3 p.m. on Friday, rather than 5 p.m. because one of the sellers was leaving to go out of town. Without his signature, we could not close the deal. I knew that I could argue that this was their problem, but that would only set us back more time. So I lost. Two hours may not seem like much, but it is when you need the time.

We needed to close the deal quickly, or the deal was off. All I knew was that we had all worked very hard for several months putting this deal together. We were also emotionally connected to the deal.

Based on all of my status updates from everyone involved, Friday was attainable. We agreed and put the deal in high gear.

We received final documents from their attorney on Thursday. Of course, there were still issues that needed to be changed. Isn't that always the case? One last issue, but it was easy to handle. Then one more argument, one more print, one more review. We are still on time.

The next issue, where is the money? The bank knew the deadline, but was not ready yet. After hours of calling, I finally get through to the banker. The deal is approved and documents are being completed. They will not be ready until Friday morning. That's okay though, we still have time.

So Friday morning rolls around and I have the final deal contracts. They look good. Soon after, I am faxed the bank loan documents. Uh-oh, they contain a major mistake. The company name is wrong. We were buying the company through a transitory acquisition company that would be merged away simultaneously with the closing. It was a structure known as a reverse-subsidiary merger. It was pretty sophisticated for a small deal, but it made total sense. And being a tax guy at heart, I loved the tax advantages it provided. It was no big deal, however, everyone involved knew the structure, and it was just a clerical mistake. It can be changed.

It is now 2 p.m. and I finally get the revised bank documents. The bankers, Paul, his wife Cindy, who was a co-guarantor, and I meet to sign the agreements. Meanwhile, the attorneys and sellers are beginning to assemble downtown for the business closing. We are still 20 minutes away. No sweat. All we need to do is sign the papers, and sign the wiring instructions. Since time was ticking, we called the lawyers to instruct them to delay a bit and to provide them with the new closing plan. Then the next bomb is dropped, the sellers do not want a wire, and they want certified bank drafts. That's just great and highly unusual. But by now, I have come to expect it.

Rather than talking them in to wiring the funds and spending countless more legal hours drafting more needless documents, I agree to go to the bank to get two certified checks. Meanwhile, Paul and his wife could drive downtown to the closing and begin the process by signing countless documents. Since Paul was the president, he could sign nearly everything. I only needed to approve a few resolutions as the corporate secretary.

Of course, the nearest bank is in the opposite direction from downtown. I weave through traffic to the bank, only to find a line out the door! Of course, it was the day that the social security checks had been received. Now what?

I try to get the attention of the branch manager, who is on the phone. She nervously hangs up and informs me that she was just on with my new business banker. He explained everything, and she was personally going to handle the transaction. I could tell that she was nervous handling a transaction of this size. She prepared the appropriate documents, and I signed and signed. Great, where are my certified checks? She can't issue them. Get this; I now have to stand in line with the branch manager to get the checks issued. Time just kept ticking.

Some poor old lady in front of me must have just received her monthly stipend from Social Security. In addition to engaging the teller in a nice neighborly discussion, then cashing her check, she then proceeds to pay nearly all of her bills. What great luck I have. Three months of work, an entire transaction is going to crap out because lonely Aunt Edna needs to talk about her roses blooming as she pays her bills! They probably weren't even due yet. That's the bills, not the roses. It just figures.

So, I finally get up to the clerk who dutifully types the checks incorrectly at least twice. Once she finally gets them both right, I am gone like the wind.

I call the conference room, to find out that a new argument has started and is being ironed out. How can this be? I guess it should have been expected since the room was filled with three shareholders, who by now hated each other, and six lawyers. Talk about a lethal combination!

As I barrel down the highway heading downtown, I continually call to give my E.T.A. We are still on time. As long as the distaste in the room doesn't unravel the deal, we should be fine. Suddenly, the traffic comes to a halt. There is an accident up ahead. I can see the building, and likely they can see me. I am less than two miles away and helplessly caught in gridlock.

I make a desperate call to the conference to warn of my plight. Too late. Sheldon, one of the sellers has already left, the remaining parties are arguing, and I am sitting in traffic with over $1 million in certified funds to close the deal. I plead with counsel to look out the window to witness the traffic. They do. The bad news is that a tractor-trailer had overturned and is blocking three lanes. The good news: I am only 1,000 feet away and will soon be past the bottleneck.

I finally arrive, ditch my car and begin to run through the building. Standing in the lobby is Sheldon. I grab him to bring him upstairs with me to sign off on the deal. He won't budge.

"You're late. I'm not doing this deal. You guys have jerked me around long enough," Sheldon said obstinately.

I can't believe this, any wonder why Paul hated working with this guy? He is being totally unreasonable. Not feeling much like arguing, I pulled the checks out of my briefcase and handed one over to Sheldon.

"Well, maybe you should be the one to tear this up," I said

Staring at the check, his mood changed. "Let's go upstairs and finish this thing," he said politely.

And that was it. The deal was done. After a short deal-closing celebration, Paul and I left to be with our families.

The hangover of the deal seemed to last for a while. There is a certain feeling that comes over me after a deal. Maybe it's relief. But mostly, I think it is more sadness. I think most would celebrate the new acquisition. Not me. For me, most of the fun was doing the deal. I'm driven by the action. But now, it is time to work. It was time to make a run at a new opportunity.

Chapter 3

Far and away the best prize that life has to offer is the chance to work hard at work worth doing.
--Theodore Roosevelt

I have a new company. It was now time to refocus my energy on the original goal. After the deal is done, it isn't always clear what the original goal really was. Through all of the negotiation, due diligence and document drafting, you tend to forget why you did the deal in the first place. Was it just the game of the deal, or did I really want this company?

I really wanted this company. It was a good company with a great deal of potential. Now it was time to unearth the hidden value and make money.

The company was born as a job shop, producing long run fabricated sheet metal products. Anything that needed to be cut, formed, and welded was the specialty. In fact, for years the company built fabricated stands, shelves and cabinets for various customer uses. The purpose of the product didn't matter, as long as it was built to specification.

Over time, the company became product-line driven, manufacturing its own line of small vending machines. The earlier merger of the two partners brought with it the opportunity to become a full-line original equipment manufacturer, or OEM. This was important in the life of the company, since job shop work was beginning to tail off in the area due to the exodus of manufacturing to overseas companies. The small line vending machines were mechanical machines. That means the product was vended from the machine by mechanical means, rather than using electronics. These machines required the product purchaser to turn a handle to dispense the item after they inserted the proper change. This is a very economical and reliable method to vend a product and is still in use today.

We manufactured two machines, a compact refrigerated soda machine, and a tabletop snack machine. The snack machine also could be attached to the soda machine and be sold as a "combo". Overall, the machines were manufactured well and had a strong acceptance in the market. We made one of the best small-line vending machines in the industry. The primary locations for our equipment were small offices or small businesses. All of our sales were to distributors who then sold the machines to the end user, a vending route company, or someone interested in becoming a vending machine operator. We did very little marketing of our product since we had a distributor network. In several cases, our equipment was branded using the distributors' brand name rather than using our brand name.

The remaining contract work was relatively captive. One of our two primary ongoing projects was manufacturing a variety of condiment stands for a large national company specializing in vending machine parts and supplies. Again, the equipment we built was the benchmark in the industry. High quality and built to last with fine attention to detail, fit and finish.

The second recurring project was seasonal. We produced large aluminum and steel shelf and cabinet systems for a national company. The systems were used by our customer for internal purposes and not sold to the general public. This was a project that we quoted annually. We typically were awarded the project provided that our pricing was in line and that we performed well the prior year. We were very good at producing these shelves; no different than our other products we produced. We were a very high quality, high volume manufacturer.

The shop was relatively sophisticated for a small operation. Most of that was a result of the product lines it manufactured. To be an equipment manufacturer, the company needed a great deal of disciplines. The metal fabrication shop was the most sophisticated area of the plant. Two turret presses were the workhorses and the backbone of the shop. Both had sophisticated tool cribs and experienced operators. Four hydraulic bending and forming press brakes were lined next to the turrets. They were the second line of production and were used to form the pieces punched out by the turret presses. A host of ancillary equipment dotted the shop, including Mig welders, spot welders, pem setters, and a full metal shop including upright milling machines, drill presses and lathes. The metal shop was used primarily to build the various jigs that were required from time to time in the fabrication and assembly process.

The quality control department was situated next to the fabrication shop. Quality control was responsible for machine set up, test runs, and machine time scheduling. The workflow started there. The idea of positioning quality control at the front of the line eliminated most of the risk of mistakes, since the initial part punching and forming was critical to every element of assembly down line.

In addition to fabricating, the company had a full paint shop equipped with two full paint booths, ventilation system and paint recapturing system. About half of the painting processes were completed in house. More sophisticated painting such as powder coating was outsourced due to the specialized recapturing systems required for powder coating.

Another separate area of manufacturing was refrigeration. We assembled all of our own refrigeration systems using purchased components such as heat exchangers, compressors and thermostats. This area was highly specialized and operated almost independent of the other departments in the shop.

Assembly was decentralized and organized in cells. For most of the year, the assembly was divided fairly evenly in making soda machines, snack machines, and condiment stands. During the aluminum cabinet season, the shop was overrun with this assembly process. The finished product was bulky and required a great deal of space. It was a good project, so it deserved the space.

The service aspect of the company was also sophisticated for a small operation. We had a full-time purchasing agent who reported directly to the shop foreman. Our shipping and receiving departments kept track of orders and material flow through the shop. Paul's secretary handled customer service. Engineering and machine computer aided design (CAD) was handled by a skilled programmer. Sales and some customer service were handled by a full-time inside salesman. Our controller cleaned up the paperwork and kept the records straight. Paul provided oversight of all aspects of the business, and essentially doubled as the plant manager. Although we did not have a great deal of depth in any area of management, we had a great team of skilled personnel. All had a long length of service with the company.

Trying to improve an already well operating company is not easy. But although we were a good company, we still had room to improve. Further, if we were going to grow, we needed better information flow. I had two primary objectives coming into the company. First, I needed to improve our purchasing procedures. Second, I needed to improve our inventory and accounting systems.

It was not difficult to improve purchasing. The first thing I did was require three supply sources for every type of inventory purchased. For the most part this was pretty easy to do; the company just didn't do it. For some specialized or custom manufactured parts we were still stuck with one supplier source.

The three supply sources were ranked 1, 2, and 3. The primary source was typically the company from where we were already buying. The second and third initially had no real relevance to our purchasing team, except to provide a back up to the primary source. Then, we dropped the bomb on our purchasing department. We instituted a bonus program based on cost reduction. It worked like this: for one month, we split the savings created by reducing our cost. For example, if our steel cost was cut by 10%, we gave 5% of one month of steel purchases to our purchasing department as a bonus. The only requirements were that the price decrease had to be for a whole year, not just a one time deal and that the quality was either the same or better.

This worked well. My purchasing department was getting everything from cold rolled steel down to the nuts and bolts re-quoted. They immediately saw my purpose for identifying three suppliers. It made it very easy to contact the companies to get quotes. The subsequent supplier ranking became a snap.

The history of profitability essentially caused inefficiency and this was especially noticeable in the purchasing department. All told, we hacked about $300,000 out of our annual cost by simply applying basic purchasing fundamentals. The amazing thing is that every company knows that this needs to be done, but success breeds complacency and this company was successful. This was low-lying fruit that we harvested within months of our taking over.

By the way, this move paid for our debt service and essentially financed the deal. The reduced salaries gained from the two exiting shareholders essentially became the company's profit. This was turning into a very, very good deal.

Chapter 4

It is common sense to take a method and try it. If it fails, admit it frankly and try another. But above all, try something.
--Franklin D. Roosevelt

Improving the purchasing and cost efficiency in the shop was pretty easy. Well inside my comfort zone, I was able to bring basic concepts to the operation and create immediate, identifiable improvements and results. Modifying or improving the revenue direction was another story.

Of our three primary sources of revenue, two were contract jobs. By their nature, we had absolutely no influence on sales. We simply waited for the orders and produced to specification on a schedule provided by our customer. It was good work at reasonable margins. The production ran trouble-free and required little improvement or modification. Over time, these jobs became relatively predictable and we could count on relatively certain production and revenue streams with some seasonality and volatility. These jobs were considered our "bill paying" jobs. These jobs we left alone.

Our third and primary revenue source was our small-line vending equipment. The machines were simple, easy to operate, easy to maintain and very inexpensive. They were, however, not very sexy. There were no lights, bells or whistles. They were purely utilitarian function over form. However, this provided for a simplified manufacturing process.

Since we sold to distributors, we again had very little influence over the sales cycle or influence over the production levels. We produced at efficient lots that were determined well before my involvement with the company. For the most part, the lot sizes made sense, and everyone was geared to the level of production, so production management was relatively easy.

Paul and I both recognized that we needed to develop another market or another product to help supplement the shop. Since we were at the mercy of other companies to drive our sales revenue, we were susceptible to large swings in production levels. The variation in production is a difficult problem in a shop that is designed for moderate to high production demands. Having a high demand in production was less of a problem for us. Typically, we could handle the extra demand by expanding our shifts, or adding a full second shift. Split-shifting our supervisors often covered production management. Basically, we would have a supervisor start with the first production shift at 7 a.m. The second floor supervisor would start at 10 or 11 am and would work late into the second shift. It was tough on the supervisors, but it typically did not last for a long duration, so it was manageable.

The real problem was the production lulls. If the slowdown was only temporary, it was sometimes welcomed since it gave us time to perform preventative maintenance on the production equipment. When the slowdowns lagged, then we lost money. There is nothing worse than having high-priced production supervisors standing around doing nothing. Layoffs were not even considered for our key people. Our staff was trained to manufacture our products. The risk of losing our key people was too great to risk a layoff.

We considered producing for inventory, but could not solve the painting issue. All of the painting had to be completed before the final assembly phase of production. Many of the small vendors we manufactured were private labeled by our distributors, so they had specific painting and decal requirements. Anticipating our distributors' demand was riskier than waiting out the lull.

Our initial idea was to sell some of the small-line vending machines direct into the market. This would allow us to build our own inventory during our slow production times allowing us to smooth out our production schedule. Since most of our distributors were selling established vending routes, they were in a completely different market. Paul was convinced that a market existed for selling the equipment directly to the small company or office. Not being convinced or unconvinced, I was game to try. We set our prices similar to the distributor-selling price. We hired an experienced salesman to head up the project.

Until then, the role of our existing salesman was to develop and maintain distributor relationships. Although this was a sales role, it really was actually more of a customer service and relationship manager role. Now we were expanding into new territory. We were now attempting to develop a sales department that could generate leads and close sales. Again, the primary reason for the sales were to allow us to level out our production by building our own machine inventory that could be sold directly.

We worked on the project for about six months developing sales and marketing brochures and pricing plans. Our salesman hit the road with leads and optimism. But the plan didn't work. The reason for the failure was not obvious, but I had several unproven theories to explain our lack of success. First, we did not understand our market. Our guess was that small companies would want these vending machines as a convenience for their employees. Since the product was vended at a profit, the machines paid for themselves relatively quickly. We even established a lease purchase program that essentially cost the company only about $30 or $40 per month to own the equipment. The price point was set below what it would cost for a water cooler or coffee service, so the actual cash flow was minimal for nearly any company. But it still did not work.

My theory was the market rejected the idea primarily because the companies did not want the hassle of filling the vending machines. If the company was big enough, they could get a vending service to provide the machines and keep the machines stocked with product. If the company was very small, they simply had a refrigerator in the break room, and the employees brought their own drinks and snacks.

Another theory was that a market was not yet created for this type of product. Since it is not customary to have a vending machine in an office, why would anyone want one or need one? I suspect that water coolers were initially not popular either. Why should a company pay for bottled water service when an employee could simply fill up a cup at the water faucet? Maybe the threat of lead in water pipes helped drive the market; maybe it was a status thing. I'm not sure, and I was not interested in researching the origins of the bottled water cooler industry to find the answer about how the market was created. But, it was safe to believe that the market for office soda machines was not well established and I was not about to spend countless dollars on attempting to make offices aware of the benefits of owning their own vending machine. It wasn't worth the effort.

My last theory was our choice for salesman. The skills and experience were not the issue, but rather the chemistry in our company. Our existing sales person felt threatened by the new guy, and I could not overcome this. And because the existing sales guy wanted to reign supreme, he did nothing to help the new guy. We tried team building, financial incentives, status incentives, you name it, and we tried it. I could not overcome the situation. The new guy was on his own trying to build a market in a difficult, if not impossible sales situation. Ultimately, he may have succeeded, but I risked losing my existing salesman, which I was not about to sacrifice. In the end, we sold some accounts, but not enough to cover the cost of the salesman, let alone the cost of marketing materials and the related soft costs. Ultimately, we killed the program and let the salesman go.

Luckily, we didn't waste much time on the direct sales program experiment. But we still needed to solve our production volatility issues, and our second idea was to expand our existing small vending machine line.

For some time, Paul was messing around with developing an electronic version of our mechanical soda vendor. It was a concept being promoted by our distributors, so we were game in attempting to develop a new look to our machine. The modifications to our existing machine were minimal. The only real change as a company was learning and understanding the requirements for electronic circuitry. We engaged a local electronic engineering firm to develop the required wiring harnesses and circuit boards.

As we were completing the final testing on the electronic machine, I became increasingly interested in an idea that Paul had for a new, revolutionary bottle vending machine. His former partners, partly because of the development cost, partly because they didn't see the market for it, and partly because conceptually it may not have proven to be as reliable as a mechanical machine that had a track record of nearly a 100% vend, had killed the project.

They weren't wrong on any of their reasoning. However, we had an understanding of electronics and were one step away from gearing up our production using this technology, which was not difficult. So I started doing some research on bottle vending machines.

A few years prior, the first full-size glass-front vending machine was introduced by a large regional manufacturer. It was primarily a captive machine for one product. Essentially, the machine was only used to distribute the product of the company for whom the machine was manufactured. In this case, the machines only distributed glass-bottle iced teas.

The vending machines had all types of problems consistently vending product, which is the kiss of death in the vending machine manufacturing business. But one of the problems was not what I expected. I figured that the glass bottles would break when they took their plunge from the delivery rack to the dispensing area. But that was not the case. They did not break. In fact, the initial market push for the vending machine was the concept of watching the bottle fall. It was a novelty for the purchaser.

The bigger novelty of the machine was the increased sales revenue experienced by the operator. Tests were conducted comparing the glass-front vending machines to a classic vending machine. The results were staggering. The glass-front machines were outselling standard machines by any where from 50% to 100% more, irrespective of the product. In fact, some studies stocked the machines with identical product, and the results were the same. More product was sold from the glass-front machines. In fact, it was theorized by the industry experts that much of the product sales were driven purely by the novelty of watching the bottle drop.

There were reliability issues, however. The glass bottles weren't breaking, they were falling down inside the machine before they would vend. Several iterations of modifications to the delivery design had the machines vending no products, two products, or more than two products. Eventually, the company that originally designed and manufactured the machines was financially strapped, and sold the idea to Standard Vending, which was a large national manufacturing and sales operation. The deal was not published, but Standard was publicly traded, so some limited information was available on the transaction. Best I could tell was that the selling price was pretty high, but was primarily a debt assumption transaction that essentially got the seller out of a sideways debt position without going bankrupt.

Standard then did the most important part of the new product development. They created the market for the machine. Unfortunately, they did not iron out all of the design wrinkles before they started mass marketing the machine. But the market was made. Glass bottle vending machines were no longer a novelty, but were on the verge of becoming the newest merchandising concept in vending.

I started comparing Paul's initial mechanical machine to the existing machine that was being reintroduced by Standard, and noticed a significant design change. The existing machine had product racks in which the bottles stood upright. When the product was selected, the bottle in the ready position slid forward and plunged to the bottom. The remaining products in line then slid forward. Gravity did most of the work. A simple solenoid would release the vending mechanism freeing the first bottle. That was it. It was hauntingly simple.

Paul's machine worked differently. His concept was to hang the bottles from their necks. The products were dispensed in a similar fashion, and gravity did most of the work. The biggest difference was that the neck provided much less friction, so the bottles slid much more freely. Further, they could not fall over and they could not be shaken loose. Finally, since the weight was in the bottom of the bottle, it actually helped vend the product, rather than causing jams like in Standard's machine. In all accounts, Paul's design was much more reliable, and most importantly, likely to be patent protected.

It did not take any convincing for Paul to jump on the idea of continuing development of the new machine. We had a working prototype in weeks, and a clean operating prototype soon after.

Since we were in our peak production season, sales were high and cash flow was plentiful, so the initial cost of development was easy to afford and cash flow. At this point, our company was posting record sales at record margins due to the benefits of the previous purchasing improvements. We were turning about a 12% bottom line operating profit after paying ourselves handsome salaries and bonuses.

The second aspect of the new machine development was learning to understand where we fit in the market place. The vending machine manufacturing industry is big business. By my account and analysis, the industry operated as an oligopoly. An oligopoly is in an industry or market that is controlled and dominated by a small number of companies or suppliers. It is similar to a monopoly, but different. The oligopoly allows for the industry to fragment. I recognized pretty quickly that the players in vending machine manufacturing were large, well-capitalized operations. The three top industry leaders were publicly traded companies with access to capital, markets and talent. Likely, their marketing budgets were more than our entire sales revenue. These companies competed hard for the bottler business. The major bottlers were the largest buyers of vending machines. To them, the vending machine was more than a way to sell product. It was a billboard and a market image. The big manufactures dominated the industry, but ultimately, the bottlers dominated everything. Without the bottlers, the entire industry was gone.

But an oligopoly allows market fragmentation and this is where we fit in. I started studying the other players in the industry. They were more like our company. They were niche providers of specialty products to a small segment of the entire market. Essentially, they lived off of the scraps of the bigger companies. They were the pilot fish to the shark, if you will. Every so often a smaller player would start to surface and gain market attention. When this happened, usually one of the bigger companies would swallow them up for a tidy fortune. This had a special appeal to me as an investor, so I was excited about the prospect of competing in this industry.

Since Standard was creating the market for glass-front bottle machines, I knew that we were on the right track, and in good company. But we needed to be different. We did not have an identity in the "real" vending market. Companies like ours were nuisance companies. We had a product line that confused the marketplace about vending machines. Our distributors were viewed as rogues, and our products viewed as inferior. Getting the attention of the real distributors in the industry was going to be difficult.

We decided to stick with our strength, and introduce the new glass-front machine as a small-line machine, most suited for offices and small businesses. This was our strength and our market, so it made sense to start there.

The machine was first introduced at a national show in Long Beach. The interest was overwhelming. No one ever saw a machine that worked like it. The initial reviews were great, and the machine worked well. Some of the bottlers were intrigued by the design and the concept. Overall, we presented well as a company and the trip was a success. We were noticed, but we didn't sell any machines.

Paul and I were not discouraged, however. What we learned was that there was room for us in the industry.

A couple weeks after the Long Beach show we received a call from a national bottler. Some of the representatives saw the machine at the show and decided that they may have an application for the machine on busses and subways.

Paul and our salesman made the trip to the bottler to learn more about the opportunity and to sell them on buying equipment from us. But the bottler had a different agenda. At the meeting, the bottler provided Paul with the machine specifications necessary for us to become an equipment manufacturer for them. The deal with them was simple: prove to them that a machine can be built to their specifications. Once that was accomplished, they would test the machine. If it passed, then they will then perform a study to determine if the machine will work in the marketplace for their application. All told, the duration of the project could take years, and there were no assurances that they would ever buy a machine from us.

We were all pretty discouraged at the news. Although this seemed like a great opportunity, we recognized that we needed faster market penetration. At this point, we believed that gaining acceptance from distributors would be the best course of action.

We worked hard on cleaning up the appearance of the machine and getting ready for the next big trade show. I spent most of my time in Long Beach taking notes on what other machines looked like and noted the features that we did not offer. Right away, we were able to incorporate most of the features of the bigger machines into our small machine. We felt we hit the mark, so we began manufacturing 200 machines for inventory.

The next show was in Chicago. We had six months to perfect the concept, and the machine was loaded with the features that were standard in the industry. We were also getting closer to the bottler specifications, which became our secondary goal. We were excited about the prospect of developing distributor relationships.

In a bold move, and in an attempt to escape our roots as a small-line mechanical vending machine manufacturer, we only brought our glass front machine to the show. Although we risked appearing as a one trick pony, we knew that we needed to revamp our image to the industry.

The show was even better than Long Beach. We attracted the attention of nearly every distributor and manufacturer. The machine was novel, and it worked perfectly. There was a buzz in our booth for the first two days.

But by the third day, we still did not land one distributor. My initial concerns about being a "newbie" company were plaguing my mind. But that wasn't the problem -- as I soon learned. Since we were having a relatively quiet third day, I started going to distributor and bottler booths to bring them to our booth for a demonstration.

In the process, I talked to a local distributor named Dale Kohn who was enjoying the product received during a demonstration of a new ice cream vendor. After a bit of convincing, he came over to our booth to witness our new invention.

After a few minutes of watching, he provided the first insight to our problem.

"John, I like the machine," Dale said. "It's novel and it looks nice. It would work well in a small office since it is compact. But I can't sell it."

"Why not, Dale?"

I was expecting an answer along the lines that we were too small of a company, that we did not have experience, or some other excuse about the nature of our company.

"The machine is too small," Dale responded.

I was shocked at the answer.

"What do you mean? It's supposed to be small."

"Yeah, I know it needs to be small, but it does not have enough capacity. It only holds 128 bottles. The operator can't make enough money to offset the cost of the equipment. The payback in total machine turns is way too low."

This was a new concept to me. I understood return on investment, and was well versed in nearly every aspect of economics, investment returns, and pricing theory. But that wasn't the yardstick used in the industry. It was profit per turn. And it was measured by how many times a machine needed to be serviced, or filled. Since the machine was expensive, it needed to be located in a high volume area to generate the sales, but since it held only 128 bottles, it would need to be serviced more than a larger vending machine. Thus, because of the extra work involved for the operator, the machine would never turn a profit commensurate with the investment in the equipment.

This was interesting since our price point for our machine was about one third of the big Standard machine. Our capacity was a bit less than one third, so the economics in a conventional sense were pretty close. But the problem wasn't the Standard machine. The real issue was the competing price of regular vending machines that could be used as a substitute to ours for the same or less investment. If the investment dollars were the same, and they only needed to be filled once to our three or four times, the economics could never be justified to an operator.

We quickly understood, but were crushed.

"Dale, are there any uses for this machine?" I asked.

"Sure. Incorporate a slave snack machine to the unit, and you will have something."

"What do you mean by slave?"

"A machine that can use the same coin and dollar bill validator, and the same circuit board. It keeps the cost of the unit down," he explained.

I was impressed.

"Dale, that is a great idea," I said.

We started to develop a rapport with Dale. His insight to the industry was invaluable. He was the first distributor to seem to want to help. I needed to get his interest and keep him involved. So I acted quickly without advanced discussion with Paul.

"Dale, if we could develop a larger machine, say the size of Standard's. A full size, 45 selection machine, would you be a distributor for us?"

Dale didn't even hesitate. "Yes. Absolutely. I love the machine and the idea."

"This could take us some time, Dale. Is there anything you can do to help us in the meanwhile? Maybe help us move these? You know, some of the bottlers are interested and it still could be a hit."

Dale smiled.

"You don't think it will be a hit?" I asked.

"No, that's not it. Don't be so quick to think you will get any bottler business. You have to meet their specs first. The timeline of getting bottler approval is long, and the journey is hard," Dale said. "Further, you are new to the business and this is an industry mired deep in tradition and relationships" he added.

Paul and I just stood there looking at each other. We didn't know what to think, but we knew that what we had was not where it needed to be. Furthermore, Dale confirmed our concerns about the long duration of bottler approval.

When we returned to the plant, we immediately began developing a slave snack machine. Since we were already manufacturing mechanical snack machines, we assumed we would incur a short development time. We were wrong. We were now working with electric motors to dispense the product. The real problem was that the power supply of the small bottle machine was not large enough to handle the additional slave snack machine. It quickly became apparent that adding a snack machine was not a small task. In fact, it required a complete engineering overhaul.

Meanwhile, much to our surprise, orders started coming in for the machine. It turned out that several small distributors started pitching the concept to their customers, and there was a niche market for the machine.

The machine performed perfectly in the field. Our vend rate was nearly 100% and the feedback we received was all positive. The machine was serving a need and the small size was only an obstacle for the large operators. But we really needed to accommodate the large operators if we were going to land the large distributors.

It didn't take long for our current mechanical small-line distributor to learn about our new invention. Within weeks they were pitching us on a new program that would feature our machine as the cornerstone of their business. But we were concerned about selling all of our products through this particular small-line distributor. Additionally, I was concerned about their reputation. I did not want the large distributors to discount our company because of a relationship with a less-than respected distributor. So I convinced Paul that we should pass on the opportunity and continue with our plan.

Sales continued over the next few months, but not at the pace that we needed. We were getting close to selling out the first 200 machines, so we began another production run. This run would incorporate a few modifications to provide for easier loading and an optional stand that would raise the height of the machine to allow for better product merchandising.

We continued to market the machine to small distributors that would each sell 2 or 3 machines a week, which was a snails pace compared to the 100 mechanical machines we would sell per week. Furthermore, the development of the slave snack machine was at a standstill.

The feedback continued to pour in from our few distributors. They loved the concept, they loved the machine operation, but they really hated the size. The consensus from the field was unanimous. We needed to develop a full size machine.

We decided to immediately stop manufacturing the small glass-front and focus on developing a full-size machine. But this was not going to be a small task. We were entering a world that we knew little about. We were now going to compete head on with Standard, a national company with very deep pockets. We were crossing over to the big time, the major leagues. It was exciting and unnerving at the same time.

Chapter 5

Be always sure you are right – then go ahead.
--David Crockett

We began working right away on the new 45-selection, glass-front bottle machine. For the most part, it was not much different than what we were accustomed to manufacturing. We were already manufacturing full size condiment stands, and we were comfortable with the new electronic delivery systems. So, building the bigger machine was simply a matter of manufacturing a bigger version of what was already invented.

Meanwhile, our core business continued to grow. The economy was robust and the orders just kept coming. The condiment stand business was posting record month after record month. The demand for snack and soda machines was peaking at the best levels in five years. And the bookcase order was on the way. From all indications, we were expecting the biggest order yet. We were on a roll and making a lot of money. Things were really looking good.

Because of the growth, the new machine development was feeling pressure. Developing prototypes was one thing. Establishing production procedures was another. The demand began causing fab shop logjams. It was becoming an increasing problem, not enough capacity.

Thinking like smart businessmen, we had to expand to a third shift. This gave us endless possibilities since it provided production capacity without a capital outlay. Keeping costs variable was a big thing with me. My experience in consulting led me to believe that most companies overbuilt their physical plants and overshot their equipment needs. Increased fixed costs drives up the break-even point of the shop.

I was always reminding myself of the sales break-even formula: Fixed costs divided by the gross margin percentage. And since gross margin is a function of sales less variable costs, a company did not increase its risk by expanding through use of variable costs. Even if the gross margin was sacrificed, as long as sales are increasing and fixed costs remain the same, the company was continuing to be profitable. And, in the event that demand falls off and sales are reduced, the company is more likely to remain profitable provided that the company keeps its fixed cost in line. To me it was basic thinking and simple to do.

In a normal economy adding a third shift was pretty simple. Since we paid pretty decent wages and offered good working conditions, getting a third shift together typically went pretty well. I was always surprised how many people actually preferred third shift to second shift. Maybe they just hated being with their spouses or family, or maybe they liked the increased pay, but third shift was usually pretty easy to fill.

But this was not a typical economy. We were dealing with some of the lowest national unemployment figures in history. And our area was no exception. Adding a third shift soon proved to be more of a challenge than originally expected.

Job openings were plentiful on first shift. Jobs were always tricky for second shift, but we were still pretty strong. The third shift was a mess.

As employment increases and less people are available, it becomes more apparent why the workers that are available are unemployed. For the most part, many of them are not hirable for some reason. Either they lack the skills, initiative, training, and desire, whatever. They are lacking. And many of them suffer from addictions like drugs, alcohol, or gambling. Something else has their attention and they are not always suited for employment.

But we needed bodies, so we expanded anyway. We had a willing third shift supervisor. Our second in command on first shift was chomping at the bit for more responsibility and recognized the opportunity. Not only was there a pay increase, but also increased status and increased responsibility -- two things employers often discount as motivators. This guy was motivated and we were pleased.

We had a few other volunteers to switch shifts to the third shift, so we were going into the third shift with primarily a rookie staff with a few veterans mixed in. Overall, it took weeks to find a workable staff. And when all of the positions were filled, it still wasn't very workable.

Oh, the wonderful great economy. To our benefit, it created demand for our product and increased sales. To our detriment, labor was scarce and we were in trouble with our staff.

It didn't take long for the problems to begin. It started with subversive passive resistance from the third shift. First it was graffiti on the freshly painted restroom stalls. "Paul s**ks". "F*** this place". You get the idea. Once the plant supervisor addressed the graffiti, it then spread to the freshly painted walls and lockers. It was a shame.

The worst part of the subversive behavior was the effect on the first and second shift employees. They were proud of our company and were happy about their jobs. In fact, for three straight years we were the recipients of an award in our region for being one of the best companies for which to work. It was our employees who nominated us for the award. We always promoted a positive atmosphere and a safe and healthy working environment. But coming in to work after a few nights of third shift, I could visibly see the morale decline. There was a force working against everything that the employees believed in and it was sour.

And the production on third shift was sub-par. Quality problems, lost and misplaced tools, and disorganized production areas quickly became the problem of first shift. So, instead of the added benefit of running machines and a running production line, each morning became an agonizing trip down "what did they do now" lane. Even when things weren't messed up, the first shift spent half of the morning complaining about third shift just because they could. Who could argue with them?

So changes came. To stop the property damage, restroom breaks were no longer "as needed", but were allowed only during break times. To improve quality, we added another floor manager, thus increasing our fixed costs. But we could not stop the theft, and it continued to get worse.

I am not sure why, but employees seem to think that hand tools that belong to the company are disposable items. So they take them home. The mutterings of "they are a write-off" always seems to be the rationale. For a theft to occur, three things are always necessary.

The first requirement is "financial need" and typically is the easiest of the three. In the instance of third shift, financial need was pretty obvious, not even considering the suspected crack habits of many of the workers.

The second requirement is "rationalization" and typically comes in the form of phrases like "they are a write-off ... no one will miss this ... they have more ... I'm underpaid ... everyone else is doing it." The list goes on and on. There was no way to combat rationalization, especially on the third shift.

The third requirement is "opportunity". They were given the chance to steal. Now, there is something that we can address.

The problem with a 90,000 square-foot shop is that it is easy to hide and even easier to steal. I am reminded of a great story of a fraud investigator who was assigned to guard the exits at a plant where theft was highly suspected. The theft was initially suspected due to significant changes in the gross profit. Further review of the out-of-balance inventory records further pointed to theft. And since several of the supervisory employees had access to the computer terminals in the warehouse, there were several suspects.

The company was a hardware store with some 17,000 stock-keeping units. Every night the inexperienced investigator reviewed the contents of the wheel barrels being shuttled out of the plant and on to the delivery trucks. And every night the contents properly matched the items that were on the packing lists. The inventory continued to be short, and the records continued to be altered to the point that it was nearly impossible to determine what was being stolen. After days of trying to reconcile, the staff investigator summoned the supervisor. After about 15 minutes of observation by the staff investigator, he wandered over and stated that he had solved the mystery. It was very simple. They were stealing the wheel barrels.

So it goes, the obvious is not always that way.

So how do you stop the theft? Create deterrence by eliminating opportunity. Within a day, I had a security camera system installed at each of the exits to the plant and office, and several more cameras pointed out to the parking lot. They weren't secret surveillance cameras, but rather they were big, blinking, visible deterrents. Monitors were installed in the plant supervisor's office that would switch from view to view. A large format tape rolled continuously recording the activity. It worked pretty well. The theft continued, but in much smaller amounts. Things like screwdrivers and pliers still disappeared, but that was simply passive subversive behavior in action.

The effect on the first shift was pretty bad, though. The morale was tainted, not so much that the "eye in the sky" was watching, but that the step had to be taken in the first place. The resentment continued to grow, and the start up time each morning increased to the point something else had to be done. We needed to ditch the third shift.

Being an accountant, I always start with the numbers. I analyzed the productivity of each shift, and the additional fixed costs that had been incurred to manage the third shift. It was a break-even proposition, if that. But we needed the production.

I started to examine what processes could be automated. There were two clear areas, the turret presses and the press breaks. Both areas were creating big bottlenecks. I suppose if we were better at managing our workflow that maybe we could have somehow restructured our plant and workflow. But we didn't even try. We had a difficult time attracting any talent for third shift, let alone any better plant management. It was a workers market caused by full employment economy.

It was getting close to the biannual machine show in Chicago. This was the biggest machine show in the U.S., maybe the world. The entire McCormick Center would be jammed full of every type of machine imaginable. Machines from around the world. Paul and I booked flights.

Chicago is always a great city to visit, but I was on a short leash. I had too many responsibilities with my accounting practice to blow a couple of days. Since Chicago has easy access and is serviced by nearly every airline flying out of Cleveland, I booked a there-and-back flight. Picking up an hour on the way always made this easy. Basically, all I lost was some of my personal time at night. What was that anyway? All I did was work, if not here, then at my accounting practice.

Paul, on the other hand, looked at these trips as a chance to play. It was a vacation away from his family and work on the company nickel. This trip was especially exciting since he had the shop foreman with him. They had not been able to travel together since I became involved since it never made any sense to have Frank along. This trip was an exception since it involved the plant. Frank's input was important.

The show was a success. And it did not take long to determine where the greatest impact could be made. Installing robotic sheet loaders on our turret punch presses made total sense. We could essentially run the turrets three shifts, seven days a week —unmanned. This would eliminate the third shift. Further, I could move the extra supervisor to first shift and beef up the assembly area.

I was pretty convinced that this made sense, but I still needed to run the numbers again. Meanwhile, we were still exploring the possibility of robotic press brakes, consequently we scheduled one more trip to visit the equipment manufacturer. Yokama America was located in Los Angeles, so this trip could not be completed in a day.

So we were off to the coast.

Chapter 6

There is never a better measure of what a person is than what he does when he is absolutely free to choose.
--William M. Bulger

Yokama recognized that selling equipment in this price range required hands-on demonstration. So they built a working factory with all of their equipment set up and functioning. It allowed a great forum for sales and training. The best part was the cost. Yokama paid all expenses, since we were a loyal customer.

Basically, Yokama had internal machine shows about every six or eight weeks. Since we were so close to the buying line, we were invited to the next available show.

We were only comped two tickets and two rooms, so Frank stayed home. This was a Paul and John trip. I already knew what equipment made sense and the costs. We were pretty much exploring the next step, automating the press brakes.

The show helped in our decision and we were satisfied with the route we were taking. Now it was time to relax.

Traveling with Paul was always fun. He could party harder than anyone I ever met. And since we were recently in LA at a trade show, we knew our way around to our favorite areas and clubs.

We started the evening at the hotel lobby bar for a few warm up drinks and some sushi. I didn't like the raw fish, but the Crown Royal was going down pretty easy. We were both feeling pretty good about our business and ourselves. The business was on track, and the new product line was a major hit. We rightfully saw the stars, and we really believed that we would soon hit them. Feeling pretty good about everything, it was time to hit the city and let off some steam.

It was real easy to talk about the future and to dream. Paul and I would have long discussions about what we will do with the money that we knew we were going to make. And we would talk about the price that we would accept if someone offered to buy the whole business.

Since the only reason I bought in to this business in the first place was to eventually hit pay dirt, it was an exciting thought. We were well on our way to making our goals. Our sales increased dramatically, but more importantly, we were making profit numbers never seen by this company. Paul and I were having fun and we were becoming good friends.

We decided that a cab ride to Hermosa Beach was in order. I liked Hermosa Beach. It was the land of beautiful people. The area was pretty trendy and the patrons were young, attractive and full of energy. Nothing like making me feel old and fat than hanging around a bunch of handsome and beautiful 25-year-olds. I couldn't wait.

Now Paul was hot for the ladies. He always felt he could score. I think that was his main goal, to hook up with some lassie for a fling. I am made from different material. I never was, and never will be, interested in hooking up. Not only did I love my wife, I respected her too much to play around. Maybe more importantly, I respected myself too much to cheapen my self-image.

I like to converse, though. Meeting new people was always fun, and I did not mind hanging out and playing the "wing man" role. I knew it would never go beyond talking, so it was real easy for me to relax, be myself and just have fun. Besides, the party is more fun when there are more involved, so I was always game.

We found a little bistro on a corner that seemed pretty happening. It was a sushi bar. They had a special going on some type of Japanese beer. I tried one, but it was no match for the Canadian brew of which I was accustomed. The one real thing I hated about Los Angeles, I could never seem to find Canadian beer. That was okay though. I switched to bourbon and kept it at that.

Now Paul, he liked to mix up his booze. Generally, he was a Jack and Coke guy, but tonight, he was drinking shots of Cuervo tequila chased by Asahi Japanese beer. Paul was lit. It did not seem like a good idea to mix countries, let alone economic systems. I was getting a bit worried about his condition, but I could not stop him.

The good thing about his drinking tonight was that no way was he hooking up with anyone. His loose tongue, however, made him a hit with the ladies. How did he do it? I could never tell. But they really liked him. He was having the time of his life. He had a girl on each arm paying attention to him. It really was fortunate, too, because if they weren't there, chances were he would be falling over.

As time wore on, I realized how late it was and that we had not eaten dinner. It's not good to drink on an empty stomach. After numerous attempts, I could not get Paul to leave, and by the look in his eye, I could not leave him alone. I needed a plan.

When Paul skipped to the can, I summonsed the ladies and asked if they would either join us for dinner or to ditch us. Either way, I could get Paul out of the bar and get some food in his stomach. Not surprisingly, and thankfully, they ditched us.

There was a great seafood restaurant across the street, so we headed in that direction. When we walked out of the sushi bar, Paul could not even stand up straight. It was pathetic. As we were waiting for the light to change, Paul was swaying to and fro. How was I going to get him into a restaurant? The light turned green and we began to cross. As he stumbled, two police officers across the street noticed us and started to make their way. I quickly turned Paul around and headed in the other direction with the oncoming crowd. I never looked back.

Two doors down from the sushi bar was a little Italian restaurant. It did not look too good, but I needed to ditch the cops and get some food. We ducked in.

An Italian woman speaking broken English greeted me.

"No food. We are closed," she hollered.

"What time do you close?" I asked.

"10 o'clock. We're closed."

I looked at my watch and it was about 9:45. I'm sure if Paul weren't smashed we would have been seated. But tonight, no exceptions would be made.

I pled with the hostess, "Please let us eat. It is not quite 10, and I will order something that is already prepared, like lasagna."

"No."

Just then, the door opened. I feared it was the police from across the street. Luckily, it wasn't. It was a man and a lady looking for a nice casual meal. The hostess now had a problem. Does she lose four dinners and toss us all, or does she succumb to capitalism and seat us.

"Okay you two, I give you seat, but any sign of trouble from him I throw you out."

"What did I do?" Paul slurred.

"Nothing, Paul. Shut up," I muttered.

I motioned to the hostess to lead us to our seats.

We were seated. After a minute, Paul popped up out of the chair and started sliding his chair in an out from under the table.

"Paul!" I quietly shouted, "What are you doing?"

"This chair is so heavy. I never sat in such a sturdy, heavy chair."

"Paul, sit down. Don't you want to eat?"

"Yup."

"Then hush up. Put on your bib and sit quietly."

Now this was a sight to see. A six-foot-two man, red as a beet from drinking, eyes glazed over, sitting with a red and white-checkered bib around his neck. It was a proud moment for me. This was my partner.

Fortunately, the restaurant was emptying out. All I could think of was eating, and getting out of there without an incident or without the interest of the police outside.

When the waitress arrived, I pulled her aside and whispered to her, "Whatever he orders for a drink, please just bring him water. He won't know the difference."

She nodded and asked me what I would like.

"Baked lasagna, please."

She turned to Paul with a somewhat startled look. He was sitting straight up in his chair with a fork in one hand and a knife in the other. He had a stupid smile on his face. It was the kind of smile you get when you mix Mexican booze with Japanese beer. He was wrecked. I was regretting coming to this restaurant. I was regretting the whole trip.

The waitress turned to me and asked, "What will he have?"

Before I could answer, Paul shouted out, "Bring me whatever *you* would order. That's what I want, whatever is *your* favorite."

The waitress winked at me, turned and placed our order. I could not imagine what Paul was going to get, seeing he was a pain in the butt. However, Italian fare is usually pretty safe, so I was not too concerned.

After about 20 minutes of waiting and trying to convince Paul that his water was, in fact, vodka and that he was just too drunk to notice the alcohol, the food finally arrived.

First, the waitress came out with a sizable portion of lasagna and a side of spaghetti, but nothing for Paul. His disappointment was obvious. He looked like a sad dog that was denied table scraps.

Then it happened. The waitress appeared with the most incredible and disgusting meal I have ever seen. It looked like a carcass of a dead animal on a plate – but not the whole animal, just the rib cage. Bones were just sticking out. The meat on the bones was glazed with some type of sauce.

"What the heck is that?" I groaned.

Before the waitress could answer, Paul blurted out, "It's venison. My favorite."

I was sick. Watching this shiny, drunk, hulking man, wearing his red and white checkered bib, stuffing his face with this animal carcass was just too much for me to deal with. So I ordered another bourbon for me – and "vodka" for Paul.

I just kept looking down so as to not get sick. Every so often I would look up at Paul. His expression never changed. Shiny and red, he just kept shoveling the food and gnawing on the bones. His dumb, drunk look never left his face.

This is my partner, I thought.

After Paul finally unstrapped the feedbag, I paid the bill and left as quickly as I could. As we walked out, I searched for a cab. Great, the cabstand was across the street on the opposite corner. That means I needed to walk Paul across two streets to clear the intersection.

The meal, although revolting, seemed to help sober up Paul. He was now able to walk under his own power, and his swaying was less noticeable. As we began to cross at the second light, my two cop friends noticed me and began to walk to the corner as if to meet me. They were walking with a purpose, and I had nowhere to hide. I was dead. I whispered to Paul under my breath to shut up and let me do the talking. Fortunately, I was in pretty good shape, so I was confident I could deal with any interrogation. They made it to the corner before us and waited patiently.

"Good evening officers," I said.

"Where are you guys headed?"

They took a long time sizing Paul and me up. I think it was obvious we were travelers and did not want trouble. Paul was still lit, and public intoxication was a crime. Knowing that they recently arrested their own mayor for drinking, I needed to remain calm. Paul stood there looking like a dope.

"To get in the next taxi, officer," I replied.

"Looks like you gentleman have been enjoying yourselves tonight. Maybe a bit too much I'd say," said one of the policemen.

"Look, officer, we haven't caused any trouble and just want to get back to our hotel. We won't be a bother. I promise. Just let us get in the cab and be on our way."

I said it almost as if I was pleading.

Paul just stood there with a stupid grin on his face. Finally, he started to mumble and I quickly squeezed his arm to remind him of his oath of silence.

The cops motioned us on and said nothing. I hailed the next cab, pushed Paul inside and jumped in as quickly as I could. As the taxi cruised through the intersection, I watched my cop friends watch us.

We were lucky. Paul was really lucky. He came close to spending the night in jail.

Paul awoke from his cab ride nap just as we pulled into our hotel. He slid out of the cab and fell on the ground. I think he was more drunk now than he was when we ate. It's funny how alcohol works sometimes. I propped him up on the curb and sat down next to him.

"Well, buddy, its time for bed," I said. "Take a minute and then we will head up to bed."

Paul sprung to life. "What?" he said. "It's all over?"

"Yes, Paul it's over."

"It's all over? No. It can't be," he cried.

"Yes Paul, the evening is over."

"It can't be over" he pleaded. "I don't want it to be over."

"Paul, let's get upstairs."

I led Paul down the hall to his room. Since he was a smoker, we were on different floors. I opened his door and shoved him in. He turned to try to come out, but after recognizing somehow in his drunken state that I was not in the mood to mess around, he turned and made his way to the bed. Then he tripped over something and landed face down on the floor.

He was out cold.

What a night.

What a trip.

Moments like this seem pretty insignificant. But Paul had hit the trifecta: a night on the town, too much to drink and incorrigible behavior. It's certainly a place most of us unfortunately have been. But there was more to this night that was not yet evident. As a company, we were well on our way to stardom, but the success was beginning to prey upon Paul. I didn't see it, though.

And yes, we bought the machines.

Chapter 7

Create a definite plan for carrying out your desire and begin at once, whether you are ready or not, to put this plan into action.
--Napoleon Hill

Borrowing money to buy equipment never bothered me. As long as the equipment could pay for itself by creating efficiency or adding needed capacity, buying and borrowing the money to purchase it was painless. It was an investment for which I could calculate a return. Even the concept of adding my personal guarantee to the note was trouble-free since we had an asset that could be sold if need be.

Adding the automation made total sense. Analyzing the numbers was intuitive, but worthy of a detailed spreadsheet. I prepared the monthly projections for one year, and annual projections for the next four. They neatly proved that the machines would easily pay for themselves by simply eliminating the cost of the third-shift overhead. Furthermore, we could easily eliminate at least one, and likely two machine operators from the first and second shifts, as well. The $5,800 a month payments looked pretty easy. As long as our volume remained the same, it was a safe bet. At this point, all indications were that our volume was only going up.

But the process of borrowing more money was always a treat. We already had some pretty hefty leverage from the acquisition and an earlier machine purchase. Within the first year, we recognized that we could use another turret punch press. And with the recession hitting Japan, equipment was plentiful. We landed a great deal on a three-year-old machine at about one half the $450,000 new price. Additionally, our production increases caused the need for more inventory and accounts receivable, so our line of credit increased over the first two years as well, so the debt was pretty high. But we were making money. A lot of money. More money than either one of us ever imagined. And the company was positioned to continue to grow and the road ahead looked clear. Besides, our cash flow already supported the previous increased debt service with ease, so this additional expansion made sense and was economically feasible.

I have been around long enough to know that in the case of most small businesses, financial projections are often more like financial "predictions". A while back, I had a client assign a sales person to assist with financial budgets and projections for a project that I was spearheading. When he was done with his work, he stepped into the office in which I was working and proudly announced that he was done with his part of the predictions.

Predictions? Well, after reviewing his work from a critical accounting point of view, he was correct in his characterization, they were predictions. Get out the crystal ball or tealeaves. There was very little substance to the projected sales. It was purely an exercise in mathematics, multiplying the monthly sales numbers from last year by 110%. Where was the substance? How was the company planning on orchestrating this leap? Was it by price increases? A more relaxed credit policy? Or was it by more volume? Who knew? They were purely predictions. The likelihood of increasing by 10% was no more evident in his analysis than the likelihood of a 10% decrease in sales. The plan was based on optimism. We will do better than last year. How? That's the question that never seems to get answered.

Without a clear measurable plan supporting the assumptions, financial projections are reduced simply to predictions. Fate will ultimately decide the outcome absent a real, workable, measurable plan. And even when the plan is real, workable and measurable, there are so many other factors that can influence the real outcome. There are factors that could never be projected or even remotely considered. Factors that are real, like increased competition from a new or existing competitor, a shortage of supply on a key raw material, the loss of a key salesperson, or an unskilled labor shortage due to a fully employed work force. The list is endless. As business planners, we tend to operate in the realm of controlled probability; we project what should happen. Then we may reduce the calculated expectation by some factor, maybe 80 or 90% so that the result remains "conservative." But what should happen and what really does happen can be vastly different. And the more complicated a business is, the more possibilities exist that can influence the outcome. So, based on my experience as a consultant, to this day, I still like the term "predictions" better than projections only because it seems more appropriate. Essentially the financial projections are the model of the likely outcome if the prediction comes true.

That does not at all diminish the need for financial projections and modeling. Projecting financial outcomes based on a set of assumptions is imperative for a successful operation. The key is being realistic in making and supporting the assumptions that drive the numbers. Additionally, the projections become internal benchmarks for performance. Comparing the actual results to the projections helps a company learn and understand not only the financial behavior of the company, but also helps it learn how the external forces affect the assumptions and plan. If prepared and utilized properly, financial projections are an important tool.

Anyway, in the case of our company, our projections were well thought out and presented an accurate financial projection within the realm of our controlled probability. I had built a pretty solid model that could be updated easily, but more importantly by using the model I could assess the volatility of the sales and production volume. Modeling the effects of volume changes is critical for an expanding business.

Another big mistake I often see made in projections is that once the fixed costs and variable costs are identified, it is assumed that the relationship of these costs will remain constant. This is not true. The fixed and variable costs may remain constant over a specific volume range, but capacity constraints will always enter into the equation. Some of the more obvious constraints are physical space, equipment capacity and capital. But a latent constraint is management. Not the availability of people, but the ability of the people. I have yet to see a model that can help here. The rigors of growth and increased volume can blindly stretch management past its capability. Not seeing it coming becomes the biggest issue. How do you project a person's breaking point?

The break-even point in sales dollars and volume should be as natural to a business owner as a phone number or zip code. The formula is simple: fixed costs divided by the gross margin percentage. The gross margin percentage should be the sales in dollars less the variable costs. Dividing the sales dollars by the unit-selling price gets you to the unit sales volume. Granted, this a bit oversimplified, but even close approximations can help arrive at a quick break-even formula.

So, as sales and production volume increase, fixed costs will increase in steps. In some cases, the steps look more like quantum leaps. Imagine the cost increase if the physical constraint is the physical space. In our case, I always tried to keep our growth at a level where the steps were small so that we could remain in control of our costs.

Further, I kept constant watch on the effect of volume on gross margin. A kiss of death for a manufacturer is to increase sales volume by lowering prices, only to have fixed costs increase due to production volume demands. Lower margins and higher fixed costs can significantly modify the break-even in sales volume amount. Without a constant review, a company could find itself in financial disaster if the sales volume falls off even just a bit.

So we increased our fixed costs to allow us to produce more efficiently and to remove the management headaches of our third shift. The plan made perfect sense with the knowledge of the volume increases that we were anticipating. We were ready to move our company to the next level. We were ready for the national scene.

Chapter 8

The amount of good luck coming your way depends on your willingness to act.

--Barbara Sher

Once the robotic loaders were installed, our production issues seemed to wane. With the shop production in order, we were able to spend our time focusing on continuing the development of the 45-select machine. The development went well and the prototypes were completed in time for the western show, which was to be held in Anaheim.

The show went very well. The new idea was well received by the market place. We had a ton of inquiries for distributorships, which was our primary goal. There was a buzz around the industry about us. We were feeling pretty good that we had a hit. It was just a matter of time. And unanswered questions about our company were overshadowed by the ingenious design. It looked as if the market would give us a chance.

However, we knew that we needed to improve the internal operation of our company in order to compete at the national level.

Not only were we competing directly with Standard with our glass front machine, we were also competing with every bottle machine manufacturer. Our focus was always the glass front market, but our customers had a different perspective. They needed to vend bottles, period. A glass front vendor was only one choice among countless styles of bottle vending machines. Most of the regular bottle vending machines could hold more capacity, were lower priced and operated relatively trouble-free. So these machines were the obvious choice. But the key advantage of glass front bottle vending was that they sold more products because of the improved merchandising. And this became the thrust of our marketing campaign.

So in addition to trying to infiltrate a dynamic market, we were reinventing ourselves as a company. But reinventing a company is not new. Plenty of companies have successfully reinvented themselves. 3M transitioned from being a mining company to a successful multifaceted manufacturer and distributor. Motorola transitioned from a television manufacturer to become a leader in the wireless telecommunication industry. Wal-Mart morphed from a small town general store to a multi-national retailer. Our goal seemed easy in comparison; we were simply transitioning from being a small manufacturer to becoming a nationally recognized equipment manufacturer.

But we were not like 3M, Motorola, or Wal-Mart. We did not have surplus capital, nor did we have significant management depth. Since we were operating under a tight budget, to be successful at our metamorphosis we needed everyone to stretch beyond his or her current capabilities. We also recognized that we would likely need to hire some new talent in key management positions. But our goal was first to allow our current staff to prove themselves before we made that jump.

Although we knew the transition would be difficult, we were confident that we could build a product that would compete with the best companies in our industry. But that wasn't enough to allow us to effectively compete with Fortune 500 level companies. We needed to rethink every aspect of our business. We could not change everything at once so we decided to concentrate on the areas that required the most improvement.

Since we had been manufacturing the small-line machines for so long, and because most of the parts were manufactured in-house, maintaining efficient inventory levels was almost second nature to our plant manager. But that would change with the new machine.

To keep our inventory under control, we developed a detailed bill of materials for the new machine. A bill of materials is like a recipe for manufacturing. Essentially, this details out every component used in the machine so that we can order the proper amount of parts in a timely fashion. We manufactured about two-thirds of the parts in-house with the remaining components being ordered from various vendors around the world. Each part then had a specific lead time and minimum order quantity. Although this may not seem that complicated, it really was. Especially when you consider that we were still in the development stage of the product. Consequently, the bill of materials was constantly changing to accommodate the numerous modifications that continued throughout development.

Because of our commitment to developing proper inventory management after the acquisition, we were able to quickly adapt to these needs. The key, however, was being certain that our staff kept the bill of materials current and that they properly utilized the software. Initially, our shipping clerk handled our purchasing functions. But with the new challenges and time commitment, we needed a dedicated purchasing person that we ultimately had to hire.

Next, we evaluated our customer service. With the small-line machines, we only had one primary customer. For the most part, Paul and our salesman maintained this relationship. And since this was a long-term relationship, there was not much interaction required. The second level of customer service involved helping end-users with equipment issues and replacement parts orders. Again, because of the long history of the product line, there was little that would go wrong, and the replacement parts needs could be predicted with ease because we already knew the wear factor of the equipment.

But all of this changed with the new market. We now had numerous distributors requiring sales support. Further, the end-users required more assistance operating the equipment. Lastly, since we did not have any real history with the equipment, we could not anticipate the parts needs, or the problems that could occur in the field. We were in completely new territory.

Our current customer service representative doubled as Paul's assistant. But with the new demand placed on her, we quickly realized that we needed additional office help. So we hired another assistant that doubled for both Paul and our salesman which, freed up time for our customer service representative.

We also recognized that developing new distributor relationships took time. Paul initially was the natural person for this task, but with his time being monopolized by development chores, he was beginning to falter at his sales duties. We were finding it difficult to find the right sales person for the job, so we decided to hire a more experienced engineer to continue the development. This allowed Paul to concentrate more time on developing our distributor relationships.

With new positions being created, office space was becoming a problem. For years, there was a company that was subletting office space from us in our building. As luck would have it, they announced to us that they were moving, so the space was becoming available. Within days of their leaving, we expanded our office space to accommodate our new personnel.

We continued to make changes to improve our image and provide better service. Of course, all of this led to new layers of overhead costs. And increased fixed overhead increases the amount of sales volume required to break-even or make a profit. The pressure to increase sales volume mounted.

The next show always came quickly after the western show. It was always held in Myrtle Beach, S.C. I was pretty excited, since I had not visited there before, and I was an ocean buff. May in Myrtle Beach could mean some beachside R&R while the others played golf. That was fine by me.

I arrived very late the night before the show. Our plane was delayed in Charlotte, which is a great airport to wait out a delay. They always had a Dixieland band, or jazz band playing in the commissary. And they have these big white rocking chairs lining the food court -- the type of rocker that I imagined on a big southern porch.

The approach to Myrtle Beach was awful. The plane bounced and shook. Worse yet, I was in the very last seat of this completely full flight. I knew the weather was bad, but this was ridiculous.

When I arrived at my beachside hotel, I could hear the ocean pounding on the beach. When I opened my balcony door, the curtains flew in and I was peppered with salty spray. It was cold. Great. I finally get to Myrtle Beach and it's cold with gale-force winds. It figures. I turned on the Weather Channel only to find out that Myrtle Beach is the lead story and that the waves are near record levels. It's not good when you're the lead story on the Weather Channel. So I closed the balcony door and went to bed. Tomorrow was a big day.

I was staying at a different hotel than the rest of the crew, so I arrived at the show alone. It was a much smaller show than in Anaheim, but it didn't matter. We generated a ton of interest. By now,

I had an understanding of the equipment as if I was an engineer. And, I could practically anticipate the next question during the demonstrations, which provided a smooth sales delivery. I was becoming a salesman.

The day was going by fast. We had trouble-free operation of the machine, which was always my worry. Late in the afternoon as the show was slowing down, a man wandered into our booth alone. He avoided the others and approached me. I remember seeing him pass our booth several times during the day. He kept watching us, but kept a distance. His behavior seemed a bit strange, but I was happy that he was paying attention to our invention. He was a tall, handsome man, maybe in his late fifties. He was much better dressed than others at the show, not just better clothes, but better style.

He approached me with a smile and firm handshake. Like most other potential customers, he opened with a casual, "How does it work?"

I proceeded to provide a detailed demonstration, ensuring to highlight the features and benefits. I had to keep remembering to, "sell the sizzle and not the steak". It was a difficult concept for an accountant. The demonstration went well and I was pleased.

After the demonstration, I spent a great deal of time fielding questions about the company and my role within it. Since we were new to most of the industry, it was not unusual to field these questions. They were fair game, especially considering the price point of the equipment. This was not an impulse purchase, and the status of our company was important to ensure fiscal continuity.

But the questions he asked were a bit more detailed than usual. I typically anticipated the "How long have you been in business?" and "Where are you located?" type questions. This new inquisitor was more adept and profound. He asked questions like, "How strong is your working capital?"

Being a financial guy working in the confidential world of public accounting, I fielded the questions with relative ease. Anyone else in the booth would have floundered or declined to answer. Not me. I could provide just enough information to share a satisfying answer without divulging the confidential nature of our operations. I immediately liked this man. I could tell he had financial savvy. He knew his stuff, and was no stranger to the industry. What I remembered most, though, was the personal side of our conversation. He asked questions about me, where I was staying, what I liked about Myrtle Beach. It was refreshing. In the back of my mind, I thought it seemed a bit uncharacteristic of a trade-show conversation. But most people were already leaving to play hooky on the links, and these are the type of questions I like to ask of others, so I responded without worry.

When we were done, his firm handshake thanked me for my time. I grabbed two business cards from my new friend, one for our salesman for follow-up purposes, and one for me. I couldn't remember his name. Cheating, I glanced down at his card, shook his hand and thanked him for stopping by. Although I didn't say it, I was hoping that we could do business together. I liked him.

Almost an hour passed, during which time Paul and our salesman, Matt were busy demonstrating the other machine in the booth. We all had stories to tell and we were all anxious to share them. Paul went first, proudly listing the names of distributors that he met. Matt had a similar list, but was less enthusiastic. But before I could reveal my newfound friend, both Paul and Matt began laughing at me. I was pretty confused.

"Ha, you got stuck with Sid," Matt said with a grin.

"He was nice. You guys know him?" I asked.

"Sure," Paul said. "Everyone knows Sid."

"So what? He was really interested in the machine," I insisted.

Paul and Matt could not contain their laughter.

"What's so funny?"

"John, he's not a customer. He's not a distributor. He's no one. He just wasted your time," Paul told me.

Matt added, "When I saw him coming, I turned away and acted busy."

"Me too. I started reloading the machine," Paul said.

At first I was shocked and embarrassed. But the more I thought about my conversation, the more I didn't care what they thought. I liked Sid. He was the nicest guy that I met at any of the shows so far.

We closed down the show. As we cleaned up, the two cacklers continued to needle me about the big fish I reeled in. I ignored them.

By the time we left, the wind was again picking up, and the temporary blue sky was replaced with thick gray ominous looking clouds. So much for taking even a chilly stroll on the beach. Rain was on the way.

Since I was a late add to the show, I ended up staying at a different hotel than Paul and Matt. Paul came with me to my hotel, since it had a better bar. He also caught wind that several companies that he was courting were staying there, so the possibility of a "chance" encounter was eminent, especially since the rain was moving in and chasing the golfers off of the courses.

He was right. It didn't take long and the bar was full, and with people he wanted to see. Paul worked the crowd like it was the tradeshow floor. He was on top of his game. Each and every compliment or sign of interest was a validation to his ego. He was rightfully proud of his invention, and thrived on the attention and accolades. I mingled, but not with the same zest as Paul.

The waves were still pounding the beach and the flotsam was swirling all the way to the closed patio bar. Every now and then a gust of wind would toss sand mixed with rain against the glass doors. It kept grabbing my attention.

As Paul worked the bar, I sat back and enjoyed the success of the day. It felt good. Even the dreary weather could not dampen my spirit. I was confident that we hit the mark with our idea, and it was only a matter of time. My mind drifted as I listened to the "Wallflowers" pound out another song on the sound system.

The bar started to empty as folks made their way to their favorite restaurants. Paul was finally finished working the floor. Good for him, too, since he had a few in him by now. We sat together, enjoying one more drink and a few more songs.

As we were getting ready to leave, I noticed Sid sitting by himself at the other corner of the bar. That's odd, I didn't notice him before. I didn't even know he was staying at this hotel. I guess I never asked him during our conversation. I tapped Paul and secretly pointed in the direction of Sid. The bar was nearly empty now.

"Why don't you guys come over here and join me for one," Sid requested.

"Sure, Sid."

Paul and I walked over and sat down. I could tell Paul was not as enthusiastic as I was. As I started to introduce the two, they both interrupted me indicating that they had already made each other's acquaintance. Paul was pretty meek around Sid, which was a far cry from the zealous confidence that he exuded earlier.

"Gentlemen, what is your plan for this new machine?" Sid asked.

Paul and I looked at each other somewhat bewildered.

"We're going to sell a ton of them. The show went great," I replied.

"Really?" was Sid's quick reply. "How are you going to sell them?"

"Through distributors. A lot of distributors are interested in carrying the line."

I paused for a moment, inviting Paul into the conversation. I could tell Paul was not really too interested in discussing any of his excitement with Sid. So I continued.

"Once we get distributors set up, it should go pretty well," I said. "I anticipate good sales. People seemed to love it."

"I'll give you that," replied Sid. "It is a good concept. It should out-sell the market. How many can you build in a month?"

I didn't know. At this point we were still building prototype machines. For the most part we are ready to go into full production. But he wanted assembly numbers? We were not far enough along to know how fast we could build them. Heck, our costing was still estimated just so we could set our initial pricing.

"I'm not sure yet, Sid," I replied. "We currently make about 250 small machines a month. This line will eventually replace it and we still have capacity..."

Sid cut me off. "Do you know how many machines Standard can make in a day? They can make 1,000 machines a day."

After a pause long enough to light another cigarette, Sid continued, "How do you stop them from copying your idea?"

"Well, it's patented, so they can't," I said.

"Really?" Sid questioned. "Patented, or patent pending?"

"Well, it's pending, but our counsel is pretty confident that it should go through."

"Well, they are probably right and you're probably okay," Sid said with a smile.

"How much working capital do you guys have?" he asked.

Before I could answer, Paul jumped into the conversation. "Sid, I think we are set with money. We should be fine."

I was immediately ticked at Paul. I could sense the initial makings of a potential deal. This was the fishing part. I had been through this before and was well aware of where this conversation may go. This product idea was good, and we could be set up for an early buy out. I tried to recover.

"Sid, we are set for now, but funding fast growth could be tricky. What are you getting at?"

"Nothing. Besides, your partner is not interested, and he makes the decisions," Sid replied.

"That's not entirely true, Sid," I countered, again trying my best to fan the flame.

"Well, I have been known to raise capital and to broker deals in this industry. If a deal is going to get done in this industry, I will surely know about it. In fact, I have been involved in all the big deals over the last 15 years."

Paul was unimpressed, but my interest was really piqued. I continued to ask questions, and Sid continued to tell of his history of deals. I liked him before, but now that I learned he was a player, I really liked him. Paul sat next to me, eying the barmaid and smoking a cigarette. He was not interested and his body language shared that with Sid.

Finally, Sid waved over the barkeep and paid for all of our drinks. He smiled and shook my hand. He handed me another card, this one different from the first.

"Gentlemen, it was a pleasure. Call me anytime, John."

Sid shook Paul's hand and turned away.

Sid stopped for a moment, turned and looked at me. "John, that number is my home office, so I can be easily reached."

With that, he turned and walked out.

I waited a few minutes to be sure that he was out of the room.

"Paul, what do you make of that?" I asked.

"Nothing. He's a gold digger. He just wants to get in on our deal to make a fast buck. He can't be trusted. I don't trust him. He has a bad reputation." Paul snarled.

I didn't reply. I liked him, but maybe Paul was right. We left and went to dinner.

Chapter 9

The difference between stumbling blocks and stepping stones is how you use them.

--unknown

The new machine was a hit, and the orders were piling up. The last two shows generated a great deal of distributor interest and things were moving forward quickly. Just the demo unit requirements for the distributors were creating a backlog in the shop. On top of it all, the rest of our products were selling well, so we again had cash flowing pretty well.

The initial wave of distributors was not what I would consider the tier one level distributors. Like any industry, there are the absolute leaders, and then there is the rest of the pack. We were dealing with the pack, which wasn't all that bad. A fragmented distributor network was better than no distributor network at all.

The problem, however, was that many of these smaller distributors did not do that much volume since they did not have that many customer accounts. But most of these distributors viewed our machine as the way to attract new customers, so they hit the market hard.

Most of the distributors initially did a good job promoting our equipment. To assist our distributors, we launched a national advertising campaign covering the two prominent trade papers. The national advertising, coupled with our presence at trade shows gave our distributors more support than they were accustomed, which strengthened our budding relationships.

The first wave of machines went out without a hitch and our distributors were pleased. Through our advertising and sales efforts, we were turning new leads daily, in addition to the volumes of leads that we generated at the show. We were cautiously optimistic.

But once the first big wave of orders had been filled, the demand began to wane. That had not been expected. We figured that there would be a lull while the customers tested the machine in a location, but we figured the lull would be short-lived. After the lull, we expected another wave of orders, maybe bigger than the first wave. But the orders didn't come, and the short-lived lull dragged and dragged. In fact, it was not a short lull. It was a complete stoppage.

We continued to consult with our distributors to find the source of our woes. The answer was not very clear, but we disseminated the information as best as we could.

My initial concern was that our distributor network was not that strong. So we continued to look for holes or weak links in the network. Further, I had our salesman step up his involvement with sales training, ensuring that all of our distributors were aware of the features and benefits of our machine.

But the feedback from the distributors varied and was worrisome. If we were hearing consistent objections to the machine, we would able to cure the objection by addressing the concerns. But there was no common objection. In fact, the objections that were given were of such a wide variety, it began to sound like a list of excuses rather than legitimate objections.

For several months, the demand for the machine declined to the point that we were only shipping five or six a week. Worse, most of these machines were sitting in the inventory that we had built in anticipation of the second wave of orders that did not come.

Since the shop was busy with our other products, we were still cash flowing, but I could see that our working capital was starting to get thin. Our healthy profits were being eaten by our heavy national marketing campaign. But we could not stop the program. We needed to continue to make the market grow and help inspire demand for the machine. We needed to continue to look strong to support our dealer network and the end user.

Time moved quickly, and before long, we were at the next trade show. This time we were in Washington, D.C. This was a city that I was very familiar with since one of my largest accounting clients had a significant operation there, so I frequently visited. This trip was important for the future of the new project and I was on a mission to zero in on the primary objection in order to finally address and overcome it.

I spent the entire show in the booth demonstrating the machine. When I wasn't demonstrating, I was carefully listening to our salesman Larry or to Paul. I was documenting as much information as I could so we could later discuss what we learned.

At the end of each day, we would get together and share notes and information. We learned a ton. Many of the objections involved cosmetic changes to the machine, which were very easy to cure. Other objections involved functional design changes that would be helpful to the operator. But none of the objections that we were uncovering could be the reason for the sales lull. Of course the objections were important, and we immediately began prioritizing the list of modifications that we felt would be important to make to the machine.

By the end of the show, I was starting to figure out the primary objection to our machine, and it was very subtle. In fact, the objection was only indirectly related to our machine.

The most common question that came up during our demonstration was, "But does it really work?"

The yardstick in this business is simple. The machine must vend properly every time. If it does not vend the product, then the machine needs to refund the purchaser their money, or allow for another selection. This is known as a positive vend. The trouble starts when the machine eats the customer's money because that always ends badly. Typically, the customer will complain to management of the business where the machine is located. The problem with this is the machine is normally not owned or operated by management; it is normally owned by a vending machine operating company that is responsible for the maintenance, service and care. So, when management gets enough complaints, they fire the vending operator and hire a new one. This is bad for the operator.

The bigger problem is when a vending machine is located where there is no management nearby. This is when an angry customer will take out their frustration on the machine by beating on it. The damage that ensues from an angry customer will far exceed the cost of the money lost in the machine, but that's how it goes. The customer wanted a soft drink and they were already willing to pay a higher price than the supermarket price for the convenience of the vending machine. When the machine eats their money, anger is almost always the result. This is much worse for the operator because of the damage inflicted to the machine from the angry customer.

So when a vending machine does not work, the vending operator, which is our ultimate customer, suffers heavily. But our machine was working well, and I had evidence of that through our few, but happy customers.

The real problem with selling our machine was due to our competitor's machine. The machine that was bought by Standard Vending was still not working well. In fact, the stories about their machine's performance before Standard bought it were legendary in the industry. Their vending mishaps involved double vends, no vends, triple vends, broken bottles, and tampered machines. For a while, no matter what Standard did to improve the delivery, another unanticipated problem would develop. This went on for years. But they were still selling the machines, mostly because there was no other alternative for a glass-front vending machine. The big-time operators lived with the problems inherent in the Standard machine. They weren't happy about them, but accepted the problems mostly because the machines out-sold the regular vending machines by a product count of two to one at a higher profit margin. The positive economics outweighed the cost. Further, the bottlers were offering price support for the machines because ultimately they benefited from higher product sales.

This was not true for the smaller operator, and the smaller operator was our customer. The smaller operator could not assume the risk of a machine failing in the field. The risk of losing an account, or the cost of the damage to the machine could wipe out their entire business. And this group was damaged by the Standard machine debacle, so they were suspect of any other machine that vended bottles. Most of them could not afford another glass-front bottle dispenser disaster. This went on for a long time. In fact, we could not convince the operators that our machine worked and did not suffer from the same problems that plagued the competition.

All in all, the show in D.C. went well and again the orders picked up. We established new distributor relationships and successfully began filling in the voids in the map.

It wasn't long after the show that a large water bottling company approached us. They were interested in having us redesign the machine to accommodate different size bottles, up to quart size. A vending machine did not exist that could do this, but our machine could be modified to handle the peculiar task.

We went right to work. It didn't take us long to modify the machine, and soon after we were in production. The initial order was for 154 machines, which was seven truckloads. This was the biggest order that we had to date, and we were ecstatic that our luck was finally running in the right direction. The value of the order was just over $300,000. This was the break that we needed and we were in a position to deliver.

But there was more to the order than the money. We were finally breaking the identity crisis. When this order was filled, we would have a customer that was real. If we had great success with meeting the production requirements in the expected time frame, we would establish ourselves as a player. We desperately needed to succeed to continue to move the company forward and to create the credibility and identity that it needed.

We worked diligently at completing the order to specification. Handling the larger bottles was tricky and required significant modification, but a more important modification was the power supply. This order was being shipped overseas, so it needed to operate using 220-volt power, rather than the 110 volts used in America. This required the installation of a series of transformers and also required modification to our wire harnessing. I couldn't believe how well we performed in making the modifications. Maybe it was because of our roots as a custom job shop, maybe it was because we had matured as a manufacturer or maybe it was just luck. But no matter what the reasons were, the machines were manufactured perfectly to specification, and the order was on time.

Since the order was going overseas, we were shipping the order using international letters of credit. The way this worked was that we would ship the order by rail to the Baltimore port. Once there, a bondsman would inspect the order for completeness and issue the proper paperwork as evidence that the order was complete. Confirmation would then be sent to the customer, our company, and our banks. Then the containers would be loaded on the boat. Once this occurred, the customer's bank would release the funds to our bank, where they would remain in escrow until the order was received in Israel, the final destination of the order. When an acknowledgement was issued that the order was correctly received, the funds would be released from escrow, and we would receive our payment.

Since this was our first significant overseas order, we were pretty nervous. So we kept calling our customer throughout the entire process. In fact, we would call them pretty much every day while the order was in process, providing them production updates and revised estimated ship dates. Everything was going as planned, and we were developing a great relationship with our new international friends.

When we released the order to ship to Baltimore, we were having trouble reaching anyone in Israel about the final shipping confirmations. Not to worry as yet, the order had at least two days in shipping and customs before it was put on the boat, which by all means, was the point of no return.

And then it happened. The first bomb went off. And it was a real bomb.

Just as the order cleared customs, we were informed as to why our overseas friends became so elusive. They were all called into military service. As it turns out, the peace was breached in Israel again and every soldier was called to arms. As it turns out, we were dealing with a military base, so the priority for them was to protect their borders and their land. They could care less about our shipment of vending machines. Once I found out, all I cared about was getting our machines back.

I was at my office when I was notified. I quickly called the bank to stop the letter of credit transaction, figuring this would protect our equipment and allow us to recover our inventory. Since the order was already in customs, however, reclaiming the shipment was not so simple. After some quick talking and pressure from the bank, the order was released back to us. Since it appeared that the order could be held up for months, we decided to put the machines back on the train and figure out what to do when they arrived at the plant.

We had just invested $225,000 in a custom order of machines that could not be used in the U.S. and they were coming back to our dock. And so the first domino fell.

Chapter 10

Our greatest glory is not in never failing but rising up every time we fail.
--Ralph Waldo Emerson

Call it bad luck, call it karma, call it anything you want, the cancelled order was bad.

To foresee the biggest custom order for the company get cancelled because a violation of the peace accord is just not something that is taught in business school. The good thing was that we at least had the inventory back. We had no idea what we were going to do with it, however.

The only bright spot was that we were busy again with orders and the small-line machines were shipping like clockwork. But the hit to working capital was enormous. The loss of the anticipated $300,000 that was due in pretty much wiped out the remaining capital that we had. And we could not ship small machines fast enough to make up the loss.

To shore up our weakening financial condition, I again went to the well. This time, however, conventional bank financing was out of the question. Instead, I contacted an old banking acquaintance that I knew was working for an alternative lender, Lake Bank. Stan was his name and lending money was his game. He had a history of working for numerous area banks and was effective at spotting deals and getting them done. I think Stan lived to close banking deals and I liked Stan.

Up to this point, we had been a profitable company, but that was changing. In the early years, we were wildly profitable. The changes we made in purchasing coupled with the demand for the small-line machines and condiment stands, enabled us to hit high marks. Enter into the equation the cost of developing the new machines, and the profit began to wane. Add to that a national advertising campaign, supporting a national dealer network, an increase in our sales force, and now a major order cancellation, and our financial statements were now turning red. Red ink, that is.

So this was not an ordinary deal and fortunately alternative financing is not necessarily based on past performance. This type of financing serves a different need. There are numerous types of alternative financing and the type we were looking to obtain is known as mezzanine financing. This type of debt actually works more like equity and it allows a company to obtain working capital.

The basics of the financing are simple. The mezzanine lender is subordinated to the primary lender. So the debt is sometimes known as sub-debt. Because of the secondary position, the mezzanine lender does not have the right to foreclose on the company, even if they are not getting paid. Furthermore, the debt is generally unsecured by company assets because typically by the time a company gets to this point, most of the assets are completely leveraged or the company did not have any tangible assets in the first place.

Because of the risk involved, the interest rate is high. Very high. And on top of the interest rate, there is a success fee that gets charged when the loan is repaid. All told, financing like this will cost 22% to 30%, which is a far cry from the typical bank rates that are indexed slightly over the prime interest rate. Since most of the fees are charged in the end as a success fee, however, the cost is manageable in the short run.

Since the lender is basically becoming a partner in the business, the loan process is difficult and long. Fortunately for me, I had a formal business plan, financial projections, a marketing plan and one heck of a story for the lender. It was pretty easy to see that we were making all of the right moves, but we were simply under-capitalized at this point. Lake Bank really liked our company. And they especially liked our new machine. After they completed nearly two months of due diligence, they approved our loan for $500,000. Our deal called for interest-only payments on the debt of about 13% per annum, which was five points higher than our bank loan. Although the interest rate was high, the deal provided us with about $500,000 of working capital to remain in business and to absorb the misfortune of the cancelled order.

The problem for me was that the entire process took so long that we had two cash calls to keep the company going. All told, I loaned the company about $85,000 over the two-month period to cover payroll. And unfortunately for me, the condition of the deal from Lake Bank was that I was to leave the money in the company for at least one year, or until they indicated to me that I could repay myself. But, at this point, it didn't matter. We were again on our way and the future looked bright.

In fact, our story and our product quickly became the poster child for the bank. As the bank told its' story to potential customers, they told our story. And why not? It was a good story. The machines were selling, production was improving, and but for the cancelled order, we were getting back to normal in terms of profit and cash flow. Life was again good and the fallen domino was stopped in its tracks.

Chapter 11

Character is the sum and total of a person's choices.
--P.B. Fitzwater

While I was spending a good portion of my summer working with Lake Bank to secure additional financing, Paul was off gallivanting with the ladies.

Paul was always a playboy on the road. Although I had a hard time understanding it personally, it was none of my business. And, as long as his antics did not interfere with our business I really didn't care. I'm not sure why people behave in this manner, and I never took any time to learn. But in Paul's case, I believe it was his fragile ego that motivated him. His yearning for constant validation seemed most fulfilled by the comfort of strange women.

A lot was changing in Paul's life. Over the last few years, we went from an average process manufacturing job shop to a national company. We were becoming relatively successful. And Paul was a handsome, outgoing successful businessman. Unfortunately, everyone deals with success differently.

As we made more money, Paul's income naturally increased. But money didn't do it for him. Earning more money just meant that he and wife Cindy would spend it. Between the two of them, they could not keep $10 in their wallets for 10 minutes. Worse yet was the way it was spent. It always seemed as if the money was blown on nonsensical ideas or products that they did not need or were of little value.

But success was not his biggest enemy. Yes, I think his ego brought out the bad side of him. For Paul, having to deal with tough financial times was worse. When cash flow was tight at the shop and things not going our way, Paul almost withdrew. Since I am not a psychologist, I cannot even begin to tell you why. What I do know is that his ego needed constant validation. When he could not get it from success in the business, he turned to the outside. He turned to infidelity.

Up until this point, Paul's endeavors were limited to out of town trips. But over the summer he brought it closer to home. And since I was so busy organizing the new financing, I did not even notice the changes occurring in his life.

And then, I got the call.

"John, I need to see you right away."

"Why, what's up that's so important?"

"I can't tell you now. Meet me at Kendal's Bar at 5 after work."

"Paul, why can't you tell me over the phone, or why can't we just meet at the shop? I don't want to go to a bar tonight. Besides, I have too much to do."

"John, I'm asking you to meet me as friend. It has nothing to do with the business."

"Okay, Paul, I will see you there."

When I arrived at Kendal's, Paul was already nursing a beer. As I approached him, I could tell it was not his first.

"Hey Paul, what's the story?"

"Momma threw me out," he said.

"What?"

"Yup, momma threw me out. She caught on to me, John. What am I going to do?"

Although I was not shocked by his statement from knowing his past indiscretions, I was however, stunned by his reaction. I wanted to say to him "And you're surprised?" But I bit my tongue. Instead, I said nothing.

So he continued on. "She found a phone number in my shirt pocket. Then she called it. Pamela answered the phone. Then they talked. John, they talked!"

I was almost afraid to ask who Pamela was, but I took the bait. "Well, who's Pamela?"

"She's my girlfriend. I have been seeing her for almost two months. We're in love."

I sat there confused. Paul has a girlfriend that he believes he loves; yet he is broken up over his wife throwing him out? I was not prepared for this so I had no idea what to say. After a few minutes of silence, I summonsed the bartender. "I'd like a Jack on the rocks please."

As we sat in silence nursing our drinks, he began to spill his guts.

"I met her on the Internet. After a few weeks of emailing each other, we decided to meet. She loves me, John. She really does. And I love her. I can't stop thinking about her and I want to be with her all the time."

I couldn't take it anymore, so I interrupted him. "Well, then what is the problem? If you love her, why do you care that Cindy tossed you out? Do you still love her?"

"No."

I knew that Paul's kids were grown, but I asked anyway. "Are you worried about your family?"

"No."

Now I was really confused. Not having too much to say about the situation, I tried to change the subject a bit.

"So, where are you going to stay?"

"Well, I have been sleeping at the shop."

Surprised by his response, I replied, "When did all of this happen?"

"Two days ago. I was afraid to tell you."

"Why?"

"Because this is going to mess everything up. You know, she owns half of my shares directly in her name. Now she wants a divorce and wants to remain a shareholder. She wants to see all of the records. This is going to be a big mess."

I looked at him, shaking my head. "Paul, you really don't do things the easy way do you?"

After a pause, I continued. "It doesn't make a difference to me, Paul, how the shares are owned or if she wants the records. She is certainly entitled to see them and I am happy to oblige. Have her call me."

Just like that, Paul's personal life became my burden. Although I seemed unfazed by any of this, I did agree with Paul that this could be a monkey wrench in the works. I was not concerned about her or the company, but rather I was more concerned how the banks would view this new tidbit of information. Especially since I just spent the last two months courting our new mezzanine lender.

I asked Paul, "So what are you going to do now? You can't keep sleeping at the shop."

"No, I can't. I have a friend that owns a couple of apartment buildings. He said he could set me up on a month-to-month basis just in case this all blows over."

Rather optimistic, I thought.

"But I don't have any furniture."

Trying to remain supportive, I gave him the name and number of a very close friend of mine, Bill Johnson, in the furniture rental business. They were specialists at short and long term rental and leasing of furniture.

With that we finished our drinks and made our way.

The next day Paul called me to get the name and number for Bill the furniture guy that he had lost the night before.

"Will this Johnson guy really help me out? And will he have everything I need?" Paul asked.

"Sure he will," I responded. "Johnson's the biggest and best in the business. He'll have your apartment furnished by the end of the day. Call him, or go see him now."

About two hours went by and the phone rang at my office. It was Johnson.

"John, Bill Johnson here. I want to thank you for the referral. Paul just left and I have to tell you, that was one interesting deal. What a nice guy, but man, is this guy insane?"

"Bill, what happened? What did he do now?"

I was almost afraid to find out. But Bill was more than happy to enlighten me.

"Paul came in here to pick some furniture and he starts to tell me the whole story about getting tossed from the house. And get this; he brings his girlfriend with him. As he's telling me the story, as if I really care to hear it, she is sitting next to him consoling him and rubbing his back. I was thinking, man, get a room."

"So that's it?" I interrupted.

"No way, it gets better. So when we were done working up the rental agreement and getting the delivery information, he turns to the chick and says, 'What do you want to get, honey?' I was surprised because he already selected enough furniture for his apartment. She then turns to him and kisses him on the nose, and says 'I'll get everything you got, big boy.' So I start to write up the order. When I asked for the delivery address, it turns out that Paul rented her the apartment right next door!"

My head almost hit the desk as I was listening. What is going on in this guy's mind?

Bill continued, "John, are you getting all this?"

"Yeah, Bill, and I'm sure there is more."

"Oh yeah, absolutely. So I had to ask him why they were renting separate apartments. His response was unbelievable. John, he told me that living with his girlfriend would be wrong because he is still married. I'm telling you, John, I was floored. That's the funniest thing I heard in a long time. He can't live with the girlfriend, but could set her up in the apartment next door."

I was floored, too. We have a company that is floundering, he is tossed out of the house and what does he do? He sets up house with his girlfriend.

Paul's behavior was beginning to show signs of self destruction and I was getting more concerned.

Chapter 12

The best ideas are common property.
                                                    --Seneca

Time seemed to move faster and faster. Before long we were back in Vegas for the national show. We had financing in place and we were continuing to build the machines and strengthen our distributor network.

We were all pretty hyped for the show. In fact, our machine was proving to be the best for delivering milk products, so we pulled out every stop to present that strong selling point. And we stopped at nothing. We had our machines painted to look like big heifer cows and everyone involved, including our distributor network wore cow-print ties. We looked like a bunch of fools, but it got the buzz going and that's what it's all about sometimes.

The show proved to be fantastic for feedback from the field. The machines had been out for better than a year, so enough time had passed to allow for the equipment users to provide meaningful feedback.

Up until then, most of the objections we heard we either trivial, like the location of the coin changer, or projected issues of failure based on the failure of our competitor's machine. But our machines were working and we were not getting mis-vend information.

But, the big objection finally did surface: our machine was hard to load. In fact, many smaller or female operators had a difficult time lifting a full rack to take it out of the inclined delivery position. Like most vending machines, gravity does a great deal of the work. Our particular design required that the delivery shelf be lifted to a horizontal position to load. Then, the old product needed to be unloaded, the fresh product loaded to the back, and then the old product loaded again to the front. This was problematic for both us, and our competitor. But the advantage our competitor had was that they did not need to lift the shelves.

For the most part, it was only a problem for the top shelf of the five, but it was a serious objection that up until now, we were not able to overcome.

I have always had the belief that you cannot be all things to all people. Although I knew that this objection would cause the loss of some sales, we still had a very good machine that worked well and was priced right.

A bigger issue that was looming, however, was the required product rotation for vending milk. Most of the milk companies were concerned that the vending operators were skipping the product rotation part when filling any of the glass-front machines. Although this was truly an issue for the operator, the milk companies were concerned because they had the product liability. What they really wanted was a foolproof way to force natural product rotation.

After listening to two days of the exact same objection, Paul and I were feeling pretty dejected. We were getting sales, but the overriding objection of the shelves was demoralizing.

But we also could not stop thinking about the milk companies' concern about product rotation. We decided to have dinner alone that night instead of entertaining customers so that we could brainstorm some ideas.

We ended up at a Japanese steakhouse that was simply fantastic. Throughout dinner, we tossed out all kinds of ideas – ideas to reduce the weight of the shelves, or the addition of levers, springs or coils. You name it; we considered it. We had numerous ideas to make the shelves lift easier, most of which would work. All we needed to do was engineer the most economical method and have it ready to go by the next show.

When we were done eating, we moved from our table to a small table in the bar. We were feeling better that we could remove the primary objection to the machine and it was time to relax.

As I sat at the table waiting for a fresh Jack on the rocks, I began nervously spinning my napkin in front of me. As if we both realized it at the very same moment, Paul exuberantly shouted, "That's it!"

And I quickly chimed in, "Bring the back to the front!"

What a fantastic idea. Have the back of the machine face the front to load. All we needed to do was install our rack system on a turret that would allow the whole delivery system to turn around. We were really on to something.

We could not contain our excitement.

For the next three hours, we sketched the concept and constructed flat models using napkins and pieces of paper. It did not take long to realize that size was going to be an issue. The space required to turn a square inside of a rectangle was going to either increase our cabinet size or significantly cut the bottle capacity. Since capacity was always a key issue, the cabinet size would likely end up the compromise. As we continued to mess around with the concept, we continued to identify more design issues. Because of the size, we would need a bigger compressor for the refrigeration. We also would need to completely redesign the wiring harnesses for the electronic delivery system. And we needed to think about the dimensions to allow the machine to get through a standard doorway.

The concept was fantastic, but we started to realize this was not simply an upgrade to what we had. We really were inventing an entirely new machine. This was going to take time and a lot of capital.

We agreed that we would not share this idea with anyone until we had completed the patent search. I left the restaurant feeling refreshed and drained all at the same time.

The next day went by quickly. Paul and I both brought our "A" games and we booked a lot of orders. I could not stop thinking about the previous night and the idea. I also could not stop thinking about just how well Paul and I worked together on projects. When we were on together, it was fantastic. We thrived off of the creativity of each other and never slowed down to determine whose idea was best. We just kept fanning the flames of creativity to arrive at solutions. We were a good team, and I began to feel good about the prospects of the future.

As the show was winding down, I was able to secure a lead for the custom "Israel" machines that sat in the back of our warehouse. The initial terms of the deal pretty much got us out even, but to recover $230,000 of cash out of inventory that was nearly unusable was a major victory. So we found the funding for developing the new machine.

I was beginning to like Las Vegas.

Chapter 13

There is nothing worse than aggressive stupidity.
                              --Johann Wolfgang von Goethe

Developing the new machine brought new life to Paul. His energy could be felt throughout the shop, and as a result we were a better company.

It didn't take too long to have a working prototype. Conceptually, all we were doing was taking the machine that we had and building the cabinet bigger to provide enough space for the delivery area to rotate. In true form, we over-built the machine to avoid failure in the field.

The initial prototype was pretty crude, but it proved that we could make it work. Paul teamed with our computer designer to make all of the parts, and the two of them worked tirelessly through the summer.

Most of the issues, including getting the wiring harnesses to work, were coming together. Once we had a second working model, we were able to test the reliability. For the most part, everything worked well. The last big hurdle was testing the airflow so that we had even cooling. Refrigeration and airflow was an area where we trailed other companies, so we outsourced most of this engineering to a specialist. The consulting company was able to specify exactly what we needed. Unfortunately, we had hoped for a different result. The refrigeration would require a completely different compressor than we were using, which was a concern because of the amount of compressor inventory we already had in stock.

We faced the same issue with the electronics and wiring harnesses. Both the electronic circuit boards and compressors were custom engineered, thus they needed to be built to our specs. Custom orders took time, and generally required sizable quantities to gain any price breaks. Accordingly, we had to stock a pretty hefty supply of both of these expensive items.

One of the many keys to releasing the new model was to be sure that we used up the entire compressor and circuit board inventory because they could not be returned for credit.

Meanwhile, production on the current model was pretty steady. Additionally, we were busy with the small-line equipment and condiment stands, so the shop was operating at a high capacity.

As the summer wore on, the development continued. Just like watching a house being built, the project took a quick quantum leap, and then it seemed to slow to almost a stop. Every small detail that pops up through the process needs to be addressed, and each one seemed to take countless hours. Every change required new computer drawings, new machine programs, and manufacturing test runs. Then, each new part needed to be added to the prototype and vigorously tested for proper operation. All in all, it is a very tedious process.

Most of the detailed drawing and machine programming was handled by Brad, our inside programmer. And while Brad was busy refining the prototype, Paul started to stray again from the shop. The biggest part of the concept design was done, and I could tell Paul was getting bored. He was ready to move into production, but I knew that would not fly since we had so many details to work out. We were at least one year away from releasing this machine.

I could tell that Paul was frustrated with me because I kept the target release date on the wall, and I made it a point to remind everyone involved of the goal. Although it seemed like an eternity to Paul, I knew that a year would go by in warp speed and we would be lucky to hit the intended date.

It was becoming time for us to get our normal bookcase order that ran for about two months. The project was pretty easy for us since we did it for at least 12 years to this point. Although it did not fit the long term plans for our company and it took up a tremendous amount of space and resources, it was a very nice project. The profit that we made from this, and the quick cash flow turn was worth the headaches it caused the production managers. And, with the tight cash flow that we were again faced because of the new machine development, the job was a welcome relief.

As time passed, I was curious as to why the job wasn't running, so I called Paul.

"Hey Paul, what's with the book case order?"

"We're not doing it this year."

"Why not?"

"We didn't get the job."

I was shocked. We had run the job for so long, I don't know why they would not have placed the order with us. So I prodded Paul for the reason.

"John, we didn't get it and that's it. I think our prices were too high."

As I hung up the phone, I though about the impact on our cash flow by not having that automatic profit.

I decided to call the rep that we used to get the job. I had developed a relationship with him over the years and felt comfortable asking him directly where we went wrong.

It took a few tries, but I eventually got him on the phone. "Jerry, I have a question, why did we lose the book case order?"

"Lost it? Paul didn't even bid it! Ticked me off to no end, John. That's an important job for me and I can't believe you guys let me out high and dry."

I said nothing.

He went on, "I had to scramble like crazy to place the job. In fact I had to eat two percent myself just to keep it. I ought to sue you over this."

"Jerry, I'm sorry. I had no idea that this even went down. I have nothing to say, but I'm sorry."

"Yeah, John, you should be. It's doing things like this that burns bridges. In business you don't get too many bridges. And I have a long memory."

It took me 10 seconds to call Paul.

"Paul, why is it we lost the job?"

"John, let it go. It doesn't concern you, this is about the shop."

"Bull crap, it doesn't concern me. How are we supposed to cash flow through the next year to develop the new machine?"

"Well, someone undercut our price. There is nothing I can do about that now," Paul lied.

"Oh really? That's not the story Jerry told me. He said you did not put in a bid."

Paul was silent.

He then jumped down my throat. "What are you doing checking up on me? It's none of your business."

"It's all my business, Paul. I have a right to be included in these decisions. Why didn't you bid it?"

"We don't have the space. We have way too much going on. I want to have the machine ready for Dallas in November."

I was stunned by his answer. But I was happy that he was finally being honest, and that he was letting me in on his secret.

"Paul, there is no way that we can have the machine ready. Even if we can have the prototypes ready, we can't introduce it yet. It will kill the orders for the current model. We have to wait until we have the machine perfected and in production. We need to test it in the field. We talked about this already."

Paul was indignant. He was dead set on releasing the machine in a few months. We were not even close to being ready for production. There were all kinds of issues with the machine that needed to be solved. Besides, sales were going well on the current model. My attitude was: Why rush?

"There is just too much going on, John. We couldn't do the book case job."

If that was the case, and the decision was arrived at with careful analysis and consideration, I would have been okay with it. The problem was that the decision was unilateral and made without considering all of the consequences.

Every decision in a company affects everything else. Small business, especially manufacturing, is a delicate balance of resource allocation and cash flow. For the last couple of years, we have been walking a tight rope of cash flow brought on by a continuing flow of uncontrollable circumstances. Now we were starting to make bad controllable decisions to sabotage our own future.

I finally responded, "Paul, so just how do you think we are going to cash flow through the development? I had the book case job in our financial projections. So now what do we do?"

"Well, that's your job, John. I guess you have your work cut out for you."

After we hung up, I reran the projections considering the newly introduced variable. We were going to be out of cash in nine months.

That evening, I reflected on the events of the day. I could not understand Paul's decision. I couldn't understand his unilateral approach. We always made these decisions together. The sudden change in behavior had me worried. We were working so well together on the new machine. Everything was coming together. We even had a rough marketing plan in the works with a new slogan..."Turning Things Around"...well, okay, it was rough. But we were on track.

But once again, the balance of our success was hanging on the ledge. And once again it will be a race to not run out of cash.

This was getting old.

Chapter 14

Real knowledge is to know the extent of one's ignorance.
--Confucius

By the end of summer, Paul's personal life got worse. He was still living in his apartment with his girlfriend living next door. On occasion, he would go home to his wife and do maintenance work around the house. And after a couple of weekends of helping, he seemed eager to move back in and start anew.

I had suggested several times that they should try counseling, but I could not convince either one that it was worth the effort.

I could tell that Paul's personal life was gnawing at him. So I did everything that I could to keep him focused on the business. The next show was critical to our success, so I needed to keep him focused on the machine development.

After a few weeks, he announced that he was moving back in with Cindy and that he was changing his life. He recognized that his family was the most important part of his life and he was going to live up to that expectation.

I was pleased about his epiphany, but didn't believe it. What I did know is that Paul worked better when he was pretending to be a family man. And we needed his focus, so I went along with the illusion.

The show in Dallas was proving to be one of the biggest yet. The industry was growing and new ideas were always rumored throughout the industry either by word of mouth or the trade rags.

Our secret was silent, though. We did everything we could to keep the new idea quiet until we arrived.

I was still ticked at Paul for forcing the issue of bringing the new machine. But at this point, I had no choice but to go along. Furthermore, I needed to do my best to sell the concept, so I completely bought in to what we were doing. Besides, we had no hope of success if there was dissension among us.

In my heart I knew that this idea would be a hit. The entire concept really was strikingly simple. My fear was the loss of business in the meanwhile.

For the show, we brought two of our standard machines, one of which was painted like a cow to attract the attention of milk companies. The plan was to set up the turret machine in the middle as our flagship. We made "Coming Soon" signs to remind our visitors that the machine was still a concept that we were developing for future release. I wanted to be sure we promised delivery far enough into the future to get buyers to overlook that machine and place orders for the machines we were producing. We needed to keep the cash flow coming and we needed to deplete the inventory of custom-built compressors, circuit boards and wiring harnesses.

Our booth location was not very good. We were at the back of the show hall. The only redeeming facts were that we were on the end of the aisle and we were close to the restrooms. If nothing else, people would see us when they took a break.

Our initial design was still receiving accolades, and we found out a week before the event that it would be showcased in the front of exhibition hall. Fortunately, that made up for our lousy booth location because everyone visited the machine showcase, which then provided the location of our booth.

The show started pretty slowly for us. To boost things a bit, I walked the show looking for our distributors to invite them to see the new concept.

It did not take long to quickly become the talk of the show.

After only an hour or so, we were swamped. Everyone wanted to see what we designed. The product rotation issue was well known in the industry, and everyone knew that whoever solved this issue would have the complete competitive edge. And we were it.

The day was going by in warp time. The interest in the turret machine provided the opportunity to introduce our current machine to distributors that had yet to see it in action.

We had the original machine pretty much perfected. The few issues that arose over time had since been solved, and the feedback that we received on our reliability was very good, and very encouraging.

But it was hard to keep people's interest in our regular machine. Their attention was always turned to the turret machine, which we gave the model name Clearview 45-R. Clearview was our product name, 45 stood for the number of selections, and the R was for revolving.

At the end of the day, Dale Kohn finally arrived. He was easily our biggest distributor. We told him that we were unveiling a new machine at the show and he was pretty excited to see our invention.

"Dale, it's nice to see you," I said as we shook hands.

"John, likewise."

Dale looked over our booth and said nothing. At the moment he walked up, we had at least 15 visitors crowded around the turret, watching a complete demonstration put on by Paul. Matt, our salesman, stood on the periphery quietly answering questions from the folks in the back of the crowd.

Dale appeared shocked.

"John, has it been like this all day? This many people?" he asked.

"This is nothing. Dale, I'm telling you, it was more crowded earlier. In fact, we have been so busy, none of us even took a lunch break today."

"I really can't see what you did. Does the whole thing rotate?"

"Yep, that's exactly what it does. If you want product rotation, rotate the product! It's that simple, Dale."

Dale looked very excited. He knew that he could sell this machine. And he knew that he could make a nice profit doing so.

"What are people saying, John?"

"You know Dale, I have not heard the feedback. I have been working the milk machines trying to get some sales. The R is not ready yet, so demonstrating it is helpful, but it's not making us any money yet. My focus is on the here and now, which is still this machine," I said, pointing to the cow-covered model.

"Yeah, but John, this is a hot idea. I'm interested in the feedback."

Dale continued to gauge the interest.

After a while, the crowd began to thin as the demonstration came to a close. Dale started to make his way to the front. I followed him.

"Paul, what's the story on the new machine?" he asked.

Paul turned around upon hearing Dale's voice. "Dale, I'm glad you're here. Check this out."

Paul was totally on his "A" game. He was happy and excited, which made for even more electricity in our booth. He started to show Dale the machine.

After about 10 minutes of explanation, Dale stood back and exclaimed, "Gentlemen, I think you nailed it. This is fantastic! It is so simple."

Paul, Matt and I smiled at each other. We knew we did it.

Dale then asked, "How did you guys think of this?"

Paul answered quickly. "It was simple, John and I just needed a couple of drinks and a steak."

We all laughed. Dale shot back, "Well, I'm buying the steaks and drinks when this thing is released. When is the release date?"

Before I could say anything, Paul blurted out, "Six weeks!"

And that was it. We were screwed.

We were really, really screwed.

Dale seemed almost as surprised by the comment as I was. I could tell by the look on his face that he was not happy with Paul's exuberant response. And why should Dale be happy? He had an inventory of Clearviews in his warehouse, marketing material, and a pipeline of potential orders. He knew what I knew. If you release the product too soon, you run the risk of quality problems. Furthermore, you can kill the pending orders.

Dale's excitement waned.

"Paul, are you sure that this machine will be ready?"

"Absolutely."

"Has it been field tested yet?" Dale asked.

"It will be. Besides, it is essentially the same machine as the 45, so the process should go quickly," Paul responded.

Dale shook his head in disagreement. "I'll start selling it when I know for sure that it works. I can't take the risk of failures in the field. I will lose all credibility with this line. It took a long time to get here and I'm not interested in starting at the beginning again."

I recalled that Dale was one of our first distributors. He was always a big supporter of our machines, going all the way back to Long Beach when we introduced the 18-select model.

He was one of the companies that agreed to field test the initial models we made. The initial models did have problems. The type of problems you cannot predict until the machine is in heavy use. We learned together and worked to fix the problems. And for that we gave Dale a discount off of the machines since he acted as a guinea pig for us.

Defending his position, Paul chirped, "You'll see, Dale. The machine will be ready in six weeks and the orders will come flying in."

Dale smiled and said, "I hope so gentlemen. The idea is fantastic. But I'm not convinced it's ready."

"It will be Dale. Just wait."

I was silent throughout the banter. I could not stop thinking about the implications of Paul's promise. There was no way the machine would be ready in six weeks. It is unlikely that it would be ready in six months. I learned that lesson with the first machine, but it was obvious that all that was lost on Paul.

The show was coming to an end for the day, and it was finally time to get off of my feet.

As I was starting to lock up the machines, I noticed a familiar face standing across the isle. It was Sid.

He approached me as the lights were dimming in the exhibition hall.

"What do you have there, John?" Sid asked as he reached for my hand.

Shaking his hand, I responded, "We have the future of bottle vending, Sid."

Smiling, he politely asked, "Can you show me how it works?"

"Sure, Sid. Let me get the key from Paul. He locked the machine already."

Paul was already walking out, not wanting to have anything to do with Sid. I shouted to him for the keys. Paul quickly turned and tossed them to me. As he walked away he shouted "Call me at 7 and we'll get dinner."

I caught the keys and said nothing.

"Sid, you are really going to like this," I said. I was smiling. Why not?

Sid could sense my excitement, but showed no reaction to my comment.

I knew that I only had a few minutes to give him the quick overview. While I was talking, I could tell that Sid was impressed with the concept.

After about five minutes of quick talking and demonstrating, I asked, "Do you have any questions?"

"Just one. When are you guys going to get smart and work with me? I could save you a lot of trouble trying to get this to market."

It was not quite the question I was anticipating. I could not come up with one of my usual quick quips. Instead I said nothing.

Sid then continued, "John, this is a great idea. But you are going to need help to get this project off the ground. You are entering a whole new game with this and you don't know the half of what you are getting into."

I was curious as to what he meant, but I was too embarrassed to ask him to explain.

I finally responded, "Well, I think we are going to do well. We had a great day today. The response has been overwhelming."

Sid agreed, "This will be a big hit."

He then handed me another business card.

"John, call me anytime if you need me. Don't wait too long, though."

"Thank you, Sid."

With that, he walked away. I finished closing up the booth and made my way back to the hotel. I could not stop thinking about Sid's comments. I recalled his comments from one of our first meetings, when he spoke about knowing everything that is going on in the industry. I began to suspect that he was right, and that he knew we were struggling financially. Maybe it was a guess, or maybe it leaked somehow. But in any event, I felt certain that he knew.

The hotel we were staying at had a fantastic pool and spa. My feet hurt from standing all day, so I decided to dip them into the spa. As I approached the door to the pool, I could hear Paul's laughter. He was already soaking in the water with a drink in his hand.

"John, you made it. I was worried that you would be stuck with Sid all night."

Everyone in the spa started laughing, as if they were all aware of Paul's disdain for Sid. I couldn't understand it, though, because I did not recognize any of the faces.

"Everyone, this is John. John, meet everyone."

"Hi, John," was the collective greeting.

Paul was excited. He could not stop telling everyone about the new machine. Most of the people in the spa were attending the show, so I suppose it was a good thing. I just don't remember Paul ever being this excited.

I wanted to confront him on his premature delivery date, but I quickly realized that this was not the time or place. Instead, I decided to have a drink and relax.

After about 15 minutes, I could tell that one of the ladies in the water was getting interested in Paul. And Paul did not hide his interest in her. Before long, they became a couple. As if the others knew what was happening, they started to leave one by one. I jumped out of the spa and sat on the edge with my feet in the water.

As the last visitor left, Paul and his new friend were completely engulfed in their private conversation of lies. I saw our salesman, Matt sitting by himself enjoying the evening, so I decided to join him.

After one more drink, Matt and I left to get some dinner, leaving Paul behind with his prey.

The next day came quickly after an easy night of dinner and relaxation. It was nice to spend time with Matt and to get his perspective on the direction of the company.

Once the show opened, it only seemed to take minutes for our booth to become full. In addition to distributors and operators, we were mobbed by reporters from the various trade rags, as well as some local newspapers that were covering the events of the show.

We were photographed and interviewed. Paul was in his glory. All of this attention was perfect for his ego. We were so busy; he did not even have the time to tell me about his exploits of the previous night. For that, I was thankful.

Later that morning, a local television news station came by our booth to get some video shots of the machine in action. They were more impressed by the bottles falling and not breaking and the cow paint job than they were by the natural product rotation our machine was soon to offer. It didn't matter. Publicity is publicity, and we would take it any way we could get it.

The morning went by in minutes.

By the afternoon, I was getting more and more inquiries as to the release date. It seemed there was a bunch of misinformation about it. Ignoring Paul, I was still telling people that it was six to eight months away in the hope of closing a sale for the standard machines. On the other hand, Paul was continuing to promise six weeks.

After a while, I was getting people back in the booth asking for clarification. Then it started to happen. My worst nightmare became a reality. Orders for the regular machine were starting to cancel.

By three o'clock that afternoon, Matt and I each lost orders. Several orders were for 12 units, one order was for 48 units. The reason was simple: they wanted to wait for the R to be released.

With Paul's big mouth spouting off, there was nothing I could do to make the deals work. I even tried price breaks and on-the-spot show specials. Nothing would work. It made sense because the R was a much better concept. But the customers did not know what I knew. There was no way the machine could be ready.

We started to slow down in the afternoon, so I finally had a chance to confront Paul. At this point, there was little use because so many of our pending deals were already foiled. But I still felt the need.

I pulled him aside and said, "Paul, we need to talk about delivery dates."

"There is nothing to talk about John, I will have to get the machine ready. They love it. They love us! We're the hit of the show!"

"Paul, I know that, but we are making a big mistake. Let's have dinner tonight and talk this through. We are losing orders."

"We're not losing orders, they are just switching them to the R. It's even better!"

I could tell that there was no reasoning with him. His ego was a five-alarm fire and no one was going to douse it now.

"What about dinner?" I asked.

"No can do. I have a date with Lisa," he said.

"Who is Lisa?" I asked as if I didn't already know.

"She's my girlfriend. I met her last night in the pool."

Some things never change. Paul was getting annoying. At this point, he was still claiming he wanted to be married, yet living with his girlfriend, who he was now cheating on with his new "girlfriend" Lisa.

I was not impressed. I was not happy. In fact, I was fairly ticked off.

The rest of the show was busy. The excitement of the new machine was overshadowed by Paul's ego and antics. At some point during the show, it became all about him. He was oblivious as to what impact he was having on the company, nor did he care. He was in the spotlight and was happy.

I tried to get excited about the prospects of the new machine. I knew it was a fantastic idea and I knew that it was our future. I knew that it would save the company. I also knew that it could be the death of us. I wanted to be happy. I wanted to be excited. But I was not.

I was disappointed that Sid did not come by to get a full demonstration. I thought I saw him walk past our booth a couple of times, but I was not sure.

By the end of the show, we had won the attention of the media, the distributors, the operators, and the competitors. But we did not have one order for our current machine that was in production. Every order we did have had been cancelled. Instead, we went home with $400,000 of orders for a machine that was not yet in production.

We were in real trouble.

Chapter 15

Occasions are rare; and those who know how to seize upon them are rarer.
                                                                  --Josh Billings

The aftermath of the Dallas show was bad. We did not hit the six-week delivery schedule as promised. Additionally, the only orders we could muster for the regular machine were deals that were already in the pipeline, or from customers that did not attend the Dallas trade show. Sales were thin and so was the cash flow.

And then a new problem started to emerge: the original machines that were sold as demonstration units were being shipped back from distributors. Since the new line was out, they were no longer interested in selling the old machines, and instead wanted credit toward a new demonstration unit. This really began to complicate things.

We were still selling the small-line machines and condiment stands, but not at the previous pace. I could sense that the economy was already beginning to slow, but it was not yet that obvious to the marketplace. No one could see it yet. Or maybe no one wanted to admit it yet. We just kept looking inward to improve sales not recognizing the outside forces that were starting to work against us.

Since most of our attention was going to the new machine, we spent little to no time working with the small machines. In fact, we simply filled the orders as they came over the fax. I would be surprised if Paul or Matt called upon the customer once a month. This was bad business, but we were left with little choice, as we were strapped for time. Our resources were as thin as our capital, and we knew the future was the new machine. The price point was higher, the profit per machine was higher, and the future outlook in terms of product demand was greater. So we pushed forward.

Meanwhile, the quality of the smaller machines was starting to slip. And the costs were starting to rise. The cash flow from each machine was thinning. Further, the warranty claims started to pile up from the quality issues. This area of the business was becoming a problem because we were not keeping our eye on the ball. The cost of the freight on a replacement machine pretty much killed the profit on the sale, let alone the return freight on the original machine. The other choice was to dispatch a repairperson. That never proved to be economical, unless the problem was previously diagnosed, which was rare. The real looming problem was the distributors unhappiness with our performance, and our seeming unwillingness to address the issues. The problems and unhappiness continued to percolate.

We were also starting to feel pressure from the distributors waiting for the R. We had commitments for orders, and most of these machines were already pre-sold by the distributors. So our neglect was causing them grief with their customers. It is never a good policy to over-promise.

We were four months past due on producing the 45-R. Cash flow was lousy and the attitude in the plant was worse. We were operating only one shift a day, so our $1.5 million of equipment sat idle two-thirds of the time. Even if we could keep the first shift operating at optimum capacity we could break-even at best. And we couldn't even keep the first shift consistently busy.

Paul finally succumbed to the pressure and started to release the 45-R without a thorough field test. His belief was that since the components were essentially the same as the current machine, not much could go wrong.

At this point, I hardly put up a fight because I knew the cash flow was so strained, I was just happy to get orders out the door. I felt relieved, yet I was pretty worried.

But the orders were small orders. The cancelled commitments for 12 Clearview machines were replaced with "trial" orders of two 45-R machines. So the economics did not match up. Because the machine was new, no one wanted to stick his or her neck out too far on unproven technology. Everyone still remembered the Standard debacle of previous years, and wisely, no one would fall for that again.

After about two months, the orders slowed down while the machines were field-tested. To my surprise, the results were actually pretty good. The machines were working and the operators were happy with the ease of loading.

The milk companies were really starting to take notice. We were gaining inquiries almost daily. We eventually got lucky and landed a large dairy in New Jersey that ordered ten test machines. If they liked the test models, they indicated that they would order about 200 machines for a new school program that they were unveiling. The optimism was starting to reappear.

But as time went on, others in the industry sensed that we were having financial difficulty. And the worries seemed to again slow down the orders, making the situation even worse. We had used most of the mezzanine debt to finance the turret machine prototypes and the ensuing advertising and marketing campaigns. Further, the sales we did have were not enough to offset the losses we sustained over the four-month drought brought on by the Dallas show.

By the time the spring Las Vegas show came around, we recognized that we would need financial help. Based on my projections, if the show was a success we would run out of cash by summer. We did not have enough working capital to support the growth in accounts receivable. And our payables were already stretched a bit from the winter slow down. All indications were that we needed to act fast, since raising capital at this stage of the game takes time. Time, which we did not have.

Over the last couple of years, we grew pretty close to several of our distributors. For the most part, they recognized that we had a great product idea, and that once we really perfected the machine, they could turn a nice profit from the sales.

In fact, several of the distributors recognized that we were struggling a bit and helped by placing orders and prepaying for the equipment. The rationale was simple, they couldn't sell our product without us, and so they wanted to help keep us alive. For that, we were thankful.

Just before the Vegas show, we received a call from Brit Brooks, a sales manager at one of our largest distributors. He suggested to Paul that we meet with a gentleman that can raise capital. Paul was receptive and summonsed me right away to plan a strategy. Since Paul always liked to meet face to face about critical issues, I drove to the plant at a moments notice for the discussion.

After our deliberation, we recognized that we had no other choices than to take the next step. I recognized right away that any deal we do now will cause a reduction in ownership. And I knew it would be a big reduction. The next round of borrowing was purely "at-risk" capital for the lender. In fact, the reality was it was capital we were trying to raise, not debt. There was nothing left to leverage but blue sky. And this type of deal comes at a great price.

Paul was unconvinced. He still believed that someone would open their checkbook, provide us with another million dollars, take a subordinated third position to both the bank and the mezzanine lender, all for an interest rate return or a minimal ownership interest position. He was not dealing in reality. He was so convinced that our product was that good, and that anyone in the industry would do it. I gave up arguing. I figured that he would see soon enough how these deals work. The angels earn their moniker for the role they play to the company, not because of some sense of greater good and generosity. In fact, most angel deals are more like deals with Satan.

I was unfazed at this point. I knew that we needed to succeed, and I recognized that we blew it financially. All the projections in the world could not predict the events that lead up to our current financial demise. I still believed in our product and wanted to be successful. I also recognized that without help we would be out of business, and likely selling at a price that would only get us out of the deal without a profit. That seemed ridiculous to me. A smaller piece of a successful business was fine. In fact, I was welcoming help from within the industry. At this point, money was important, but we also needed an identity. For two years we fought our identity crisis. It was time for industry support.

I arrived in Vegas a day later then the rest. Typically, I would try to travel on different flights from Paul in the off chance one of our planes went down. The company couldn't risk losing both of us in a catastrophe.

I never liked having the shows in Vegas. It was too much of a party town, and very impersonal for conducting business. In other cities, we always would have dinner appointments, stops at nightclubs, and maybe even a show with customers or distributors. None of this seemed to happen in Vegas. Everyone just wanted to gamble. And sitting at a gambling table was not conducive to business.

I also am in the minority in that I don't like to gamble. That may be because I am not good at it. But more likely it is my conservative accountant nature that keeps me thinking of the stacked odds. The buildings in Vegas were not built with house losses. I know that I can't win, so I never play. That's bad thinking for casinos. I mostly watched the others win, only to lose their bounty later, or the next day, or the next trip. Ultimately, you cannot win at gambling. The rush of winning causes you to keep playing. The more you continue to win, the more the odds work against you. It's a lot like being an entrepreneur. Maybe that's why I don't like to gamble; it's too much like work.

When I arrived at the show, I was stymied by the great booth location that we had. This was the best exposure ever. We were two booths over from Standard and across from Coke. This was great. We would get the best traffic and high exposure.

As I walked to the booth, I stopped off at Standard's booth to witness a private demonstration being provided to some Coke executives. I could tell the Standard brass was performing the demonstration, since they were wearing suits. Typically, the trade-show sales floor attire was a sport shirt donning the company colors and company logo. This demonstration looked important. I ducked behind another machine to remain partially obscured since I did not want to appear nosy.

Standard had been working on a new product that was actually financed by Coke. The plan was to reduce the amount of fizz that was created by the product delivery process. It was a real problem for vending carbonated beverage bottles. The slightest agitation causes the product to spew like a volcano. Ultimately, it was because of physics. I learned it was a combination of the light entering the bottle and the plastic that caused the carbonation to escape at a faster rate than aluminum cans. So that the product would not go flat, the bottles were over-carbonated to compensate. This also caused for more rigidity in the bottles, so that they would not get crushed in the vending machines.

How much of this was true, I am not sure. A lot of tales get told in this industry. I am not very scientific, so I cannot confirm the stories. I do know from drinking soda that there are more bubbles in bottled soft drinks than there are in canned soft drinks. And, I knew that little could be done to eliminate fizz in warm soda. This came from experience and testing.

The new Standard idea was pretty good. Instead of the bottle making a plunge to the bottom of the machine into the delivery area, an elevator lowered the bottle. In addition to the sizable costs involved with the machine, there were other issues. The primary problem was that the bottle still had to be shuttled to the delivery area. As I watched the demonstration, I could see that the idea was not going to work well. The bottle was still agitated as it plopped onto the elevator, and then was sent skidding to the delivery area where it received a final couple of shakes and jolts as it was properly positioned for the waiting customer. As I watched, for the benefit of Standard, and the person that was going to open the bottle, I was hoping that the product was cold. That would at least reduce the likelihood of an explosion. But, I was not optimistic for their success, especially since most of the sample product vended at shows was warm simply to deter passers-by from drinking the display product.

As everyone gathered watching in anticipation, the selection was made, the elevator was dispatched, the product bounced onto the track, the track lowered to the delivery area and the bottle shuttled to the delivery area. Everyone was amazed and excited. Then, without any hesitation, the Standard executive removed the bottle and quickly twisted the cap. Soda spewed out everywhere, soaking him and a Coke executive. Everyone else jumped back, scurrying to stay dry. Coke spent five million bucks and the soda still exploded. It was back to the drawing board. I slid out behind some machines unnoticed and headed to our booth.

Our booth looked great and the machines displayed well. I was quietly satisfied that the new Standard machine wasn't working. I felt bad for them because it was a good idea, but it helped prove that our method was still a good solution. I knew that our machine would cause agitation and hence the product would fizz. But that was a small problem, since mostly our machine vended milk and other non-carbonated refreshments. The fizz problem was an industry gripe that likely can never be completely cured. And even if it were cured, the industry would find another complaint. There is always a complaint. It is human nature.

I was excited waiting to see Brit. He always had something funny to say and had a great perspective on life. He liked calling me a bean counter and I liked that he called me that. Throughout this project, sometimes people would lose sight of what really made me tick. Not Brit. He never let me forget that I was an accountant. He would drop a new accountant joke on me every chance he could. This proved useful to me, since I would like to pass on accountant jokes every chance that I could. I especially enjoyed doing it when teaching a class to accountants. It always woke up the room.

Through out our early discussions, he had kept his contact confidential, so I was in suspense as to our potential suitor.

"Brit, how are you this fine morning?" I asked.

"Oh my! It's the FBC!" Brit exclaimed as he turned to the nearest person to gain their attention. Jokes are only funny if there is an audience.

"Hey Matt, do you know what an FBC is? A Friggin' Bean Counter! That's what." The Brit inspired laughter ensued.

I was delighted at the warm response. I always believed that if someone cracked a joke about me, they liked me. Maybe it's because I only make jokes with the people I like. I was happy that Brit liked me. I liked him.

"So FBC, did you get Paul's receipts from last night? He sure was spending the dough," commented Brit.

"Where at Brit? The tables?"

"Heck no. Come on John, where do you think he was? He was at the girly bar," Brit chuckled.

I was a bit surprised. I know that Paul was a player and would hit the clubs on trips, but on this trip? How could he? This trip may have been the most important trip of his life.

"How late did you guys stay?" I asked.

"We didn't stay late. But I didn't go with Paul. We ran into him there. He was with the other boys. I was jet lagging. I think they stayed pretty late though."

"Great. Who was he with?" I asked.

"The boys from Northern. He was schmoozing them, I guess. Look, they are never going to sign up with you guys. They have an exclusive contract with Standard. One of their salesmen worked with me eight years ago at AMD. He told me about their deal. Paul's just wastes his time, and your money. I keep telling him that. Get his receipts!"

With that, Brit was pulled away by one of his customers. He was all smiles, handshakes and back slaps – the consummate equipment salesman. I would buy from him.

I couldn't stop thinking about Paul's foolishness. We were in a financial world of hurt and we were in Las Vegas on a mission to save the company. Instead of getting prepared for maybe the most important meeting of our business life, Paul is out spending money on a distributor that has no use for us. Shame on him; and shame on them.

As if on queue, Paul walked into the booth looking like death warmed over. This was not good. What a great first impression this will make.

"Paul, did you get any sleep last night? We have a big day today." I asked the question as if I didn't already know the answer.

"No. The Northern guys took me out last night. What a night."

"The Northern guys took you out? I didn't think they wanted to distribute for us? Why are they suddenly interested in taking you out?"

"Well, I took them out. What difference does it make? They are signing with us," Paul quipped angrily.

"Who is signing with us, Northern? You're dreaming, Paul. They just wanted a free night. They have an exclusive deal with Standard. We are out, no matter what."

"Where did you hear that?" Paul asked.

"It doesn't matter. It was a valid source. But I get the feeling you know all of this already."

I was already starting to feel stress with Paul. The anguish of the money trouble at the business, coupled with the turret machine release date debacle was starting to strain our relationship. Several times now, we had words. I like honesty. And I was getting the feeling that Paul wasn't always giving me the straight story. That bothered me.

For the most part, however, I ignored it since it seemed to be stress induced. If we could just get by the next six months, we would be all right and our relationship would go back to normal. For now, I just bit my tongue.

My mind drifted back to our big meeting later today. Brit had it all arranged. I was hoping to ask him for any early predictions, just to calm my nerves. The opportunity never came.

People began filing into our booth for demonstrations. For the most part, word was out in the industry about the machine. Most people read the industry trade rags, which provided us plenty of good press. Plus we ran monthly full-page promotional ads. Couple this with a growing distributor base, and we were pretty popular. Still, many operators had not seen the machine in action, so I was happy to provide the full demonstration to any willing listener.

Every time a new person entered the booth, I had to wonder if this was the one, the angel. But no one seemed to fit the description that my mind conjured up about the mystery financier. I was disappointed, but the day was going great and orders were pouring in.

It was always our plan to have a trade show special. It would be an "incentive to act today" type thing. This particular plan was giving a great price incentive off of the second machine purchased. And why not? We needed sales. Selling two at once had incredible savings on shipping, so we didn't lose too much giving nice price breaks.

The day was busy. It was nearly as busy as the Dallas show where we first introduced the turret machine. I was getting tired and my voice was beginning to give out. Not good since this was the first of three days. And I still had the big meeting to attend. Oh yeah, the big meeting. I nearly forgot about it we were so busy.

Throughout the day, Brit came into our booth to demonstrate the machine to groups of his customers. It was customary for distributors to work the floor and use the equipment manufacturers booths to make their pitch. It worked well and I invited the help. Listening to Brit taught me a great deal on how to deal with sales objections. There were always objections. Most of the gripes were just that, the handle was too stiff; the door was too heavy, the keypad too low or too high, or not centered. It didn't matter; there was always a complaint. Brit knew this and worked around the complaints as if they were benefits. He was a good salesman. Usually when Brit arrived, Paul took a smoke break while I stayed back and listened. I liked listening to Brit.

Eventually the crowd steadied and time slowed down. The pace was easy for our salesman Matt to handle. I finally got a chance to take a break and walk the floor. I was always interested in what other companies were up to. Someone always had something new and exciting to see. The show was smaller than past shows, and after one quick pass, I didn't see anything new besides Standard's elevator machine. I guess that was good. We were still fresh and front running in the "new" department.

The one thing I learned about this industry was that there weren't a great deal of break through ideas. This was a mature industry and a mature market. The cash cow days were long gone. The only real innovation was in the circuitry and electronic data capturing software. Even this innovation was pretty pale compared to other high tech industries where quantum leaps were the norm.

Dispensing a bottle or a bag of chips was pretty mundane stuff. The most important aspect was reliability. Redundancy had to be built into the delivery system so that if the purchaser did not get their product, they had another choice, or their money was returned. It was ATM quality level and beyond. The real problem with mis-vends was that often the angry purchaser takes out their frustration on the machine by beating it up. It seems pretty foolish when you think about it, but I have been there. I don't like when a vending machine eats my money. Stories of the damage that operators encountered due to mis-vend were legendary.

The other great part of the show was the free snacks. Vending machines were only half of the industry. The vending stuff was the other. There were booths for candy, chips, drinks and sandwiches. You name it, if it could be vended; it was represented at the show. I always looked for new products since it was safe to try them here. No cost, and there were plenty of garbage cans around to discard the stuff I didn't like. And there was plenty of that happening.

I was strolling along stuffing my face with some type of candy when I heard a familiar voice behind me calling my name. It was Sid. I turned around to see his charming smile and receive his firm handshake.

"Mr. Davis, how is the show going for you today?" he asked.

"Very well, Sid. It is nice to see you. I figured you would be at one of the casinos by now. The show is pretty much winding down."

"Nah, I was up late last night gambling. I will go again later. I didn't get to your booth today. Really, did it go well?"

"Sid, I am telling you, we have the hottest idea out there. It needs a bit more refinement, but I think it is there." I responded.

Sid looked at me curiously and asked, "How's cash flow? You know I hear everything, John."

"Well, not as good as I would like it to be. The small line machines are down and the orders aren't shipping as fast as I would like. We'll pull it out, though. I am sure of it. The machine is too good to fail."

"So what time are we getting together tonight?" Sid asked.

I surprisingly answered, "Oh, I don't know. I didn't know that we were getting together."

Sid looked at me surprised and confused. "Brit did talk to you, right?"

At that moment, I realized that Sid was the angel. I should have known.

"Oh that meeting. Brit didn't say what time," I responded.

"Did Brit say that you would be meeting with me?" he asked.

I stalled my answer, not knowing if there was some other message involved in this discussion. "No, Sid. He did not say that we were meeting with you. I just knew that we had a meeting."

"Good. He was supposed to keep this quiet. Brit is a good man."

"Sid, I am really glad that we are meeting. But I had no idea that you would be involved."

Sid interrupted. "John, I told you earlier, if a deal is going to happen in this industry, I will be involved.

"I am staying at Paris. Meet me at my room at 7 o'clock. I am on the penthouse floor. You will need a pass to get up to my room. Call me when you are on your way and I will have someone waiting for you."

"Great, Sid. I will see you then."

We shook hands and I made my way back to the booth.

When I returned to the booth, Matt and Paul were beginning to close everything down. Paul didn't look too happy. I grabbed him by the arm and pulled him aside from Matt to tell him about what I learned. We had to keep business issues quiet around Matt. First, because it was good business to keep executive matters between executive management. Second, because Matt was like a broadcast system. He was one of those guys that could turn a sound byte into a novel, simply by filling in the blanks. And that's a lot of blanks. The stories would end up sounding like fish tales.

"Paul, you will never believe who we are meeting with tonight," I said.

"Oh, I already know. Brit came by while you were walking the floor. I'm not going." Paul chimed.

"What? Are you nuts? We have to go."

"No way. I'm not doing a deal with him. No way."

I was floored. I knew that Paul did not like Sid because of what he heard about Sid. I was not convinced that any of what he heard was true. Brit was a great guy and a very good friend of Sid's. Besides, I felt a connection to Sid the first time I met him and was excited that he wanted to be involved.

For a long time, Paul had a strong connection with a company that did not have a strong opinion of Sid. And I think they prejudiced Paul's opinion over the years.

"Paul, we need to go tonight. We have no choice. Let's go back to the hotel and relax a bit. The pool is probably still open. We'll have a cocktail poolside and talk this over."

"All right." Paul replied.

The show went great, and I was optimistic that we could strike a deal with Sid. This could turn out to be the best trip ever, the best sale ever. Now I needed to be sure Paul was on board. I believed that if Paul would just meet with him, the deal would come together. I looked forward to a swim and a drink. My feet hurt.

Matt, Paul and I walked back to the hotel in silence.

Chapter 16

Let go of your attachment to being right, and suddenly your mind is more open. You're able to benefit from the unique viewpoints of others, without being crippled by your own judgment.
--Ralph Marston

I didn't know much about Las Vegas. In fact, the times that I came before this one, I never left the hotel where I was staying. Typically, I would stay at the Hilton that was connected to the Convention Center. This was the most convenient location for the show, and they offered discounts for show participants. That was important to me since I did not gamble nor get comped like a high roller.

I still remember my first visit to Las Vegas. It was in April, just after tax season. I remember saving a few bucks to gamble. Since I like to go native when I travel, trying my hand at least at the slot machines was a requirement. So I saved $100, maybe $200, thinking that this would hold me over for the trip. I also figured it would be no big deal if I lost the money. Initially, I was pretty excited about the idea of the slot machines.

When I got off of the plane, I was pretty shocked at the opulence. If you're not in the mindset to gamble and party, the initial view of Vegas can be pretty intimidating. I had been in casinos before, in the Grand Bahamas and in Windsor, Canada. I even watched the Travel Channel specials on Vegas to be prepared. Nothing could have prepared me. My first thought was 'How can anyone here think they can win?'

When I got to the hotel, I was even more amazed at the number of people that were sitting at the slot machines. The casinos have it so figured out, that you don't even need to put money in the machine. You simply slide a card in a slot and start hitting the button. You don't even need to pull down the big handle on the side of the slot machine anymore. That's how I remembered playing slot machines. A great deal changes I guess when you are busy trying to build a business.

But the people gambling amazed me. There were old ladies, as far as I could see, madly smacking the button. They would hardly wait to see if they lost. As soon as the second wheel stopped and they could tell they lost, they recycled the machine again. Another dollar was lost. I never did gamble on that trip. I put the money away and bought some petunias for our garden when I got home.

Paul and I met at the pool for a drink. I sat at the side with my feet in the water with a drink in my hand. I arrived one drink ahead of Paul. He swaggered into the pool area as if he owned it. You could never tell that this man was president of a failing company. Maybe it was confidence, or maybe it was denial. It was difficult to tell. Besides, how can anyone really predict the thoughts and psyche of another person? At this point I didn't care; my feet felt better.

Paul needed some coaxing to even attend the meeting. He was not at all happy about the prospect of being a partner with Sid. I really couldn't understand his objection, though. I kept reminding him of the alternative.

I wasn't wild about doing a deal with Sid, either. Not because of Sid, but rather because I knew that any deal we would do would reduce my equity. I also knew that it would mess up the voting stock situation. Although I only had a 25% equity stake, I had a 50% vote by virtue of a voting trust that we formed. The trust was a pretty useful mechanism to even out the votes when there is a disparity in ownership equity. To me, the vote was more important than the equity amount. The vote meant a voice.

The way the trust worked was pretty simple. The votes were removed from our shares and assigned to the voting trust. The trustees of the trust then voted the shares based on the trust agreement. In our case, Paul and I each cast one vote. We had simple rules for deadlocks. First there was a one-day cooling off period if we could not agree. If we still couldn't agree, then we used tiebreakers. If it were a matter of accounting, finance, computer systems, or business operations, I cast the final vote. If it were related to design, production, shop management, or personnel, Paul would cast an extra vote. If an issue that crossed over our respective domains caused the deadlock, we could either use an independent third party to help mediate, or we would simply toss a coin. Our intention was simply that if we couldn't agree, and believing that we were smart, well informed businessmen, that fate would decide. This way, we could not be mad at each other for the outcome. We each had an equal opportunity to be right, or wrong.

Paul eventually agreed that it was best for the company to keep the meeting with Sid. I was relieved because I did not want to have to exercise my right under the voting trust and "out vote" him, thus forcing him into a deal. Not that we had any real alternatives.

When we arrived at the hotel, we were escorted to the private elevators that took us to the high roller suites. The bellhop escorted us all the way to the door and quietly knocked on the door.

Shortly, the doublewide doors both opened and Sid greeted us warmly. The suite was more of a penthouse. There were five rooms that I could identify. The main living room windows opened to the Las Vegas strip below. The water show at the Bellagio was dancing in the night sky. The room itself was decorated in a combination of shades of red and gold. The portion of the floor that was not carpeted was made of marble. The bedroom was off to the left side. Just before the entrance way to bedroom was a fully stocked wet bar. Sid offered us drinks, which Paul was way too eager to have, and I was willing to accept. The suite also had a sunken whirlpool tub, a spacious kitchen, and a sitting room. I was amazed at the opulence.

Sitting on the couch was a lady that I recognized from the trade shows, but I did not know her name. Sid quickly introduced us. He indicated to me that she was just a very good friend and that they were having dinner after our meeting. He asked if she could stay through our conversation. I wasn't wild about the idea, but I agreed. I had no choice; Sid held the cards and could deal them any way he chose.

"What do you think of this room? I was comped the whole thing for a week," Sid asked.

I nodded in approval and we all sat down in the neatly arranged chairs and sofas. Paul sat down across from the lady with Sid to his right. I sat across from Sid with Paul to my right. Paul kept staring at the lady.

There wasn't much small talk, Sid got right down to business.

"So, my friend Brit tells me that you need money."

Paul quickly answered, "Yes."

I added, "We need money, but we need more than that. We need an identity in the marketplace."

"Tell me more about that, John," Sid asked.

"Well, right now we are floundering. We have some good sales, and then we go stale. We have some good distributors, but they really don't seem too interested in promoting our product. I think the distributors jumped on the bandwagon just to say they carry our product. We only have two or three nationwide that really seem to work to move machines," I added.

Sid politely interrupted me. "But do the machines work?"

Before I could answer, Paul defiantly retorted, "Of course they work. Who said they don't work?"

Sid looked a bit astonished by Paul's defensive answer. Sid knew he hit a nerve with Paul.

I tried to pick up the pieces and added, "We have had some difficulties with the design. But that is true with any new design. You cannot create an environment in the shop that will test for every possible thing that will go wrong in real use. How do you anticipate college kids pranks, or devious employees trying to steal a soda? We have had our share of miscues, but so has Standard. We keep learning from them and making the necessary modifications. There hasn't been that many, though."

Sid seemed pleased with my answer.

"So where do you see this company going, Paul?" Sid asked.

"I think that we will sell a ton of these and we will make a ton of money," Paul blurted.

"John, where do you see this company going?"

"Nowhere fast if we can't access more capital. The R&D costs are killing our working capital. We raised some mezzanine debt about eight months ago, but the sales haven't kicked in fast enough to build the working capital. I am worried now that our growth will kill us. We will not be able to carry the receivables. If we can get over the hump, however, I think we can build a nice profitable company that we could easily sell for a high return."

I could tell that it was obvious to Sid that I had the business training and Paul did not.

"So, what is your current arrangement?" Sid asked.

"Well, we have two banks involved..."

Sid again politely interrupted me. "That's not what I mean. What it the arrangement between you two, you are partners, right?"

"Oh, okay. Paul and I are the only shareholders. Paul owns 75% of the shares and is the president and the "idea" guy. I own 25% of the shares, and am the financial guy. We have pretty specific domains within the company. The shares are voted 50-50 by using a voting trust."

"A voting trust, what's that?" Sid asked.

"It's a trust whereby the votes are removed from the shares by a corporate resolution and put into a trust. The shares are then voted by the trustees of the trust, in this case Paul and me. It works well."

"Interesting. So how can I help you?" Sid asked.

"Well, Brit indicated that you might be interested in investing in the company." I explained.

"He did?"

"Yes Sid, that's why I thought we were here."

"Well, John, I told you years ago in Myrtle Beach, and again today, that a deal doesn't get done in this industry without my involvement. That's why were here. I may be interested in putting together a group to invest. Or maybe the company should just be sold right now. I don't know yet. What are your thoughts, John?"

I thought about the answer for a moment. The room became silent awaiting my reply.

"I think it is too early to sell. The company has not built enough value. The brand has not been built and the company lacks identity. We need to improve the company and it's image before it can be sold for a reasonable value. It will take some time, experience and industry knowledge. But we can't continue with our finances in this disarray. We won't make it three more months under this pressure. Even less if we get a big order at this show." I explained.

We spent a great deal of time discussing the financial situation of the company. Particularly, we discussed the current banking arrangements and possibilities of raising capital from other sources. It was becoming evident to Sid that we were on our last lifeline. Throughout the entire conversation, Paul had been sitting quietly listening. He seemed almost disinterested in any of our conversation. He seemed happier staring at the young lady's legs that were sitting across from him.

"Well gentlemen, this has been interesting and informative. I like the machine. I told you that years ago, and I still like it now. It is the best idea that I have seen in this industry in a long time. But you are right. You need help. You are making mistakes that are costing you countless dollars and time. I could help you. I told you that two years ago. If you would have accepted my help then, you probably would both be millionaires by now. So be it." Sid paused while he was refreshing his drink at the wet bar.

I was reminded of our "chance" meeting in Myrtle Beach. Sid was right, we have blown it so far and we really need his help now.

Sid continued, "But I am wondering if this is all too late. The company may be too far-gone to save. I will need to look at the numbers to decide that. But presuming that it is worth saving, how much money do you think you will need?"

That was a tough question and I knew that this was the key question in the negotiation. I had been in this situation many times before. And as an experienced negotiator, I knew a quick response was death. This question could not be answered directly. In fact, it needed to be answered with a question to test where the negotiation would be headed.

Getting capital at this stage of the game comes at a huge cost. And this question set the price on the deal. I wanted to take my time to answer as to not give up any more equity than I needed to, but enough to satisfy both sides of the deal. I was thinking quickly as to the question that I wanted to lead with so that we could enter the negotiation phase.

But, before I could even process the entire question to frame my response, Paul blurted out "One million dollars."

Just like that, the negotiation was over. Paul blew it. I was fumed.

Sid, being the professional that he was, jumped on the fumble and responded, "Okay, fine. I will invest one million dollars for fifty percent of the company."

Paul now came to life and decided that he would negotiate the deal. What an absolute jerk. I just glared at him as the words spilled from his lips.

"I'm not giving up half the company. No way," Paul shouted.

"Well, then I am not interested in the deal," Sid said calmly.

Sid and Paul just sat there staring at each other. I should have known at this point that the contempt between these two was dangerous. But I really liked Sid. I liked him from the start, and I liked him even more now. I shouldn't have liked him because I thought this deal was way too low, but I admired him. He jumped on the fumble, just like I would have done. He was polished and skilled. We needed him in the company. I would be happy to give up half of a sinking ship at the hope of making a pile of money with Sid. And I knew that he could do it. His resume was impressive and included two prior deals going public. That doesn't happen by accident.

There was little I could do, but I just couldn't sit there and watch the opportunity fade away. So I tried to get the genie back in the bottle.

"Sid, I have a problem with this deal. It won't work," I said.

"Why not John?"

"Well, I don't have a problem with 50 percent. In fact I am surprised that you don't want control, over 50 percent." I paused for a moment to see if Sid would take the bait and open up a new negotiation. He didn't, he was way too skilled. He sat quietly, waiting for me to continue. So I did.

"The problem I have is the amount of money. I think we will need more than a million dollars to do this right. The amount is probably closer to two million."

Sid didn't respond. He just sat there, staring at Paul, knowing that he was the weak link.

"Do you agree Paul?" Sid asked.

"I'm not giving up half of my stock," Paul insisted.

"Well gentlemen, I need to get to dinner and I have kept this young lady waiting long enough." Sid said.

I tried everything I could to keep the deal alive.

"Why don't we talk again tomorrow, Sid," I said. "A lot has been discussed and this was a good first meeting."

"Why bother? Paul doesn't want to do it and it's apparent that he is the one in control here. I can't help anyone that doesn't want to be helped."

I didn't know what to say. I knew Paul's behavior was incorrigible and I could tell that Sid had him sized up pretty well. But I also knew that this deal was far from over. Sid did like this deal and he wanted to get it done. We both needed to step away and plan round two. I knew it wasn't over.

As we were making for the door, Sid asked where we were dining. I knew that this was not an inquiry that would lead to an invitation to join him. That would be improper deal etiquette, and Sid was way too polished at deals. Besides, he already introduced his lady friend as his dinner companion.

I safely responded, "We are not sure. We didn't make any reservations."

"Well, I will call my driver. He will take you anywhere you want to go in the city."

"Oh, that's not necessary, Sid."

"I insist, John. Take the car. We are dining downstairs in the hotel, so we don't need the driver. I will call down right now. When you get off the elevator, take a right turn to the concierge desk. He will be expecting you."

"Thank you, Sid. So I will see you on the show floor tomorrow?"

"Sure, John. I will be by."

We all shook hands and we parted.

When we got downstairs and into the limousine, Paul's mouth was running on and on about how bad it would be to do a deal with Sid.

"I can't believe the nerve of this guy," he said. Fifty percent of the company for one million dollars! What does he think I am, an idiot? I would give him 10 percent for a million dollars and that's it. Nothing more."

Paul was rambling while living in dreamland. The fact was the company was pretty much worthless to an investor. Paul did not understand any of the principles of business valuation, nor did he understand the categories of business buyers.

After all of my business valuation training and all of the theory that has been developed, discussed and debated involving the intricacies of valuing closely held businesses, I can summarize the entire process very simply. A businesses value is based on the cash flow, or the expectation of cash flow that the business can produce. There is no other reason to buy a business. At the end of all of the analysis and explanation, cash flow or the expectation of cash flow is all that matters.

The complication is in the details. For example, what is the true cash flow of a business, and how should it be measured? What is the proper return on investment that a buyer should expect? What are the probabilities of the future cash flow differing from the current cash flow? The list of details goes on and on. But all of these variables are addressed differently by the category of buyer.

There are several categories of business buyers. In this case, we were dealing with an investor type buyer that was making the investment to yield a return. The primary objective of the buyer is to yield a return from the business. The form of the return can be in current cash flow, or in future growth of the business to be harvested later in the eventual sale of the company. Typically, an investor type buyer will not be directly involved in the daily management of the company. But in the true spirit of an entrepreneur, the investor will likely remain involved in the executive management of the company. This is the key feature that attracts investor buyers into a closely held business rather than just investing in publicly traded securities. Involvement with a closely held company provides a level of control over the possible outcomes of the business. The only real control an investor has in a publicly traded company is when to buy or sell the shares. There is really very little opportunity for any influence on the company.

I signaled to Paul to stop talking and pointed at the limousine driver. I was suspicious of everyone involved in any deals. I wasn't sure if the driver was going to convey information back to Sid. And with Paul's mouth spewing, I couldn't take the chance. I finally got Paul to stop talking about the deal.

I was reminded of a deal that I worked on in Texas a few years earlier. I was hired by a firm to perform due diligence on a company that they were interested in acquiring. It was only a $25 million company with one location, so the initial due-diligence was only going to take a few days. My client and an associate accompanied me to assist in the process. When we arrived, the conference room where we were working was jammed with papers. Computer reports of financial details were stacked high, cross referenced with large handwritten numbers to a master control document. It was information overload, which made me immediately suspicious. As we sifted through the documents, we had several conversations about facts that we could not uncover in the documents that we had. Mysteriously, the next day new reports were neatly arranged on the tabletop, specifically answering the questions we raised, which conveniently provided plausible answers to each secret inquiry. The following day, much of the same occurred, and as expected, the required reports were on the table. Knowing that none of us requested the documents, we were suspicious that the room was bugged. It had to be. So I had some fun. During the course of our workday, I laid a tidbit out to the room.

"You know, Ken the president would be so much more believable and presentable if he would just shave his shaggy beard."

The next morning, Ken the president arrived at work with a neatly shaved face. From this point forward in my career, when involved in deals, or any high stakes game, I have always assumed that someone is listening somewhere.

After a long silence, Paul started up again. "That chick was into me."

"What?"

"She was into me. She wanted me," Paul continued.

"What are you talking about, Paul. I didn't see any such thing."

"John, I'm telling you, she wants me. She's wanted me for a long time. That's probably why she was there. She wants me."

I looked at Paul in disgust. Lately, every woman he met wanted him -- at least in *his* mind. He needed constant validation of his bravado, even if it came in the form of self-validation.

Paul droned on. "Man, I should have jumped at the opportunity. Did you see how she looked at me? We connected. She wants me."

I tried to ignore him. I stared out the window as he continued to mumble about his brief imaginary encounter.

The limousine stopped in front of club Rio. We hopped out as if we were some type of fat cats. But once the doors opened and we popped out, the illusion was ended for all of the bystanders. We were just a couple of mopes hitching a limousine ride on someone else's dime.

We wandered into the casino. We did not talk much about the prospect of the deal, even after we left the limousine. It wasn't long though, before Paul ran into some folks that he knew from one of our suppliers. They were all a bunch of playboys and I wasn't too interested in joining them for dinner. I really did not fit in. They acted like a bunch of big-shot players, but they weren't. I did not like hanging around pretentious people.

I split from Paul and walked through the casino, observing the action at the tables. Excitement was everywhere. At each table, dreams were beginning or ending. The occasional cheers from the craps tables made it all the more exciting. The gamblers were having fun. I was lost and out of my element. My dice roll happened an hour earlier on the penthouse floor. That was my element. That was the action I liked.

Too bad Paul had opened his mouth. All he had to do was sit quietly and let me work the deal. It didn't matter now. It was too late. I had to work the new deal that started and I was ready.

I had enough of the casino and made for the door. I didn't feel like waiting in the cab line, so I walked out to the street and hailed a passing cab.

When I got to my room, I started outlining my next day's conversation with Sid. I wanted to be prepared. It was game time again and I was ready.

Chapter 17

Never confuse motion with action.
--Ernest Hemmingway

The show the next day started off busier than expected. Paul rolled in about an hour after the show opening, bragging about his wild night that ended at 2:30 am. Once again, he was not prepared for the importance of the day's events.

The day went by fast, and just like that it was 3:00. The show ended at 4:00 so I only had one more hour on my feet. For most of the show demonstrators, the shows went by slowly. For the most part, the industry did not have many new ideas or new products. In fact, most of the booths were more social visits than real business transactions. Our booth was different, though. We always were busy. The concept of our machine was very different from the other machines in the industry. Everyone wanted to see it, potential customers, competitors, and those not even remotely involved in bottle vending, would come by for a demonstration. By now, I had demonstrated the machine so many times; I could do it in my sleep. Even the jokes seemed stale; all they needed was some canned laughter.

I was disappointed that the show was nearly over and I had yet to see Sid. He said he would come by. I began to think about last night's events. He had to be turned off by Paul's behavior. I certainly was, so I could understand.

The shows always seemed to slow down for the last hour. I was already closing down the show when Sid came by the booth. Paul was out on a smoke break and I was there with our salesman. Sid pulled me aside and spoke quickly and quietly.

"Here is my card again, just so you have it," he whispered. " Talk to your friend Paul about this deal. Your company needs help, and I want to provide it. But I won't go forward unless he wants me too.

You are the voice of reason for the company. I know that. Talk to him and call me."

"Sid, we have one more day here, can I talk to him tonight and meet with you tomorrow?"

"No, I am leaving tonight. I will be out of the country for a week or so. We can talk when I get back."

"Okay, Sid. Thank you."

Sid quickly turned and left. Before long, Paul was back in the booth. I pulled him aside and told him about Sid's quick visit. Paul was unimpressed. Before I even had a chance to talk to him, I felt a hard slap on my back and heard a familiar voice. It was Brit.

"Okay FBC, what did you do to my friend Sid?"

"What do you mean?" I asked.

"You guys didn't come to terms. And he's leaving tonight. Boy did you guys screw that up!"

I didn't want to get into the details with Brit because it wasn't his business, nor was it proper. I knew the reason Sid was cooling on the deal was Paul's attitude. But I could not split the company. We had to present a unified front. As much as I wanted to blame Paul and make him out to be the goat, it was not right for business. Paul was my problem.

"I didn't think that we screwed anything up, Brit. We met, shared our views and ideas, and discussed potential terms. That's a lot for a first meeting."

Brit looked at me with disgust, shaking his head. "That's not the story I heard."

"Well, Brit, what did you hear?"

"That you turned him down."

"I turned *him* down?"

"Well, not you specifically. But that Sid's offer was rejected."

Brit spoke in a very serious tone.

I was silent. It is amazing how fast information flows, correct or not. Now I knew that we were not quite on the same page, but I still felt that a deal was brewing. I tried to spin the information.

"Brit, I just spoke with Sid. We are set to talk again in the next week or so."

"Yeah, yeah. If this big buffoon over here gets his head and butt wired together. What is your problem, Paul?"

Brit was nearly in Paul's face by now.

Paul stared back at Brit. "What's my problem?"

"You blew the deal," Brit said.

I cut in. "Brit, the deal is not dead. We are taking the discussion to the next level. Don't worry."

"Yeah? Well leave a-hole home next time. I worked for a month to get you guys together and he blows it. FBC, I am ticked, buddy. You need to straighten this out."

"Don't worry, Brit. If a deal was going to happen, it still will happen. If it doesn't happen, it won't be because of our first meeting. I will assure you that."

Brit walked away, disgusted. I was stunned at how much information was on the floor about our meeting. I was also shocked at how Brit got into Paul's face, but after some thought, it made sense. Brit liked our machine and saw the potential in it. He was plugged in to the major dairy market and could make a ton of money if we could stay alive as a company. He took the initiative to make the contacts with Sid to set up the rendezvous. And we did blow it.

More was riding on this deal than just our company staying in business. Several other companies were at risk, too. I was suddenly feeling more pressure than before.

Now I was really worried about Sid. The delay caused by this set us back at least another three weeks because of Sid's travel schedule. I needed to think of a way to move up the timeline.

Now all I had left to look forward to was the Saturday show. This was trick-or-treat day. Well, that's what we called it. Over two thirds of the booths at the show were passing out samples of candy, chips, popcorn, sandwiches, etc. If it could be vended, it was. And Saturday always seemed to attract the small, regional vending companies, many of which were mom and pop operations. They walked the show with several plastic bags that were handed out to collect samples and show materials. The trick-or-treaters spent most of the show filling their bags and wasting our time.

Most of the equipment that we sold was to large distributors or to very large national vending operations. In fact, our machine was not really designed with the small vendor in mind. Since our machine was a bottle vendor, the price was significantly higher than a standard can vendor. This forced our equipment into very high traffic and usage locations that were typically serviced by larger institutional operations. But many of these smaller vendors were our indirect customers that bought our small-line machines through our other distributor. So, we always obliged by providing them a demonstration of the 45-R, even though we knew that they would never buy the machine. So, for the most part, Saturday's did not turn up much business. We were always busy and worked hard, but did so pretty much for nothing.

I was happy the show ended. We came into the show hoping to gain support from a new partner, but we accomplished very little. We got mostly a handshake, a friendly face, and the potential for another meeting. It wasn't much, but it was something. We were running out of time.

Chapter 18

Our real blessings often appear to us in shapes of pains, losses and disappointments; but let us have patience, and we soon shall see them in their proper figures.
                                              --Joseph Addison

We were always busiest after the shows. A good show would lead to a two dozen or so orders that would keep the plant busy for the next two months. This show was no exception.

My goal was to figure out how to continue to cash flow the business until we could gain some industry help. Convincing Paul that Sid was the answer was another problem. He did not like Sid. It was that simple. I could never figure out why, nor would Paul tell me. He didn't like him and was being close-minded and stubborn.

But at this stage of the game, Paul did not have any skin in the game. He was still drawing his salary, he still had his truck, and he was still the boss. He never once had to put up more money. The only thing that he had at risk was his investment in the company, which amounted to not much more than fifteen years of sweat equity.

That may seem like a lot to most people, but sweat equity is not equivalent to real equity. Money is money. Sweat is not money. If you never had money, you have no idea the advantages that are created by having money. When you have money, and make a choice to invest it into a business, and the business begins to lose your money, it feels much different than losing something that you never had. When you lose sweat equity, you still lose value. But it is not the same. What is really lost is the dream or the opportunity for money. It is still not the money. Maybe it's because the value was never cashed in. Maybe it's because the advantages of money were never realized. Let's face it; you cannot spend the inherent equity in a small business. You can't even borrow against it. It is nothing more than potential money.

What's worse is investing more money in an already losing proposition. Now that separates the want-to-be's from the players. To be that confident in the business when everything is falling apart around you takes nerves of steel. Or stupidity. It's tough to tell the difference. A lot of people have died trying stunts in the name of courage, and when you break it down, they were just stupid. Writing a check and depositing it into the bank account of a failing business does not feel good. It's like increasing a bet already placed on a team to win when the game is nearly over and they are losing by three touchdowns. Is that confidence or stupidity? I still believe that losing money that you never had is not nearly as bad as losing money that you did have.

After demonstrating to Paul through my financial projections that we were going to be out of business in a couple of months, and recalling the purpose of the Las Vegas trip, Paul began to waiver and finally relinquished to the fact that not only did we need the help, he realized that Sid was likely our best option.

I instantly left a message for Sid to call me immediately when he arrived back to the country. I was excited to get this moving forward since time was ticking.

About a week after the call, Sid called me back. After a spirited conversation about the show orders and further show prospects, we agreed to get a confidentiality agreement in place and move a step in the next direction. After our agreement was in place, I sent to him a complete financial history, sales data, tax returns, accounts receivable and payables aging reports, and copies of our bank agreements.

After about a day of Sid having the information, he called me back.

"John, where are you generating all of your sales?" was his greeting.

"Partly though the condiment stands, our small line sales, and the new machine," was my reply.

"I didn't realize that you guys were doing this much volume. How big is your facility?"

"About 90,000 feet or so. Maybe more."

"What is the value of your equipment?"

"Maybe $1.5 million."

There was silence. I finally spoke up. "Sid, are you not interested in dealing with all of this?"

"No, I am fine with it. We just have a better start than I was expecting."

At that moment I was convinced we could do a deal. "You" switched to "we". We were now working together.

"Sid, do you want to see my projections?"

"Yes. Please fax them over to me."

"I am assuming that you are going to Myrtle Beach, John?"

"Sure, are you going to be there?" I asked.

"Of course. Let's meet when you get there. I have a lot of questions."

Not wanting to wait another 10 days to meet, I tried to convince Sid to come see the operation. "Why don't you come to see us at our plant?"

"Nah, I have too much going on this week. I have several deals that I am closing and I have been out way too much. I will see you in Myrtle Beach."

Now I had to scramble. I wasn't planning on going to Myrtle Beach since the show was pretty small, and our budget was cooked. Now I had no choice. To top it off, I would have to pay full airfare since I was not booking two weeks in advance. Just great. I am spending more money that we don't have.

Ten days went by in warp speed. Shuffling my schedule to allow three days off is always difficult. And on top of it, I had a physical exam scheduled that I knew that I could not blow off. I had not seen a doctor for 16 years and suddenly I was feeling the need. My frequent chest pains had me scared since a close friend recently had a heart attack.

It didn't take long for the doctor to diagnose my overriding problem: Significant stress. He ordered a stress test and sent me home on a portable heart monitor to determine the condition of my heart. I knew that I could not get the full walking stress test in until after the show. The thought of wearing this wired contraption had me a bit concerned. What if my heart was failing? That's just what I need right now, a heart attack. Worse, I could not soften the doctor's concerns with my wife. The monitor and wires blew any chance at concealing a secret.

Before I knew it, though, I was on a plane to Charlotte, connecting to Myrtle Beach.

The weather was much better than my first visit. Sunny and warm with light ocean breezes. I was feeling pretty good about this trip.

I wasn't on the floor for five minutes when Brit hunted me down.

"Don't blow it this time, FBC."

He chortled and winked.

I didn't respond, but I had brought my game face. I was ready.

Within an hour of the show starting, Sid was at the booth. He immediately pulled me aside.

"Hey, everyone I talk to in the industry tells me that this machine doesn't work."

"What?"

"It doesn't work. The bottles don't vend ... they hang up."

Now, I knew that we had problems with that. For the most part, we had the problems solved. But the industry had a long memory. Once a machine was branded inoperable, it was hard to overcome. In fact, this is one of the reasons we got into the bottle-vending game in the first place. Our competitor's machine that was leading the industry was not vending well, so the industry was willing to try our machine. Even with our hang-ups, it still vended better than Standard's machine. But try to advertise that. 'We stink, but not as bad as the other guy.' That never works.

"Sid, that's true. But we are passed that. The hang-ups were fixed. We needed to change the angle on the rack system, which has been done. Any machines in the field that had problems were retrofit with a kit we sent out. It was only on a few types of bottles that didn't slide well."

"Well, I heard it was more than that. Come walk with me."

Sid walked the floor introducing me to just about everyone. I knew some people in the industry, but Sid knew everyone. I suppose this was his time to demonstrate to me what he brought to the table. But I already knew.

After a couple of hours, he wanted to leave.

"Have you ever been to Paul and Mary's on the beach?"

"No."

"Let's go get Paul. It's almost 1:00. Your guys can handle the booth?"

"Sure they can. Brit is working it with Matt."

We left the show. We dropped our rental car at Paul's hotel and left with Sid.

Sid was staying at the north end of the beach, which by my account was the exclusive end. We went straight to the bar, which was packed. It was an interesting place. The bar was amidst a very large winding pool. The swimmers floated around in the pool on round inflatable tubes, jettisoned by water streams. It was fantastic and I wished I could jump in. It was mostly women at the bar and in the pool. Apparently, the husbands leave for the day to play one of the many championship golf courses during the day, while the wives spend the day poolside. Paul was in his glory.

We found three stools together and we ordered up.

The conversation was entirely about business. Sid asked question after question that Paul and I handled with relative ease. As Paul became more comfortable, I was beginning to feel relieved. I knew that we needed to do this, but I wanted Paul to buy into the deal. If he didn't like it, the deal would never work.

As the conversations continued, I could tell that Sid wanted to do the deal. I also knew that Paul was beginning to like Sid. And why not? Sid was a charming man. He was bright, polished handsome and polite. Furthermore, Sid made it clear to Paul that Paul would remain in charge. The plan was to work together to make the business succeed. Sid recognized that Paul was an integral part of the company and that his abilities were required for success. Sid was smart. He knew that the company needed more than money, it needed direction and identity. Both were items that he could bring. We needed to be the soldiers. Paul was to continue to run the operations, and I was to continue to maintain the financial and banking aspects of the business. Paul was buying in.

As the day progressed, we roughly outlined a plan that would allow the company to grow based on assumptions of a new and revamped sales and marketing effort. It was apparent that this was our weakest area. Sid's plan included bringing in an industry sales person as a senior vice president to oversee the distributor network that we had put together. He recommended that we search out a long time industry player to help create our identity and help establish credibility. Sid was right. But this would all take money, significant amounts of money.

At this point, I had already been feeding the company. In addition to the eighty-five thousand dollars that I put in at the end of the year to keep the doors open, I was now into covering the bank notes. I had put at least another $50,000 into the company in the past few weeks. The thought of the expansion scared me, but Sid was bringing in ample capital. I was still concerned that his initial offer of $1,000,000 was not enough.

After spending the afternoon together, dinner was in order. More business plans were discussed, which took us right into the evening. I cannot even remember where we dined the first night. All I remember was that we never stopped talking about the company and its potential.

By now, I was pretty tired and ready to head back to my room. Sid and Paul had other plans, though. There was a party at a local club being co-sponsored by some of the big industry players. All of the exhibitors from the show were invited, so off we went. All I could think of was sleeping, though.

The place was packed. Apparently the location was one of the hottest nightclubs in the area. We were late, so the hors d'oeuvres and complimentary drinks were long gone. The remaining participants of the closed party were mixed in with the club regulars and vacationers. It was a great atmosphere and I came to life a bit. Sid spent the first hour introducing Paul and me to everyone he could meet. Although we were trying to keep the deal quiet, the industry was keen at picking up on the ensuing deal. I didn't mind, though. I wanted the potential customers to know that we were on the right track and that we had proper financial backing. I also wanted the competitors to know that we weren't going away. I was finally feeling pretty optimistic about our future.

After we lapped the club, Sid hooked up with his dear friend from the Las Vegas trip. She was enjoying the night with her husband.

Sid didn't seem to mind being the third wheel since they were all good friends.

"Sid, I am spent. I need to get back and get some sleep. Paul is leaving with me. Do you want to meet for breakfast tomorrow before the show?"

"No, John. Let's plan on meeting at the show. I have a feeling tonight may run a bit late."

"Great. We'll see you at the show then."

Paul and I left Sid. We decided to make one last round through the club.

"Well, Paul, what do you think?"

"John, I feel a lot better about Sid. He has it together and his plans make sense. We need a strategy, though. We need to be sure that we get the right deal. We need to sit down and plan this out."

At this point, I could tell that Paul was into the deal. Now all we needed to do was close the terms with Sid.

Paul interjected, "Since Sid does not want to have breakfast, we should meet instead. We could lay out our plan."

"Okay, Paul. Plan on picking me up tomorrow at my hotel at 9 a.m. There are several restaurants near me. We can pick one tomorrow."

Since I made late reservations, I was stuck in a really cheesy hotel at the very south end of the beach. I didn't mind, though. The trip was working out well.

"Let's have one more drink to celebrate, John."

"I don't know, Paul. It has been a long day and I am pretty spent."

"Come on. There are two stools at the bar. Let's grab them quick."

We sat down at the bar. Paul was pretty excited about the prospects. In fact, this was the most evidence of spirit that I had seen in a long time. The future was feeling good again. He ordered a double Jack and Coke; I ordered a tall ice water.

Before long, Paul's interest turned away from business and to the lady sitting next to him. Soon, they were engulfed in deep conversation. I was tired and could only think about going to bed. Paul ordered another drink for himself and his new encounter. I could tell that he was not leaving with me. In fact, he wasn't even trying to include me in the conversation. I needed to leave.

I continued my pass through the club on my way to the door. I paused for a moment to take in the activity. It was pretty sad. The bar was filled with middle-aged men wearing wedding bands and toupees. Most of them were on the make. What were they thinking? I am not kidding, though. These old, fat, concealed bald guys actually thought that they could hook up with all of these young pretty ladies. My first thought was who would want them? My second thought was why are they acting this way? Don't they have wives and children? I left sad. I just hoped that I didn't end up like that some day.

The next morning came quickly. I was up at 6 a.m. to exercise and to make some notes preparing for my meeting with Paul. It was nearing 9 o'clock, so I went out to the street to meet him to save some time and to get some fresh air. Ten minutes went by, then 15. I needed to call Paul.

I tried calling his cell phone, but there was no answer. I didn't know the number to his room, so I went back up to my room to make the call. The phone rang twice before a lady answered it. Uh-oh, I rang the wrong room, I thought.

"Hello."

"Hi, is this Paul's room?"

"Who is calling?"

"It's John, his partner."

"Oh, hi John. Paul told me all about you."

"That's nice. Who is this?"

"I'm Maria."

"Maria, let me speak with Paul."

I could not believe this. It may be the most important day in the life of our business, and Paul is shacking up with some broad. This is just perfect.

"Hi, John," Paul mumbled.

"Paul, what are you doing? We were supposed to meet this morning."

"What time is it?"

"It's nine-thirty. We were to meet at nine."

"I'm late."

"No kidding. We need to meet Paul. Don't you understand?"
"Okay. I will pick you up at 10 o'clock."
"Fine."

I hung up the phone in disgust. I could not believe his behavior. It just never ends. Just when I think we are on the verge of building this thing back up, he acts like an idiot. I hope that Sid did not see him last night. I hope that he had the sense to leave the club and go to his hotel.

I spent the half hour watching the sunlight on the water from my ocean view room. I was back downstairs at 10 o'clock, waiting for Paul. Again 15 minutes passed and no sign of Paul. Again, there was no answer on his cell phone. This time I brought his room phone number with me. Again, the phone was answered on the second ring.

"Paul, where are you?"
"Hold on, John. Someone wants to talk to you."

After a moment, Maria was on the phone. She moaned to me, "John, Paul is unbelievable. He is dreamy. Oh-oh, I can't let him go."

I was sickened. His behavior is bad enough, let alone providing me with details. This was too much.

"Maria, put Paul back on the phone."
"He can't come to the phone right now. He's busy."
"Is he in shower?"
"No," she said in a low voice.
"Is he in the bathroom?"
"No," she whispered.
"Well, where is he?"
"He's under the covers."

I immediately hung up the phone. This guy is unbelievable. I had enough. I called a cab and went to the show, which started a half-hour ago.

When I got to the show, Sid was already in the booth. He was having a talk with Matt the salesman. I could see Matt yakking away and Sid just listening. Brit was also in the booth demonstrating the machine to a potential customer.

"Good morning, John. How was your night?"
"It was quiet. I slept well."

"You are a bit late this morning. I figured you would be here earlier."

"Oh, I was supposed to meet with Paul this morning, but our plans got messed up. I used the time to put together my thoughts about our meeting yesterday."

"Did the planning mix-up have anything to do with the lady that Paul picked up in the bar last night?"

I was stunned. Sid knew about Paul's encounter.

"I'm not sure. Probably, though."

Sid turned to Brit, who was now done with his demonstration. "You should have seen Paul last night. This chick was all over him, and he was all over her. He is quite the playboy."

"Yeah, he's like that all the time. The guy gets laid at all of these shows. He's remarkable." Brit said.

I just stood there taking it all in. I didn't have anything to add. The story was a bit blown out of proportion, but that's how those stories go. They are like fish tales; they just continue to grow bigger with time. And Paul encouraged the legend. He liked people thinking that he was a Casanova. It helped stroke his damaged ego.

I turned the conversation to business. "So, what do think, Sid? Are we still going to work this out?"

"Should I? Your partner hasn't convinced me that I should put up a million dollars. "

I knew that Paul was a problem. When he was on his game, he was as good as I have ever seen in small manufacturing. I think the pressure of the company's struggles brought out the worst of his behavior. I didn't think that he was too far-gone, however. He still had very creative ideas and led the shop employees with ease. His stubbornness and ego were a problem, but not insurmountable. At this point, I believed that if we pulled this out, he would snap back into and produce ideas like he historically had. I was confident of it.

"Well, Sid, Paul is Paul. He is a work hard, play hard type of guy."

"Well, if that is true, John, where is he right now?"

A good question that I could not answer, so I said nothing.

Sid then chimed in, "Let's go for a walk."

We started to walk the floor, stopping at the booths of our direct competitors. After watching the salesmen work the floor, Sid opened up a new conversation.

"John, what's the story on Matt?"

"What do you mean, Sid?"

"Tell me about Matt."

Sid was great at asking open-ended questions that required a detailed response.

"He's a decent salesman. A bit of a talker though. He's the kind of guy who turns a sound byte into a story. All he needs is one piece of information and he could write a book. The problem is that he fills in the blanks with whatever information he can fabricate that sounds good. You know the type. He's a blabber mouth."

"Well, he had some interesting things to say about Paul," Sid said.

"Like what?"

"Well, you should know, John."

The problem was that I didn't know. I did know that Matt liked to talk, and Paul gave Matt a big discussion topic. I knew that Paul and Matt were not friends. I knew that Matt was not part of the long-term plan for the company, especially in the model that was discussed yesterday. I was not afraid to sacrifice Matt for Paul. Now Paul and I had disagreements, and I was especially ticked at him for his behavior last night and this morning, but in no way was Matt more important than Paul.

"What I do know is that Matt doesn't fit the long-term plan of the company. I recognized this a while back, and yesterday confirmed my initial instinct.

"Regarding Paul, he can be irresponsible and a pain in my butt. However, he is my partner and we've chewed through some tough dirt together. I believe that he can still run this company. We just need to fix the financial mess. He doesn't function that well under this much financial pressure."

I couldn't believe that I was defending Paul. But deep inside, he was my friend and I really did still believe in him. We needed to get back on track together.

"Well that explains a lot," Sid said.

"What does it explain?"

"Matt had very little good to say about Paul, or the machine for that matter. That's not good for business when your salesman does not have confidence in the company and its leadership."

Right then, I knew that Matt's days were numbered. At that very moment, I decided to terminate him. Sid was right. I was ticked at Matt that he would try to submarine our deal with Sid. Although we tried to keep the concept of the deal quiet, it was becoming pretty obvious that a deal was pending. Matt had to recognize this and had to flap his gums anyway. I took it as a personal shot at me. This was after everything I did for him and the protection I gave him behind the scenes at the plant when money was tight and his numbers were off. I thought maybe I developed a level of loyalty with him. It was apparent that I did not. You can't buy loyalty. And, he was an idiot. The termination decision was made; it was not a matter of whether or not he *would* be let go, but rather a question of *when* he would be let go.

I focused on Sid's comment and replied, "Well, there is no love lost between the two. Matt doesn't matter anyway. He's gone at the first chance I get."

We continued our tour of the competitor's booths and eventually wound up back at our booth. Paul was finally there. He was giving a demonstration to a group of distributors. I could tell they liked Paul. After a late night on the town, ironically, he was on his game. Sid and I stood back a few yards and observed Paul's presentation. Just when I expected the worst, Paul came through like a champion. I was relieved.

After his demonstration, Sid and Paul left for a smoke break. I'm sure this is when Sid would take the opportunity to interrogate Paul about me. I didn't care. It needed to be done. Besides, I was happy to have a moment alone with Matt. I quickly pulled him to the back of the booth out of the earshot of passers-by.

"Matt, what are you thinking?" My question caught him by surprise.

"What?"

"What are you trying to do with Sid? Are you a moron or do you hate me that much?"

"What? John I like you. What are you so upset about?"

"Matt, I am referring to your discussion with Sid."

"I didn't say anything to Sid," Matt replied.

"That's not what I heard, Matt. I heard that you had some pretty choice words about Paul, the machine and the company."

"All I did was answer his questions."

I stood there looking at him in disagreement and said nothing. The silence was killing Matt and I knew that he would talk. He always did.

"Okay, so I told him that Paul can be a pain in the butt, and that the machine doesn't always work, but that was it. I swear."

That was it. In one brief encounter with Sid, he nearly unraveled the deal that I had been working on for more than a month. It is difficult enough trying to put together a deal, let alone have a human wrecking ball on your own team. I was reluctant to share any details with Matt about the potential deal with Sid for fear that it would end up published in the trade rag, or announced over the public address system at the show. Matt had a way of spreading information. But I needed to be sure he knew of the importance of a positive presentation to Sid.

"Matt, do me a favor, if you really do like me, please keep it positive. I know that we have all been through a lot the last few months. But Sid may be an important part of our future as a company. Respect him, respect me, respect Paul, and respect the company. That's all I ask. Use your head."

"Okay. I understand."

The rest of the show went by quickly. Again, Sid, Paul and I left early and headed to the beachside bar. Sid had more interrogatories for me and I handled them with ease. This was his way of performing due diligence and it was very effective. Typically, he knew the answer before he asked the question. The test was my effectiveness and honesty in answering them. I had no motivation to lie, so the process was pretty easy.

I also enjoyed learning his method. I was much more financially driven in my due diligence approach. Sid recognized that deals were all about the people involved. He connected every aspect of the deal to the people. He sized us up pretty well.

By now, our company was pretty predictable. We had a talented, but lacking team. A creative, ego-driven, control freak of a manager that employees either loved or hated led the company. An accountant was doing our marketing. Our sales effort was headed by an over-weight, loud mouth that was stifled under Paul's shadow. A glorified supervisor with absolutely no engineering or management training or ability managed our plant. The only area that we excelled was our financial reporting. In this area we were covered, and we were losing money precisely and accurately to the penny. But our distributors still liked us for one simple reason. We had a great idea. Our product filled a specific need. Remove the machine, and we were out of business. Another "once was" company that could not manage the pains of growth.

Sid was coming around to making his pitch. We were set to have dinner that night at a quiet local restaurant off of the beaten path. It was a townie restaurant unlike the trendy tourist spots dotting the area near the beach.

I was getting tired of answering questions, and was ready to move on to the next level. I knew that this would be difficult to accomplish since Paul pretty much set the price when we were visiting Sid at his posh Las Vegas hotel room. One million dollars for 50% of the company kept ringing in my ears. How could I renegotiate the number without losing the deal? It would be tricky, if not impossible. But I had to try.

I was pretty concerned about the money that I kept feeding the company in recent months to keep the doors open. My plan was to be sure that I was reimbursed for the money that I had in above my initial capital contribution. I was also pretty concerned about diluting my ownership beyond where I currently was. Reducing beyond 25% was not a very good feeling, especially since I still believed that this company was going to be successful and eventually pay handsome dividends.

We weren't at the restaurant very long when Sid began the negotiation.

"Okay gentlemen, you have my attention. Are we going to do business?" was Sid's opening.

I looked at Paul. As much as I wanted to answer for him, I couldn't. I knew that he had to want to do this, or the deal would never work. I could tell Sid was waiting for my reply, but I remained quiet deferring to Paul.

Paul sat quiet for a moment looking at me and then at Sid. I knew that Paul was going to go along with this deal. But I could tell that he was uncomfortable with me forcing him to respond. Paul knew that his answering first erased any chance of a future "I told you so" back in my face if the deal did not meet his expectations.

Paul hesitated, and then finally answered.

"Yeah, Sid. Yes we are."

"John, you are in agreement?"

I responded without hesitation, "Of course, Sid."

"Good, gentlemen. Let's work out the terms: one million for 50 percent of the company. The initial funding will be in the form of debenture notes. The notes will contain stock options that can be exercised at my election to buy 50 percent of the company. The option price will be $1. The notes will have a preference on any transaction. In other words, they must be paid off before any shareholders receive any benefit of a sale, or dividend. You will not be able to sell your shares as long as the debenture note remains outstanding. I will be able to sell my shares with board approval. The board will consist of Paul, John, me and another person appointed by me, if I choose."

Sid paused for a minute as if he was thinking of any other term that he missed. He then continued, "I think that summarizes the key points. I am sure I missed some points. And, of course, this is subject to a due diligence study period. I will want an exclusive study period for 90 days. If everything is in order, we can close soon after."

I sat quietly, awaiting the addition of any terms. Nothing was added.

"Well, John, what do you think?"

I sat quiet for a few minutes, and then responded, "It's pretty much the deal I expected. However, I am not convinced that $1 million is the right amount of money to make this work. I'm just not convinced."

"Paul, your thoughts?" Sid questioned.

"Am I still president and am I still in charge of the plant and development?"

"As long as you continue to perform, yes."

"Will you put that in writing?" Paul asked.

"Yes, you will both have employee contracts. And non-compete agreements."

"Fine." Paul replied.

"What about the current bank guarantees? Are you going to sign on as a guarantor, Sid?" I inquired.

"No. I will not."

"The bank may require you to sign."

"I won't. Besides, the bank will agree to anything that I ask, provided that more money comes into the deal," Sid said.

I was quiet.

"John, you still seem unconvinced."

"Well, I have a lot of reservations. Ultimately, I get screwed in this deal."

"How do you figure?" Sid asked.

"Well, for starters, I will be reduced to a 12 and a half percent owner, but I will shoulder 100 percent of the bank guarantee. That's not fair."

"What about Paul? Aren't you both signed on the notes?"

"Sure, but Paul can't cover any of the note, so it's my responsibility. We are signed joint and several. You know, 100 percent each."

"I understand," was Sid's only reply.

After a few moments of silence, Sid inquired again. "That can't be everything. What else is bothering you, John?"

Sid was very perceptive.

"Well, here are my issues with this deal. First, I think it will take more than $1 million to make all of the improvements that we already discussed. I can see most of the million being used to fix the current financial backlog and barely being enough to cover the cash flow shortage of the next six months. Second, I can live with the dilution. I would rather have 12½ percent of a successful company than 25 percent of a failing company. But I don't like being the only guarantor. Third, I have at least $135,000 in the deal in the form of notes. When I add all of this up, the deal is not fair. I have more skin in the game proportionately than anyone else."

That mouthful stopped the conversation. Luckily, the waiter came by and took our order, allowing all of us a few minutes to mentally prepare for the next round.

After some small talk about the great food while waiting for our drinks, we finally got back down to business.

Sid got us back on track.

"When did you make the loans, John?"

"Eighty-five came in right before the mezzanine deal about a year ago. I had to subordinate this note to Lake Bank. The remaining $50,000 has been recent. Mostly within the last two months."

"Okay, John. What if I paid off your notes? I will pay $85,000 in addition to the $1 million. The other $50,000 will come out of the $1 million proceeds at closing."

"What about any additional notes that I need to make to keep the company cash flowing between now and closing the deal?"

Sid thought for a moment. "How much do you think you will need?"

"I'm not sure. Maybe none; maybe $50,000 more. If it's much more than that, I will have a problem raising the money."

Sid thought for a moment, and then said, "You will be reimbursed for any notes that you have in the deal going forward. So you are covered."

We all grew quiet. Up until now, I really figured that Paul would be the one to challenge the deal. He sat there, apparently content on remaining the president and making a salary. I was struggling with the money issues, but I understood that this was the best deal I could manage, being that the price was firm since the fateful first meeting.

"So, do we have a deal?" Sid asked.

"I'm in," said Paul.

I still wasn't sure.

"I need time to think about this. I am still concerned about the bank guarantees."

As if on cue, the first course of our meal came, providing a natural break in the negotiations. We all ate quietly, enjoying our meals.

After a while, Sid started again.

"John, you are not at any more risk under this deal, than you are now. Actually, you are better off. The company will survive. We will make a lot of money. Do you think I am investing $1 million to lose? Come on."

"It still bothers me, Sid. I have all of the downside risk, but only a sliver of the upside benefit. The deal is upside down."

"John, if we could work out something regarding the bank notes, would you be in?"

"Like what?" I questioned.

"Well, we may be refinancing the notes anyway, so that would eliminate your guarantee. There are other ways, too. I will talk to my attorneys, Finagle and Huckster; they will come up with something. I want this to be fair and you to be comfortable."

We all laughed at the "Finagle and Huckster" comment.

"All right, Sid, if the bank issue can be solved to my satisfaction, I am in."

Sid and I stood up and shook hands. Then Paul joined in. We all shook. We had a deal.

When I got back to my room after dinner, I couldn't even think of sleeping. I was still caught up in the terms. I had agreed in principle and details were still forthcoming, but largely the deal was spelled out.

I decided to take a walk on the beach. The cool night ocean air was just the trick. As I walked on the beach, I could see the shadows of lovers walking hand in hand, as carefree as the ocean breeze. They didn't care about my bank guarantees, or about my cash-flow problems. They only cared about the here and now of the surf, the moonlight, and the romance in the air. I cared about none of those things. All I cared about was straightening out the company, and keeping our deal fair.

As I stared out into the blackness of the sea, my thoughts turned to the traders of old, cast adrift on the ocean. They were risk takers. They left all they knew behind and sailed the vast sea. They did it for money. They did it for trade. They did it for the dream. They were seafaring entrepreneurs, with a belief so strong they could face any level of danger with courage and grace.

I then thought of the shipwrecks and the souls lost on sea. They were taken in by all that surrounds them because their confidence overtook there abilities, or simply because their luck ran out. Either way, they were just a memory to those that knew them, and an illusion to me. I could not see them, but I understood why they did it. I felt a connection to them, a kinship. I knew them as the glorious ghosts of the night sea.

Two seagulls noticed me and swooped down to gather a closer look in the hope of me offering them some food. I had none to offer. They then turned their attention to the dark sea. They would run from the lapping waves trying to stay clear of the water, only to chase the flotsam in hope of finding a fish or some other sea creature for dinner.

As I walked, I realized that I had no choice in this deal. Without a deal, I was likely doomed. With a deal, I stilled carried the risk of loss, but I gained some upside. It didn't take me long to mentally agree that this was the best I could do. By the time of my epiphany, I was back at my hotel.

The next morning, I was awakened by a ringing telephone.

"John, it's Paul. I will be over in a half hour."

Not wasting any time, I hastily got showered and dressed for my unscheduled meeting.

A sudden pounding startled me. Bam. Bam. Bam. It was Paul at the door. "Hey, did you talk to your wife about the deal?" he asked.

"No. It was too late when I got in to call her."

"I talked to Cindy this morning. We both agreed that you should not have to dilute so much, so here is what we want to do. If the company ever sells for a profit, we will give you some of our share. It will be enough so that you'd be a 17.5 percent owner instead of 12.5 percent. What do you think?"

I was puzzled by the offer. "Well, that is very kind of you Paul. I thank both of you. But why are doing this?"

"Well, we know that you have saved this company over and over. We just want you to feel like you are being treated fairly."

"Fine, Paul. I am okay with this. If you want to cover the five percent, that is fair. Thank you."

I never could figure out why the offer was really made. Maybe Paul was feeling guilty for spending the night with Maria. Maybe he was just buying me off. Maybe he wanted to be sure to keep me on his side, so to speak, since we were inviting a new partner to the game.

Maybe it was all Cindy's doing just to get back at Paul. I didn't know and I really didn't care. I also didn't give it any more thought.

We arrived at the show early. I was leaving that day, and was looking forward to a short day. Sid arrived shortly after and sought me out immediately.

"John, you are one heck of a salesman. What did you get me to agree to yesterday?"

"What kind of welcome is that, Sid?"

"You really pulled the wool over my eyes, John. I feel like I was fleeced!" Sid said.

"I'm not sure where you are going with this Sid, but I thought we worked out a fair deal and shook on it. We still have a deal, right?"

"Of course."

At that moment, Brit came strolling past.

"Well gentlemen, I take it that last night went well since we are all so happy this morning?"

"Yes, Brit, I think last night went fine." I said.

"We have a deal." Sid added.

"Man, did you see that chick in the FastCo booth?" Paul chimed in.

We all stood there laughing at Paul. The rest of the day went great.

Chapter 19

People of mediocre ability sometimes achieve outstanding success because they don't know when to quit. Most men succeed because they are determined to.

--George Allen

I wasn't home for more than a day when I received a call from one of our competitors. To maintain the confidentiality of the parties, I always referred to them, and will continue to refer to them as XYZ Company.

XYZ was a direct competitor, though a much bigger operation than we were. Based on industry rumors, they ranked in the top five manufacturers of soda machines. They had a strong industry presence and a long history of successful operations.

Recently, however, they had suffered a financial blow from a large customer. They were contracted to design and build a new machine for a large bottler, only to lose the actual production contract within months of completing a brand new factory. It was a pretty horrible story. It was one that was upsetting to me, since I could relate to the whimsical nature of the customers in this business.

I was anticipating a letter of intent from Sid. In my world, my word was my bond, and we had a working deal. However, a lot had to still happen to close a deal. I had also been consistently screwed on deals in this industry thus far, so I was feeling a bit less concerned about others and was more interested in what was best for our company. Besides, I couldn't resist returning the call of XYZ out of curiosity. So I did. Since I had a direct cell number, I was confident of a direct contact with the president who originally called me.

"Glen, John Davis returning your call."

"Hi John. Thank you for calling back. I am glad that you called. How was the show last week?" he asked.

"It was fine, Glen."

"I wanted to get over to your booth to meet you. My people tell me that you were doing very well with your new machine. Congratulations." Glen added.

"Thank you, Glen."

"I am interested in meeting with you and your partner. When can we get together?" inquired Glen.

"What is the purpose of our meeting?" I asked.

"Well, I like your machine and I like the direction that you are going with your company. And, you probably already know that we are in need of a new project. I figured that it may make sense for us to meet."

I thought carefully about this conversation and I had to be careful with my response. I wasn't sure where this was going, or where this call was coming from. I knew a bit about XYZ from the industry rumors, but I also knew that this could be a set up to pump us for information. I provided a guarded response.

"I am interested in meeting. However, you will need sign a confidentiality agreement, Glen."

"Fine. E-mail me the agreement. I would like to come in on Wednesday. I am bringing my vice president of sales and my head engineer. Be sure your partner is there, too. We will arrive at your plant at 10 a.m.," Glen said.

"Okay, Glen. Be sure to return the signed agreement, or your trip will be for nothing."

Glen understood. "If you send it today, you will have it back today. I will see you Wednesday," he said.

Just like that, we were in play. It's hard to keep the lid on a pending deal, especially when the primary negotiation occurred at a trade show. I knew the cat was out of the bag about our pending deal with Sid. Let's face it; the industry knew that we were in financial trouble. There was no way to hide it. Sid spending the entire show in our booth was all the industry needed to make the rumor fact.

I spent the rest of the day performing some cursory due-diligence on the gentlemen joining us for our Wednesday rendezvous. I was a bit nervous about the meeting, especially since we came to initial terms with Sid. However, I needed a deal and was receptive to anything. I needed to find out where Paul's head was regarding the meeting.

"Paul, XYZ wants to meet us on Wednesday," I told him.

"Why?" he asked.

"Well, it's pretty obvious they want to talk to us about a deal. Word is out that we are working with Sid. I think this is there attempt at sliding in before Sid. What do you think?"

"Did Sid get us his letter of intent yet?" Paul asked.

"No. I haven't seen it, nor have I spoken to him since the show. What about you?" I said.

"No, I haven't heard from him." Replied Paul.

We were both quiet.

Paul jumped in. "I think that we should keep the meeting, John. What is our risk? Until we have a letter of intent, we are fair game."

"I agree, Paul. We need to move quickly, though. When Sid comes up with the agreement, we will have to honor it. It is only fair."

When Wednesday came I felt like a cheating husband en route to his first bout of infidelity. I was nervous and excited at the same time. I liked deals so much, and the advent of a bidding war for the company was pretty exciting. But I kept thinking about Sid's letter of intent that I had yet to receive.

By now, most of the people at our plant knew that something was in the making. The office personnel were always the first to know. In a small company, it is hard to keep anything a secret. All you can really hope for is that they won't share their knowledge and suspicions with the customers and vendors. It is hard to stop the talking inside the company. I did try to keep all of the conversations confidential, but when the top three executives of your competitor from across the country walk in the front door, it's hard to convince anyone that it is a social visit.

The meeting went very well. We shared just about every detail about the machine and they were impressed. Normally, I would be skeptical sharing this level of detail with a competitor. But in this instance it was pretty risk free. First, we had a written, signed confidentiality agreement. Of course, these types of agreements only work between honorable parties. Since the visiting president was also a

CPA, I felt a bond of honor. Second, several patents protected the equipment. Third, if a competitor chose to, they could simply buy one of our machines and reverse engineer it in the comfort of their own plant. Essentially, there were few secrets in this industry and fewer ways to protect them.

After a half-day of meetings, they were off. The plan was they would get back to us with a plan and a proposal.

A few days later, Sid finally called me with instructions regarding the letter of intent. Apparently, his legal counsel was vacationing so the process was slowed. Within two days of the call, his version of the letter of intent was sent to me. It contained all of the oral agreement terms that we discussed. It was refreshing to read.

To be true to XYZ, I called Glen and informed him of a pending deal with another entity. He congratulated us, and wished us luck with the deal. I then signed Sid's letter of intent. We were finally moving forward.

Now that we came to terms, the real work was just beginning. Sid visited the plant several times. Each time he would bring with him experts from the industry that he had worked with in the past. And each time, he left with more questions than answers.

Our fabrication department was as sophisticated as any in the industry. Our assembly process, however, was another story. It was obvious to Sid's experienced professionals that we were a real project. It also was becoming more obvious that my instincts about the amount of money that we would need may be correct. I could tell that $1 million was not going to be enough money.

Still, we moved forward. The orders were pouring in from the Las Vegas and Myrtle Beach shows. The condiment stand business was also flourishing, keeping the fabrication department at full capacity.

Another problem was brewing in the shop, however. Through all of the adversity that we faced, we always seemed to keep the company afloat with the small line vending machine lines. This was changing, however. The orders had been slowing over the last few months, and now we were starting to get alarmed.

The decline in small line vending seemed to begin with the departure of our original salesman Larry. He was always active in selling the small machines. It was a comfort zone for him and because of his success, the money rolled in for him and the company. It was a staple item for us. We had been making the machines for 10 years, 256 machines at a time. Our plant was geared up to produce the machines, and they took little management time.

Sid was not pleased with our involvement with the small line vending machines. Not because of our ability to manufacture them, and not with the cash flow they provided. He didn't like our involvement because of what they meant to the industry.

For decades, small time distributors ran scams using small line vending machines. These distributors would run advertisements in the local business opportunities sections of the newspapers. They would advertise a vending route for sale, complete with accounts and equipment. They would then sell these routes to unsuspecting budding entrepreneurs for very high profits. Some of the routes were legitimate, but most were not. About every five years, the Fed's would jump in with covert operations like "clean sweep" which temporarily eliminated most of the crooks and sent many of the boiler room operators to jail.

We were not involved with the scam artists that ran these cons. We were equally concerned about the ill will they caused the industry. We also were not interested in doing business with criminals.

Our primary distributor had been in business for over ten years. They did sell the machines as a "business opportunity". However, they would sell the equipment to their customers after the customer had an established vending route. The distributor helped find the route locations, provided equipment financing, and taught their customer how to operate a vending business. All this came at a high price that they would roll into the cost of the equipment.

I felt comfortable being the manufacturer of the equipment. We provided a high quality machine and unmatched service and a lengthy warranty. We were regarded as the finest manufacturer of small line vending machines and were proud of our accomplishments.

At about the time of doing our deal with Sid, the demand had begun to wane. I suspected that the slow death was caused by the information flow available through the Internet. The scams were being uncovered and published on the Internet by the victims. This essentially tainted the operation of the few legitimate distributors in the industry. Additionally, most of the equipment was now available through pure equipment distributors that offered equipment for sale without all of the cost associated with our primary distributor that offered more services.

Sid wanted us out of the small line all together, but I resisted since we needed the cash flow. Sid's concern dated back to "operation clean sweep" in which he was called to testify on behalf of the attorney generals office against several companies that were running scams. I could not convince him that we were not partaking in the scams. He didn't care, though. He did not want his reputation harmed, nor did he want a Federal investigation.

Fortunately, or unfortunately, we never had a chance to debate manufacturing the small line machines. One day, our distributor dropped us without any notice. Of course this violated the terms of the agreement, but what real recourse did we have? Did we really want to continue to manufacture and sell equipment to a company that did not want to business with us? They would certainly stick us with the receivable, and that was the last thing we needed right now. It was easier to work out a deal whereby the contract would be set aside, provided that they paid the entire amount due to us. They honored the agreement and we received our money. Sid was happy that we were out. I was bummed because we just lost $140,000 of sales per month. Even though that was historical lows for the small line machines, it was still sales and cash flow that we desperately needed.

Ultimately the reason our distributor left was directly related to Larry our ex-salesman. When Larry left our company, he left on decent terms. He told us that he had an opportunity to go into business with his father-in-law, and that it was an opportunity of a lifetime. Not being one to stand in the way of someone's dreams or opportunity, I wished him well and helped him transition from our company to his new found opportunity. His opportunity, as he described it, was completely out of the vending machine industry. Since he had a non-compete agreement, I was completely comfortable with his reasons.

As it turned out, from the moment Larry left our company, he began contracting with a company in China to provide an identical knock off of our equipment. Even the artwork and decoration was the same. Within a couple of months of the expiration of his non-compete agreement, the Chinese machines were being imported at less than half of the cost of our machine. Naturally, he gained the entire attention of our distributor who gladly jumped at the cost savings. And just like that, we were out. We never even saw it coming. We were so busy and preoccupied by the new machine, that we did not even recognize the warning signs. All along, though, we knew the day was coming when we wouldn't be manufacturing the small machines, but it would have been better to go out on our terms and on our timetable.

Since sales were down even more, we needed more support from my bank account. It now became a race to see if we could stay in business long enough to even get the deal done with Sid.

Nearly every week, I was writing a check out of my personal bank account to cover the payroll and the payroll taxes. It was getting pretty tiring.

It just seemed like the deal was taking forever. It was now the end of June. I had returned the 25-page due diligence questionnaire to "Finagle & Huckster" weeks ago. I was still awaiting news on the next step.

Just about the time that we were ready to fund the deal, I received a call from Lake Bank's lawyer inquiring to the terms of the new deal. I provided to him a copy of the letter of intent and a quick written narrative in my words what the deal meant to the company, and more importantly, what the deal meant to both of the banks.

Suddenly, the deal was put on hold. Lake Bank decided that the new deal violated the terms of the mezzanine deal that we put into place 15 months earlier. The problem had to do with the reorganization of the voting trust and the naming of directors. As it turns out, the Lake Bank agreements required that Paul and I maintain control, defined as 51% of voting control while our debt was outstanding with Lake Bank.

Our new deal called for Sid having a "swing" vote if the company had a negative equity position. Essentially, the voting trust was reconfigured so that Paul and I voted as one vote, and Sid voted as the other vote. This eliminated me from having swing vote power to overrule Paul. So, Paul and I would have to first agree, and then we would vote either with or against Sid. All of the same tiebreakers were in effect from our first agreement, except one new one was added. In the event that the company had negative equity, Sid would receive two votes. This made sense since if we were losing equity, which at this point was all his, he would get control of the company until such time that positive equity was restored.

Personally, I liked the idea because it removed the stigma of me losing Sid's money. Once we started to eat into his principal, he had a chance to stop it irrespective of what Paul or I wanted. That was very fair in my opinion.

The bank's lawyer disagreed. While we tried to come to some rational solution to the deal, the cash flow continued to worsen. It was becoming like a scene from the old Batman shows where Batman and Robin needed to escape before a 4,000-pound cleaver fell from the sky to decapitate them. I was worried that I was out of ideas, and I was certainly out of money. Meanwhile, I had stretched our vendors so long, that most of them would not sell us any more materials, so our plant was running into constant stock outs. We couldn't even fill the orders that we had so the prospect of new cash from accounts receivable was out of the question.

Finally, I proposed a solution that would solve both Sid's lawyers and Lake Bank's lawyers. Now it was a matter of approval from the bank president.

I had a pretty long history with Peter, the bank president, through my accounting practice, and while putting the mezzanine deal together. He liked our deal and I was confident that he would go along with it, provided his counsel was satisfied that the language and the agreement made sense. All we needed was his signature.

That became the problem. While we were all debating on the right words, the bank president skipped out of town on vacation. Worse, he was fishing in Northern Canada, far out of the range of cell phones and faxes.

Meanwhile, Sid is ready to fund the deal, but won't until the deal is signed by the bank. At the plant, we are out of money and cannot make payroll on Friday. I am losing the little remaining hair that I have. Paul was pretty much a basket case. At this point, 90 days after working out our new deal with Sid, Paul had pretty much given up on the deal. He was spending his days searching for porn on the

Internet or maintaining one of his many on-line romances in which he was engaged.

Frantically, I kept calling the bank president's cell phone. He should never have given it to me. Finally, after four days, he went into town to get more food and bait. Luckily, his phone notified him of my numerous messages and he called me.

"Peter, I need your help," I said.

"Yes, John. What do you need? You do know that I am on vacation in Canada?"

"Yes, but this is pretty urgent." I begged.

I explained the entire convoluted mess to him.

"Okay, John. Get a copy of the language faxed to me. I need to read it. If it makes sense for the bank, I will sign it and fax it back to you."

Within minutes I had the document faxed to him. He called me right back.

"John, I need to talk to my lawyer before I sign this. I will call him right now and will call you back." And like that, Peter hung up the phone.

All I could do was agree and wait.

I didn't hear back from him, and hours passed. I finally called the bank's lawyer. He was in court all day and missed the call. I am running out of luck. I leave several more calls with the banker and the lawyer, begging for action as to not lose the deal.

Meanwhile, Sid is getting restless. He too knows what is riding on the deal. Paul meanwhile is still searching for porn.

At 4:00 on Thursday, I finally hear from the banker. He agreed to sign off on the deal. He instructed me that I would be receiving a fax from the local bait and tackle shop, which had the only fax machine in town.

Within a half hour, my fax began to ring. It was coming from Canada. Just as I was sighing relief, I noticed that the fax was coming in blank. It turns out that they put the paper in the wrong way. Things couldn't get much worse, but in fact they did. The banker was long out of cell phone range and I did not have the phone number to the bait shop to inform them of the miscue. So I did the only thing I could. I faxed them back a desperate message and my phone number. Again, all I could do was wait.

At about 6:30, another fax came through with signatures and apologies from the bait shop. I immediately broadcast the signature pages to every party involved. Now, all we needed to do was get our signatures on the documents and the money wired.

Anticipating a long distance closing, I met at Badger Bob's office for a signing party. Badger Bob as I called him, was my fantastic and brilliant attorney. As Paul and I signed documents, Badger Bob would attest verbally to our signatures, and then would fax the signature page to Sid's lawyer. After about an hour of signing, we had the deal closed. By 2:30 the wire hit the account and the payroll was covered. We used another lifeline and we were running out.

We had to make this deal work.

Chapter 20

Surround yourself with the best people you can find, delegate authority, and don't interfere.

--Ronald Reagan

Now that the deal was done with Sid, it seemed as if we could breath a little bit better. We now had additional capital and a strong industry leader on our side. At this point, I really felt as if we made it. I was comfortable in Sid's ability and contacts to make the deal work, and work well. It was new life, a whole new game.

Sid was eager, too. He had already been working on sales deals by calling in years of favors and relationships. He was magnificent. Companies that never would even take our calls were lining up to place orders. His influence was immediately felt and the buzz in the industry was that we were now on our way to success.

Sid did not waste any time coming to the plant. In fact, he was on the first plane Monday morning. I was excited to see him and get to work. It was my job to pick him up at the airport. As I circled through the arrival area, I could see his smile a mile away.

"Hi Sid"

"Hi partner," he said, as he offered me a firm handshake.

We didn't have too much to say as I navigated through the rush hour traffic on route to the plant. In fact, Sid was very quiet. Too, quiet in fact.

Finally, Sid broke the silence. "So, when were you going to tell me that Matt quit?"

"What?" I replied.

"Matt, your salesman. When were you going to tell me that he quit?"

"He didn't quit." I replied.

"Come on, John. I told you that I know everything that's going on in the industry."

I was shocked by the news. I didn't even know that he quit. This was a big problem. Not so much that Matt quit, since I was planning on replacing him anyway. The problem was that I did not know. Nothing good could come from this. I will either come across to Sid as a liar, since I denied knowing about the event. Or worse, I will come across as an idiot for not knowing what is happening within the company.

The real problem was Paul. I knew that Matt was tired of working with Paul. Further, Matt had to know that I was pretty down on him for not supporting the company during the pending deal with Sid. During the due diligence process, it was becoming apparent to the employees that some type of major change was looming. If Matt had any sense of his future, he had to realize that he probably did not fit the future plans of the company. In fact, I had a sense that he was looking for a job. I always can tell when an employee is leaving. It is as if they let off a scent. But, his sense of timing could not have been worse. Further, I was pretty disappointed that he didn't even talk to me about it.

I finally responded. "Sid, I did not know about this. When is his last day?"

Sid jumped on that and retorted, "His last day was Friday. What is going on, John?"

With that response, I knew that Paul was the problem. This could not have happened without his knowledge. And he didn't bother to tell me about it. That really ticked me off. Paul had this way of concealing things that he knew would make me go off. Further, I would have investigated the reasons for Matt's leaving during an exit interview. I felt that Paul was covering something up by denying me access. I needed to learn more, but now was not the time.

"I don't know, Sid. I was so busy getting everything in order trying to get the deal done. And I was supposed to be of town on Friday, so I was scrambling after signing to get home and pack up the family to get away for the weekend. We haven't had a vacation for years. How did you find out, Sid? Did Paul call you?"

I knew that Paul would not have called Sid without calling me first. I was curious as to the answer.

Sid replied in a disgusted tone, "He called the media! He actually called one of my friends at a trade rag to say 'good-bye' to her. He then told her to keep it quiet, since Paul did not want anyone to know yet since it could end our pending deal."

Sid stopped talking, and let those words just hang there. I did not know how to respond. I was shocked and angry with Paul. I could feel my face get warm. I knew that my blood pressure was rising. I wanted to kill Paul.

But what about Matt? Unbelievable. I knew that he was like a broadcast system, but how stupid could he be to call the media and ask them to keep it quiet. This was the most unbelievable part of the drama. How could he make that call? How could I not know what was going on. I started to recall a conversation with Paul about Matt about six or seven weeks back.

"Well, Sid, I remember Paul telling me some time back that Matt was not happy and wanted to talk to us about his future with the company. I put it off since I was uncertain about his future. I never figured that this would happen."

"Are you telling me that you really did not know?" Sid questioned.

"I was suspicious that he might be planning to jump, and I knew that he was unhappy. And I was certain that he did not fit our future plans, so I let the situation unfold. I didn't stay abreast of it. It was my fault. I had no idea that he was leaving now, though."

By this time, we were at the plant. I immediately stormed into Paul's office.

"Paul, did Matt quit?"

"Yes."

"Was his last day on Friday?" I asked.

"Yes."

"When were you planning on telling me?" I asked.

At this point, Sid walked into the office.

"You knew already." Paul responded.

"Did you tell me?" I asked.

"I don't remember if I did, or if Matt did. I thought I did, but maybe I left it up to Matt to tell you. I can't remember." Paul said.

That explained a lot. I knew that Paul did not tell me, likely in fear of my response. Matt would never have told me. He was too afraid to deal with me directly since I would have challenged him, especially in an exit interview.

I continued my interrogation of Paul. "Did you tell Matt to keep it quiet?"

"Sure I did. I didn't want rumors started. You know, with Matt's mouth and all, he could have started something. I just wanted him to leave quietly." Paul explained.

Sid stood there looking at the two of us in disgust. And I didn't blame him. This was a ridiculous situation and the story seemed unbelievable. I was embarrassed and mad at the same time. Sid turned away and started to walk down the hall. As he was leaving, he motioned for us to follow him, so we did.

When we got into the conference room, I felt like a student being summonsed to the principal's office for a reprimand. I was worried. Sid motioned for us to take a seat, and he slowly closed the door behind him. He then calmly walked to the end of the table. Paul and I were sitting across from each other.

Sid stood quietly for a few minutes, and then he spoke. "Gentlemen, let's get something straight right now. If we are going to continue as partners, we will always tell the truth. There will be no lies or deceit. Do you understand?"

"But Sid" I started to reply.

Sid cut me off and continued. "No more lies. I don't care what anyone has to say. Do you understand?"

It was too late for explanation or reason. I could not defend myself. So, I just nodded in agreement.

Sid continued. "Paul, do you understand?"

Paul just sat there leaning back in his chair. He then took a long drag from his cigarette, and smugly replied. "Yea, I understand."

After a few minutes of silence, Sid said, "Okay, gentlemen, this is behind us. Let's get to work."

And we did. We spent most of the day introducing the key people to Sid. Sid would then interview each person as if he was sizing up his team of players to determine what he had to work with. The level of questions was interesting. Not only was he interested in their abilities and skills, but also he asked questions about their ages, families, wives, and children. All of the questions that I learned were either taboo or illegal. Sid didn't care. He needed to know his team and he dissected the group his way. I liked it.

Getting the crew organized and the company moving in the right direction was the easy part. Sid was pretty organized in his approach and it was obvious. I could tell, however, that Paul was not as enthusiastic about Sid's approach. Although it was not intended to be, I could tell Paul viewed it as a shot against his ability to manage. It was a definite shot to Paul's brittle ego.

It is interesting to observe people in this situation. Ultimately, this could be the best thing for Paul and his career. Long ago, Paul recognized that he is not a good manager. I disagreed to a point. I thought he was a good manager for the size company that we once were. But we were a bigger company now. Not necessarily by sales volume, but rather in complexity. We needed more than good shop fundamentals. We now were building a brand, a company identity, and to some degree, an entire market. This was no small task, and it required a great deal of management skill. Skills that were beyond those that Paul possessed. For better than a year, Paul and I had discussions about the eventual need for a more effective business manager. In fact, we discussed the possibility of me joining the company in a full time capacity to help bridge the management gap that was developing. I declined as to not want to disrupt my successful accounting and consulting practice.

So as this new situation unfolded, it should have been viewed by Paul as an opportunity to step back and let someone else deal with the areas where he was not effective, and ultimately did not enjoy doing. What he liked doing, and where he excelled, was design. Paul had good visual mathematician skills and a fundamental understanding of mechanics. He lacked true engineering training, but that ultimately led to him arriving at answers that were creative. He was not bound by the restrictions of theory.

But Paul didn't act as if it was an opportunity. In fact, almost immediately he acted with contempt and disdain for Sid. Paul let his ego get in the way, and it was obvious to me. So instead of spending more time designing and improving our product, he began to spend time gossiping with the shop personnel. His actions become subversive to Sid's goals.

I, on the other hand, remained in my role as accountant. I was still active in all aspects of the business and remained involved at an executive decision-making level, but my primary purpose was to keep the cash flow positive. But right from the beginning, I knew that this was a more difficult task than anyone ever expected it to be.

Back in Las Vegas, when the concept of $1 million was shouted out, I was concerned about the ability to make the deal work. Again, during the Myrtle Beach negotiations, I stressed my concerns about the amount of money required to orchestrate the turn around. And I was right. I could already see a cash call on the distant horizon, and we just started the new deal. This was not good.

Money flowed out of this company like water from a fire hose. The problem started before the deal even closed. The original deal called for the money that I had loaned the company to be paid back to me at closing. Additionally, Sid agreed to reimburse me for any additional cash that I needed to inject into the company to keep it cash flowing while our deal was finalized. Well, the time frame to close the deal extended to over three months. And they were painful months. Throughout this period, we had difficulty manufacturing the orders that we had on the books. Our working capital position was so weak, we could not keep enough inventory on hand to keep the production moving. This ultimately caused all of our problems.

Maintaining the right production and inventory level is a tricky proposition. Countless books have been written about the subject. You could fill a room with the theories and methods that have been developed to track the inventory usage and ordering levels and quantities. Ironically, I was well versed in most of the commonly accepted theories. Further, I instituted several mechanisms over the years to aid in keeping pace with purchasing and production. They were simple, but generally they were effective.

But you can throw all of the theory out the window when you run out of money.

Like any company that was hurting for cash, we fell behind payment terms with our vendors. Typically, most vendors understand if the slow payment situation is temporary. The overriding problem, however, was that we abused our payment terms so often that we used all of our goodwill. Worse, when we were slow in the past, our payables clerk, as well as Paul, hid from the problem and avoided the collection calls. This never works since the vendors just get angry and eventually cut you off, or put you on cash on delivery. And we were there with most of our vendors.

Our company was purchasing about $225,000 of raw materials each month. And typically, our 30-day terms were stretched to 45 days. But as our capital eroded due to our monthly operating losses, the 45-day period was pushing 60 days or better. So, essentially, we had close to $450,000 of accounts payable outstanding, assuming a 60-day payment period. When we were put on COD with our vendors, we now needed to pay for the purchases upon receipt, which in theory, required an additional $225,000 of cash. So, essentially our working capital was immediately $675,000 in the hole. Even worse, many of our custom item suppliers put us on cash upon order terms. And, on top of it all, we lost our small machine distributor, so that cash flow was gone

Since we did not have enough cash to buy the required inventory, we could not maintain efficient levels of production. In fact, we couldn't maintain any level of production. Without production, we could not ship product, without sales, there were no new accounts receivable. Without any additional accounts receivable, there was no increase in working capital. Further, the machines we did manage to manufacture were costing us more money to make than for which we could sell them. The reason is simple. The overhead to manufacture 30 machines was the same as it was to manufacture 300. If we covered our costs at 200, we were spitting up blood at 30 machines.

During this period, I injected as much cash as I could to keep the production moving, but it was not nearly enough to keep up. All told, I loaned another $125,000 to the company, bringing the total owed to me at closing to about $210,000.

So, the economics of the deal after closing went like this, $1.085 million comes in. $210,000 was paid to me to satisfy the personal money that I used to carry the company. Another $40,000 was paid to the lawyers to draft the deal, so that left $835,000 for working capital and to finance the growth and development of the company. Since we were already close to $675,000 behind in our working capital, we were still in trouble. It doesn't take an accountant to figure out that a cash call was near, unless we could turn the corner very, very quickly.

Chapter 21

Here's a rule I recommend: Never practice two vices at once.
--Tallulah Bankhead

I was working early at the shop one Thursday morning when I noticed Paul come stumbling through the door. It was about 7:10 a.m., which was very early for Paul. His clothes were disheveled and his hair was a mess. It looked as if he did not sleep a bit.

"What happened to you last night?" I asked.

Paul was surprised at my presence. He laughingly responded, "What? Do I look bad?"

"Paul, not only do you look bad, you smell bad too. What did you do now?"

He tried to keep a straight face, but he started cracking up like a teenager. "I slept in my truck last night." He said proudly.

"Why?"

"I couldn't go home. I was busted."

Now I was confused. I knew that Paul had moved out. I knew that he tried to make a go of it again and moved back in. Then, I knew that Cindy tossed him out again. I wasn't sure, but I thought he was living with his girlfriend again. I could not keep up. Beside, curiosity got the better of me so I had to ask.

"I thought you moved out and were back in with your girlfriend." I was almost afraid to hear the reply.

"I did move out. I'm back in my apartment with my girlfriend. But I got busted last night so I couldn't go home. So, I slept in my truck in the back parking lot."

"I'm confused Paul. What are you talking about? How are you busted?"

"Well, John, it's a long story. Are you sure you want to hear it?"

"I'm not sure, Paul. Ah, what the heck. Lay it on me."

"Well, it all started last week. I was feeling guilty about Cindy so I decided it was time to introduce Cindy to my girlfriend."

"Whoa, stop right there Paul. Why did you want to do that?"

"It's simple. I was feeling bad that she was feeling bad, so I thought maybe if she knew that I was happy and was being taken care of that she wouldn't feel so bad. She wouldn't be worried about me."

"Wait a minute," I interrupted. "You thought her worries were about you and not her situation?"

"Look, if you want to hear the story, stop interrupting me. If all you are going to do is lecture me, I'm not telling you the rest." Paul quipped.

"Okay, Okay. Continue. I'll be quiet."

Paul continued, "So, I got this great idea to invite both of them to breakfast on Sunday. Except that I would not tell either of them that the other was going to be there. Once they both arrived I could then introduce them. Then I wouldn't feel bad about Cindy, because she would know that I am with someone that cares about me."

I sat there in amazement. Now, I have heard it all.

Paul went on, "So the plan was set. Momma was to meet me at 10 a.m. I didn't want to drive there with Pamela, so I told her I was going to church and asked her to meet me for breakfast at 10:00."

I interrupted Paul, "Who is Pamela?"

"My girlfriend, you know, the chick I'm living with."

"Of course. Sorry, I couldn't remember her name."

"That's okay.

"The plan was perfect. I got there early so that I could get a booth in the back, but one where I could see them both arrive. Cindy arrived first, so I waved to her to come back to the booth. Her back was to the door which was perfect because she would not see Pamela walking toward us."

Paul took a break to light a cigarette, took a drag and then continued. "So a few minutes later, Pamela shows up. I got her attention so she came back to the booth. Then I introduced them to each other."

Paul took another puff and sat there quietly as if he was done. But wanting to know more, I had to ask, "So what happened next?"

"Well, it went well. At first Momma was pretty ticked and she started swearing at me. Pamela was confused wondering why I did this. But then everyone calmed down. After a few minutes, I could tell that they wanted to talk. They both ordered breakfast. But not me, I ended up leaving."

"You left them there together? Why?"

"I figured it would be easier to talk about me when I wasn't there. So I left."

"So that's it? What happened?"

"Well, that's not all. I went to the truck to sit outside and wait. But then I got a phone call from a girl I met on the Internet. She was out for a run and was wondering what I was doing. I told her nothing, so we decided to get together so I left."

"You left completely?"

"Yep"

"What was the outcome of the two meeting?"

"Well, Momma hasn't talked to me this week, so I don't know. Pamela said that she liked Cindy and that they had a nice chat."

"So that's it?" I asked.

"Well, not quite. Here is what happened. I met Toni at her house after she was done with her run. When I got there, she was just getting into the shower. So I joined her in the shower and then one thing led to another, and, well, you know."

I sat there in amazement. This guy had lost his mind. He is cheating on his wife, he then introduces his girlfriend to his wife, and buys them both breakfast. And then leaves them to visit a new girl he met on the Internet. This story sounds like a script for a bad movie.

I had to ask, "So how is it you came to sleeping in your truck?"

"Oh yeah," Paul continued, "That was on Sunday. Well, I was so into Toni, that I met her again for drinks after work on Tuesday. Man, she is hot. I really like her. Whew, is she hot. Well, that ended well, too. But I had to leave to go home to Pamela. When I got home it was pretty late and Pamela was in bed. The next morning she was asking me where I was and I lied to her. I told her I was out with you."

Perfect, now I am sucked into this maze, I thought. But I said nothing.

"So, yesterday I get an email from Toni about getting together after work again. I then called Pamela and told her that I had a meeting and would not be home again until late. Well, it turns out that she didn't believe me. So, she decided to follow me which was bad because we did not meet at a bar, we met at Toni's place. About ten minutes after I went upstairs my cell phone rang. I figured it was you because you always call at the end of the day to see what happened at the shop. I didn't even look at the number, I just answered it."

At this point, Paul snuffed out his cigarette and shifted in his chair. He then continued, "I panicked when I heard Pamela's voice, but my voice remained calm. I tried to act like nothing was up and that I was in a meeting. She kept asking me questions, though. Finally, after telling lies for every answer, she told me that she was outside the building and that I should look out the window. I was busted. I looked out and there she was. I couldn't go home, so I drove back to the shop and slept in the back lot."

I had to ask, "Why didn't you at least stay with Toni at her place?"

Paul looked at me bewildered and said, "Well, that would be wrong, wouldn't it?"

Chapter 22

It is the unhappy people who most fear change.
--Mignon McLaughlin

Now we were pretty caught up with our past bills, and inventory started flowing again in the plant. Activity was getting back to normal and it looked optimistic that we would be shipping completed units quickly. We set modest goals at first. The plan required us to ship only 80 units a month to break-even, which did not seem like very many when considering we could produce over 200 small soda machines and another 300 or 400 hundred snack machines in a month. Since the small line equipment was gone, we had plenty of resources to concentrate on building the 80 units that we needed to break-even.

I was pretty worried, though. Four completed machines a day seemed difficult since we our production procedures had not been fully developed. And I was even more worried about not having the small line equipment. I knew that Sid did not want to be in the small line business because he did not like the market that it serviced. Further, I knew that Paul was relieved that were no longer required to manufacture the small equipment, especially since he believed it to be very low margin work compared to the new machine. It was, in fact, low margin work.

But margin analysis can be misleading, especially in manufacturing. I like to analyze cost in several levels. First there is the cost of the raw materials. This represents the bare bones cost of the product. The costs are tracked in a bill of materials that includes all of the component parts. Then I like to look at the direct labor cost, which includes taxes and fringe benefits. I like to consider this cost from the perspective of daily or weekly cost of direct labor compared to the daily or weekly completed units of production. I prefer analyzing the cost like this because it factors in the unproductive time and settles in on a practical production model. The result of these two factors becomes the contribution margin. To me, this is the most important aspect of profit analysis. This factor represents the amount of money that will be available for covering overhead costs. I prefer this analysis because in contract manufacturing, you cannot always control your product mix. But, if all of the products that you manufacture contribute positive to the margin, then profitability becomes a function of plant utilization and not necessarily production volume.

I study the remaining overhead costs separately. Essentially, there are two components of overhead. First, there are the fixed overhead costs, such as rent, equipment leases or debt service, plant management, accounting, purchasing, customer service, etc. Then there are the semi-variable overhead costs or sometimes referred to as indirect costs. Typically, I consider these to be the shift supervisors, shipping and receiving, utilities, and other such costs. They are semi-variable in nature in that they may fluctuate with volume, but for the most part, they are constant in amount. In my experience, most manufacturing plants attempt to burden each manufactured product line with a component of indirect costs and a component of overhead costs. Typically, this analysis only works if the plant is functioning at a constant level of production and the product mix does not vary. The reason why it only works under those conditions is simple. Allocating the indirect and fixed cost requires some basis of allocation. So how should they be allocated? Over units-of-production? But what if the production volume changes? If the product volume goes down, does that mean that the parts cost more to make because they have to cover more of the overhead? Maybe they should be allocated over production hours. But what happens if the plant temporarily produces using overtime hours? Does that mean that our fixed costs have increased? Based on the allocation of hours, it would suggest that they have!

Numerous theories and volumes of books have been written about the subject, and I have yet to see one method that works effectively for factories with variable production. So, I like to keep it simple. I analyze the contribution margin separate from the indirect and overhead costs. Once the indirect and overhead costs are known, it is simple to determine the company's break-even point based production. The primary variables that then need to be monitored, in addition to basic actual cost verses budgeted costs, are the production volumes and the production mix.

In any event, I remained very concerned that we could not cash flow without the small line equipment. Basically, the deal we had with our distributor was cash upon shipment. Nearly every other Friday we shipped, and nearly every other Friday a wire transfer hit our bank account. Essentially, this increased our working capital turn by an easy 45 days. Removing these sales from our company had a very silent, but very damaging effect. Not only did we lose the sales, and profit that the sales contributed to the margin, we lost the immediate cash flow that was essentially keeping us alive.

But that wasn't the problem that was most pressing. It should have been, but it wasn't. Right now, we needed a new salesman. Luckily, Sid was heading up the search. He knew everyone in the industry. Who was better at handpicking the most important person in the company? It didn't take long for Sid to zero in on several very good candidates. Fortunately, I knew each of the candidates and could offer my opinion from personal experience. I liked all of them, but one stood apart from the rest, Brit Brooks. I couldn't believe that he wanted to work with us. He was an accomplished salesman in the industry selling at the distributor level. He was known and respected by nearly everyone in the industry. The only people who did not like Brit were the people who had to compete against him in the same sales territory. I liked Brit, and I was excited that he was a candidate. He would add immediate credibility to our product and company.

In the end, it came down to two candidates, Brit Brooks and Dale Kohn. Both were big supporters of our company, and both were very good salesmen. They were both from other cities, which offered our company a bit more national coverage. Essentially, the way our industry operated, it was not essential to have a salesman operating out of the same city as the plant. So, I was comfortable with the out of town aspect of the decision.

When it came to decision time, Sid consulted Paul and me. Sid liked both, but was leaning towards Brit and presented a very good case for hiring Brit. Much like Sid, I also liked both, but was also in favor of Brit. I also presented a powerful case from a completely different perspective than Sid, in favor of Brit. Paul, on the other hand, only liked Dale. I couldn't understand this since Paul seemed to get along so well with Brit. Paul never did give a reason for his choice. He did not present any argument as to why Dale was the better candidate, and why Brit was not. He just stated his position and said nothing more. Paul wanted Dale, and that was final.

The decision never really came down to a vote. It could have, but it didn't. Sid pretty much took the poll, listened to the reasoning that I offered and left the room. I really like this approach and I was glad that our relationship was starting off as a team with all of us having an opportunity to provide input. About fifteen minutes later he came back into the room and announced that Brit was our new salesman, and that he would be in town on Monday morning to get started.

Paul was ticked. He didn't say anything, but I could tell by his actions that he was not happy. He just leaned back in his chair with a cigarette in his hand, staring at Sid. He said nothing. After a few minutes, he ashed his butt, stood up and left the room. He said nothing to either of us.

I think this was the moment it started for Paul. This was the defining moment for the rest of his relationship with Sid and the company. From the beginning, I knew that Paul did not want to work with Sid. Although he came around when doing the deal, I believed that it was only a front. At that moment, I realized that Sid was not the problem. It truly was Paul. His ego was wounded, so he acted like a child.

It was a shame, too. We all had very different perspectives and skill, so we had the recipe for a great team. Sid had industry experience, a finance background and was an experienced executive. I covered the accounting, costing and finance areas. Paul had production and product design covered. With the addition of Brit, we now had experienced sales and marketing. We had all of our bases covered. But if everyone isn't pulling together, a business this size just cannot survive. Sure we had the skills at the top level to match any company. But we did not have the depth. Our management was one thin layer of talented people, a group of individuals who had to work together. It was four people tied together in a five-legged race. The only way to win is to work together. But Paul was defiant and it was the start of his dissention.

So, we had the sales position filled and the focus again became production. We were still struggling to get the machines made and we fell further behind the daily minimum production of four completed machines.

It didn't take long for Sid to realize that we were having problems in the shop beyond cash flow woes. All along, Paul was informing me that the production issues were purely due to inventory stock outs. Basically, all it would take is being short one component, and the production would break down. Being a witness to the cash flow problem, I gave no additional attention to the problem. But when the money was available the production should have improved, but it didn't. In fact, it seemed to get worse.

Sid made it clear to us when he invested that he did not have a manufacturing background and that he was relying heavily on Paul's experience. But he could not sit on the sidelines and watch. The shop was not producing, and we were all smart guys, so it was time to trouble shoot. Sid started by bringing in a friend of his that recently sold a vending machine manufacturing company. Steve Smith was his name, but everyone new him as Smitty.

Smitty knew everything about building vending machines. His company produced nearly 100 machines a day in his facility before he sold out. From all accounts, Smitty did pretty well with his sale, and was now living comfortably in California with his family watching his money grow.

I could tell when I first met him that he was a no-nonsense guy. There was one way to build vending machines and only one way to run a factory. I was eager to learn from Smitty. Any guy that can build a successful business and then sell it for a pile of dough is worthy of respect. So, until he proved to me that he didn't know what he was talking about, he remained the expert and was in charge.

Smitty spent a day understanding our processes and learning the key players of the plant. He studied the procedures from ordering the parts, all the way to the size of the pallets that were used to ship the final finished machines. By the time he was done, he had reams of notes that he wanted to share with us.

After a full day at the plant, we decided to go to dinner to hear the Smitty report. I was pretty interested in what he had discovered. I had a hunch what one of the primary problems would be, but I was always prevented from discussing it with Paul.

Since the time I did the deal with Paul, the shop was his baby. He had his people and his way, and there was nothing I could ever do to affect what he was doing. Initially, that made sense. I was not a production expert by any stretch of imagination. But, over the years, I developed a keen awareness to the production process. Let's face it, I already had a detailed working knowledge of the production process from studying and understanding the costing and developing our bill of materials inventory. Additionally, I'm a pretty fast study. Since being in the business, I spent countless hours reading about production and manufacturing. I had no problem learning from reading. I did not need to make the parts to understand the processes and problems involved. In fact, my perspective added a whole new level of thinking because I was not constrained by physics or engineering. But I wasn't a metal bender, and because of that, Paul never listened to any suggestion that I would have concerning the shop.

On my drive to the restaurant, I anticipated the diagnosis to the problems. My first guess was that our plant manager Frank was the primary problem. I never liked Frank. He was arrogant and fat. The fat part I could live with, because I am over weight too, but the arrogance was unacceptable. He would treat everyone in the plant like he was the czar and everyone else were his subjects. Further, his skills were weak. The only reason he remained in power with Paul was because Frank had an ability to derail any attempt to bring in someone with more skills.

Several times over the prior five years, Paul and I experimented with bringing in an experienced production manager to fill the gap between Paul and Frank. The idea was to bring in a plant manager with engineering experience to build a production line. Paul and I always seemed to be in agreement that we needed to improve this area and we both recognized that Frank was really not the answer. I also always believed that Paul wasn't the solution either. His lack of engineering and cost accounting were natural constraints.

For a while, I tried to help Paul and Frank improve their collective skills. I installed a great inventory management and bill of materials system for tracking inventory. I trained everyone how to use the ordering features so that we had a simple method to identify when we needed to create the purchase orders. I even purchased books for them that I found helpful about effective manufacturing processes and plant management techniques. But nothing worked. In fact, the books sat on Frank's shelf unopened, and his computer was not even turned on. It was a total waste of effort and resources. Some people just do not want to improve, or they are so arrogant that they think that they know everything and there is nothing else to learn.

But Paul and I were so serious about improving this area of the plant, at one point we paid a headhunter a small fortune to find us a plant manager from the industry. As luck would have it, he found a guy right from one of our competitor's plants. He was pretty skilled and experienced. The guy moved his family here from across the country to take the job. Additionally, he convinced his number one foreman to do the same. So we were set. We had the experience that we needed.

But it didn't work. Frank sabotaged the whole plan. I immediately recognized that Frank was a problem and was destroying any hope of the new guy running the plant. Frank was a subversive snake that controlled his domain effectively. Worse, he had Paul's ear. So no matter what happened in the plant, Frank did everything to blame the new guy. Unfortunately, Paul only listened to Frank. And why not? Frank was Paul's drinking buddy. They were chums. Frank would never do anything to hurt Paul or the company. Paul was just that gullible to believe that and as blind to not see what was happening. Paul was a sucker for Frank.

I should have known. Three times we tried to bring in a plant manager to take a position above Frank. And three times it failed. All three times it was blamed on the incompetence of our new hire. Never once was it the fault of our close-minded, fat, lazy, subversive control freak, Frank. I did not like him then, and I still don't.

When we got to the restaurant, Smitty immediately challenged me about our operations?

"John, how do you know when to purchase? What systems are in place?" Smitty asked.

"Well Smitty, right now that is controlled by Frank. He works with Sheila in purchasing. She creates the purchase order." I answered.

"Well, how does Frank know what he needs?" he asked.

"I don't know. I have attempted to put systems in place, but I can't get anyone to use them. They use the inventory system for ordering parts, tracking orders, and creating the payable. But they only use 10 percent of its capability." I said.

The inquiry continued, and it continued to be directed at me. I was a bit confused by this since I was an outsider to the shop. That was Paul's domain and he should be answering these questions.

I looked across the table at Paul. He was leaning back in his chair, his eyes staring up to the ceiling, a lit cigarette in his hand. He seemed unfazed by the inquiry. His body language said it all. He was not interested in hearing anything that Smitty had to say. My guess is that Smitty sized up Paul pretty quickly, so he directed the conversation to me.

After about an hour of answering questions, Smitty offered his first step to a solution. "The problem is simple, you need a plant manager that has a clue about manufacturing."

I knew it, and was relieved. Sid stared at me a long time not saying a word. We both knew that this was going to be a power struggle with Paul. I looked over at Paul. He was still staring into space smoking his cigarette. He added nothing to the conversation.

Smitty continued, "Your plant is unorganized. You have a poor layout. Heck, you are moving the machines all over the place. The parts don't fit right. In fact, half of the parts don't even have drawings. I can't understand anything that is going on out there. There is no flow. And the machines don't fit in a truck. Your shipping costs will be too high. You can only get half the amount of machines in a truckload."

Smitty paused for a moment. I sat still staring at my drink. I was embarrassed. Sid looked pretty angry. His anger was justified. We were so far from being a good manufacturer. All along I thought that we were good. Not great, but good. I thought that we had some capability, but we didn't come close to what was required to produce 100 units a day.

All along, our plant appeared efficient mostly because of the small line vending machines. We were very good at building these, and the production systems and lines were in place for a long time. And since this production utilized most of the shop, it masqueraded the inefficiency that had developed in building the new machines. Once the small line production stopped, all that was exposed was this inefficient mess of an operation.

Smitty continued. "Gentlemen, we have a lot of work to do. John, I want you to run an ad for a plant manager. You need to get a highly qualified guy. It should be pretty easy with all of the recent layoffs in this area. Decent plant managers are a dime a dozen. By the way, how much are you paying Frank?"

"Eighty thousand," I replied.

"Heck, you could get a decent guy right now for fifty. Get rid of him. You need someone new. And get rid of anyone that complains about Frank being let go. You need to create a unified team, not like the mess you have out there right now." Smitty added.

I looked at Sid and asked, "You are okay with this, Sid?"

"Absolutely. Whatever Smitty says, goes. Consider his words gospel. We will all do what he says." Sid replied sternly.

"Do both of you understand?" Sid said while looking directly at Paul.

"Yes, Sid. What ever we need to do, I will do." I replied.

Paul said nothing.

"Paul, are we in agreement?" Sid asked again.

"Yes." Paul answered.

We spent the rest of the dinner meeting detailing the requirements for our new plant manager search and tossing around ideas on how to improve the plant. It was pretty exciting and very spirited. Once the problems were discussed, the hard part was over. Now we needed to work on fixing the problem. The plant needed to be rebuilt, and we were going to do it. The pieces of the puzzle were coming together, and again, we were on the right path for success.

I never felt more assured of our success as I did at that dinner meeting. Sid was a quick study to manufacturing principles. But, I expected that. Sid was smart. He just needed a good teacher, and Smitty was just that.

Two important things that I remember more than any other thing discussed at the meeting had to do with how vending machines should be manufactured. The first amazing fact was that most of the refrigerated vending machines manufactured did not contain any welds, screws or rivets in the cabinet. In fact, standard refrigerators are made in a similar fashion. To build the cabinet, pieces of pre-painted steel are assembled in a form. Various bends create an interlocking form of two walls, an inner wall and exterior wall. The two walls are taped together inside the form with masking tape. Once all of the pieces are assembled, an insert is placed inside the cavity of the cabinet. Then, foam insulation is injected through holes into the one-inch space between the inner wall and the exterior wall. The sticky foam expands creating a rigid, insulation barrier that holds the entire structure together. When the insulation dries, the walls and the insert of the form are removed, leaving a completed rigid, insulated vending machine cabinet.

I was amazed. It took us days to weld, assemble, paint and insulate the cabinets. Using the "foam in place" method, as it was known, an entire cabinet could be made in about 30 minutes.

The second key thing that I learned was even more important to our current process. It was a concept of "fit-up." The concept had to do with the stacking of parts in an assembly process. Since parts are stacked on top of other parts during the manufacturing process, tolerances had to be adjusted to allow for parts to "fit". In simple terms, the more parts stacked on top of each other, the more opportunity for parts not to fit correctly because the part to which it was being attached may be out of tolerance. Since I am not an engineer, I had only a crude understanding of the concept. But it made sense. If one part were a smidgen too big or too small, it would affect the next part, and possibly any other part that was being attached. I understood it, but we needed someone that could implement the engineering to correct the "fit-up" problems that Smitty discussed in great detail.

Eventually, we all grew tired and we knew that much work had to be done, so the meeting was concluded. I was relieved that we had a plan in place and was excited about the next chapter in our company's history that we were about to write.

I walked out with Paul. We spent a few minutes in the parking lot recapping the meeting. I knew that Paul was not buying into the evolving program, but I wanted to hear his objections first hand.

"So, what do you think of Smitty?" I asked.

"He's a jerk. He doesn't know anything." Paul replied.

"How could you say that? With his background, his experience, how could you even..."

Paul cut me off. "Look, I can see where this is going. It is just what I expected. Everyone thinks they know everything. And I have no say in what's going on."

I jumped in. "Paul, you have a say. You chose to sit quietly. You added nothing to the meeting. You said nothing!"

"That's right. I said nothing. What would it matter? Sid's going to do what he wants and Smitty knows everything. So why do you need me? I'm quitting."

I looked at Paul and was shocked. We are finally dialing in the company, getting all of our ducks lined up. We are finally in a position to really make this thing work, and he is acting like a child. His fragile ego was becoming his worst enemy. I had no compassion for him. I was willing to take the leap of faith with Sid and Smitty. They had a history of building companies. They were smart and successful. Instead of Paul seeing the opportunity to advance and learn, he viewed the entire process as a threat to his domain. A direct shot against his ego and manhood.

I finally responded, "Fine, quit. That will leave more funds to buy a better plant manager. Maybe we could hire two with the money we save from your salary."

I was ready to duck. I really felt that Paul would swing at me with the last dig. But he didn't. After a moment he added, "If I leave, you still have to pay me. I have a contract."

"Paul, have you read your contract? That's only true if you are fired without cause. If you quit, you get nothing."

Paul stared at me and said nothing.

After a few minutes, he opened his truck and drove away.

As I drove home, I knew that we were losing Paul. He was not adjusting to the new company and the new level of thinking. This was no longer a garage shop pushing low volumes of equipment to a small market. We were now working with professionals that knew how to market, sell, manage and produce. There was no room for anyone that was not interested in improving the company. We had failed in our attempt. The methods and approaches that we used did not work. We needed more change, and it was in sight. I was excited about the prospects of where we were headed. I wanted to get better and I wanted to be successful. I welcomed the changes.

Just for a moment, I felt sad for Paul. He just didn't get it. This was not a shot at him or what he built. But he took it personally. He could not accept that we had failed, nor could he accept that there is a better way. He just didn't get it. He let his ego control his emotions and his decision-making. Yes, I felt bad for him.

Chapter 23

It's not that some people have willpower and some don't. It's that some people are ready to change and others are not.
--James Gordon, M.D.

Smitty was right about hiring a plant manager. It did not take long. We ran one add in the local newspaper and turned up at least one hundred resumes. Sorting through them to find suitable candidates was my job. I then handed off to Sid the one's that I thought had the closest match to the experience that we needed.

Sid handled all of the interviews. I sat in on some of them to learn. Sid was very good at conducting interviews. His charm made it easy on the candidate. It's a skill to get a candidate to explain their experience without embellishment. And Sid had the skill, so he was able to get to the real facts. He had the field of ten narrowed down to two in a matter of days. He then made the decision with input from Paul and me. We were all in agreement on the choice, so we moved quickly to a start date.

Within two weeks of Smitty's visit, we were up and running with a new plant manager. Of course, it was Paul's responsibility to break the news to Frank. Sid insisted on that. He insisted, maybe because it was punishment for not actively participating in the Smitty meeting, or maybe just because Paul knew him best. But for whatever reason, the responsibility rested with Paul, and Paul did not do it.

Sid arrived a week after the new manager started, giving a week for the new guy to get his impressions of the shop and the task at hand. When Sid arrived, he was stunned to see Frank still working in the plant.

"John, what is going on? Why is Frank still here? Where is Doug, the new guy?"

"Nice to see you too, Sid" was my reply. "I think you need to talk to Paul. He seems to think that we can work with both and that Frank is vital to the plant."

"Well, that's not how this is going down. We agreed on this."

"I know, Sid. Paul was to let Frank go, but he didn't do it. I'll gladly do it, just give me the go ahead."

"No."

Sid stood in his office, calmly turned to the door, and walked out. As he was leaving he said under his breath, "I will take care of this with Paul."

I followed Sid down the hall to the engineering office in the back. Doug, the new guy, was in the office working on testing parts and reviewing the drawings. He was happy to see Sid.

"Hi Sid, it's nice to see you again," was Doug's welcome.

"Well, what do you think about the project?" Sid questioned.

"The idea is fantastic. But the machines have a lot of engineering issues. For one, they are over-built. They need some weight taken out of them. They also can be a bit smaller, too. I can fix all of this."

"Well, what about the plant and production? What are your initial thoughts on how many of these we can manufacture?" Sid quizzed.

"I'm not sure on that yet. I have not been given any opportunity to work in the shop. Frank put me in here and that has been it."

Sid was fuming mad. I could see his face turn red with the increase in his blood pressure. Without saying a word, Sid retreated from engineering and swiftly walked down the hall to Paul's office. The door was open, and Sid marched in. Paul was talking on the phone, laughing and joking it up with the unknown party. Sid was in no mood to wait, so he signaled to Paul to hang up.

Paul was being stubborn and kept talking. Sid was getting more impatient by the minute. He then walked out to Stacy's office to find out if she knew to whom Paul was speaking. She did not, so Sid decided to wait until Paul was done; otherwise, I suspect Sid was ready to hang up on the caller. Sid paced back and forth.

Sid was back in Paul's office the moment the phone hit the cradle.

"What the heck is going on? Why is Frank still here?"

Paul looked at Sid defiantly and responded, "If you want him gone, you fire him."

"That's not how this works, Paul. If you want to be in charge, you need to behave like you are in charge. Further, you need to put the company ahead of your personal friendships. If you cannot do that, tell me and I will relieve you of your responsibility."

Paul did not say anything. I remained quiet as well. I was not interested getting between these two in this mess. Beside, this was Paul's fight. I was in favor in letting Frank go. In fact, I was eager about it.

After a few minutes, Paul finally spoke up, "Sid, I think we need Frank. He can still work in the plant. He can work for Doug."

Sid did not respond.

I decided to weigh in with my thoughts. "Paul, we tried this three times already and every time it ended up in a disaster. Frank cannot let go of his control. We need to make a clean break. We need help out there, and Doug is our best solution. We need to make this change. Frank has to go."

Paul glared at me.

Sid seemed to calm down and started to reason with Paul, "Look, we cannot afford both guys, and we need Doug. I know that Frank is your friend and he has been with you for a long time. But Frank has had his chance and he has been unsuccessful. We cannot continue to wait for him to change. He will not take direction and he does not have the required skills to get these machines built."

Paul sat down behind his desk. He knew that Sid was right, and he knew what he had to do. The problem was that he was Frank's personal friend. They did a lot together outside of work, and it was a real problem now. After a few moments of silence, Paul finally said, "Okay, I will take care of it today."

I walked out of the office following Sid. He was eager to learn more about what Doug had to say, and so was I.

Sid and I were with Doug for about an hour or so, when we heard a knock on the door. The door slowly opened and behind it was standing Frank.

"I need to get some of my things out of here, can I come in?"

This was pretty awkward. Up until now, I was gung ho on firing Frank. He was not getting the job done and he deserved it. Furthermore, he sabotaged every attempt we made at improving the plant just to save his own job. To me, nothing could be worse than an employee in a management position that puts the needs of the company behind their own. But having to face Frank at this very moment was tough. No matter how much he deserved to be fired, I could not help feel compassion. Seeing him saddened me. But I had to shake it off. I knew that we made the right decision.

Sid motioned for Frank to enter and suggested that we all leave and take a walk through the plant. But Sid was not going to allow Frank free reign in the engineering department, so he whispered to me to stay behind to observe that Frank only removed his personal items and nothing more. I agreed and stayed behind with Frank while Sid and Doug went into the plant.

I did not say a word while Frank was gathering his items. I tried to look as if I was not watching, pretending to read some blue prints that Doug was redrawing, but I did not fool Frank. He knew that I was watching him. But I knew that I needed to. Disenfranchised employees cannot be trusted under any circumstances. Unfortunately, I learned that lesson years ago.

It did not take long for Frank to gather up his stuff and leave. He said absolutely nothing to me as he walked out of the room.

After a couple of minutes, I could hear Frank leave out the side door. Knowing that the coast was clear, I left to catch up with Sid and Doug. As I popped out of the office, Paul was standing in the hallway.

"Are you happy now?" he asked.

"I just want what is right for the company. I've had enough of the petty games, Paul. We need to move on."

Paul did not respond.

"Are you coming with me to walk the floor with Sid and Doug. I think it would be a good idea."

Paul stared at me and replied, "No. Have fun." Then he motioned to the plant door.

I walked into the plant alone. I could see Sid and Doug having an animated discussion in the assembly area. I was eager to join them so I double-timed through the plant. I did not give the Frank incident another thought. Instead, I shook off all of the controversy and began to focus on the future of rebuilding this company.

Chapter 24

Only two things are infinite, the universe and human stupidity, and I'm not sure about the former.
--Albert Einstein

After only a few days, the plant was going through a major overhaul. The new plant manager was quick to make changes. Within a week he had a whole new team of supervisors and a new purchasing department. Some positions were filled with current employees, but most were filled with people Doug knew from his prior employment. The former plant he managed shut down about six months prior, stranding about fifty employees. Some were able to relocate to another factory that the company ran down south, but for most, they were left unemployed. They were all eager to work and they all worked well with Doug.

Doug initially tried to work directly with Paul, especially when it came to hiring decisions. However, the attempt proved futile because of Paul's disdain for Doug. It quickly became apparent to Doug that if he were going to get anything done that he would need to work through Sid.

At first Sid seemed frustrated by the situation. But after a while, Sid seemed to embrace it. Soon, Doug and Sid were working closely together at improving the shop and implementing the plans and ideas that were developed by Smitty. The plan was really coming together and our production was increasing.

Meanwhile, Brit was busy increasing our distributor network and developing new sales.

But problems were looming with Paul. His lack of authority, which was brought on by his own doing, was beginning to gnaw at him. He slowly began to retreat from management and from the daily company activity. Instead, he spent most of his time in the engineering department working on fixes to some of the nagging delivery problems that continued to occur. Since the machine was never properly field-tested before going into production, it did not have the reliability factor of the earlier model, and this was becoming an increasing problem. Since the problems needed to be fixed, I was happy that Paul was focusing his energy on these issues.

For some time, every morning started with a call to or from Paul. Even through this tumultuous transition, Paul and I still managed to talk daily about what was happening at the shop. Our conversations were more vague and his perspective was narrowed to the engineering on which he was now focused. But because of my commitment to other activities, I was not noticing Paul's depression being brought on by the damages caused to his fragile ego.

This morning was an exception. I called several times and only would get Stacy, the customer service rep. She had been with the company for a long time. In fact, she was the first person I ever met at the firm. Back in the day, she was in charge of paying bills and invoicing, as well as nearly every other office management task. When the computer was on the fritz, she called me for my initial meeting with the company. She was loyal to the company, and very loyal to Paul.

Usually she was pretty open with me about Paul's whereabouts. On occasion Paul's behavior would keep him out late, rendering him useless first thing in the morning. Stacy did a good job keeping the other employees and customers in the dark about his antics, but she usually was square with me.

"Stacy, where is Paul?" I quizzed.

"I don't know," was her curt reply.

"Come on, Stacy, it's me. Is he still at home?"

"Honestly, I have not heard from him. I've tried his cell and home. He's not answering either one."

"All right. Have him call me right away when you hear from him."

I went back to work, not giving this a second thought.

A couple of hours went by and I was deeply involved in a meeting with a client at my office. I could hear the phone frequently ringing in our office in the background, which was a bit unusual for this time of year. But I did not pay attention to the need that was building, impatiently waiting for me to conclude my meeting. I have a simple rule that I follow with my accounting practice; I will not accept calls when I am involved in a client meeting. I devote my entire attention to my client during my meetings. Only in very, very rare circumstances, and only if pre-arranged, would I interrupt a scheduled meeting. This is my mode of operation, and nothing will influence me to change.

When I emerged from the conference room and escorted my client to the door, my secretary was waiting for me a bit panicked.

"You need to call Stacy immediately. She said it was urgent. She has called four times already."

"Did she say why?"

"No, but she sounded upset."

"Have we heard from Paul yet?"

"No" she replied.

As I walked back to my office with the message in hand, I could not stop wondering what had her so upset. Obviously, it had to involve Paul. We have not heard from him for several hours.

I quickly dialed. Our bookkeeper answered the phone. Upon hearing my voice, without hesitation or small talk, she immediately transferred my call to Stacy.

"John, we have a problem. Paul's in jail."

"What?"

"Paul's in jail. He needs your help. He needs bail."

"What did he do? Don't tell me it was a DUI."

"No, he said they arrested him for hitting Cindy. But he said he didn't do it."

"What? He hit his wife? Why? Is he out of his mind?"

"John, he said he didn't do it. She was knocked over as he was leaving the house. She was supposedly throwing him out. He was mad and pushed by her on his way to the door."

I was speechless.

Stacy continued, "He said he didn't do anything."

"Which jail is he in?" I asked.

"Well, now he's in the county jail by his house."

"What do you mean by *now*? Where was he before?"

"Well, he was originally taken to the city jail. He was arrested here after he shot off his gun in the plant."

"What?" I was horrified.

"I guess he came here and shot his gun. Then he got arrested."

I knew that Paul was a gun buff. He used target practice as a hobby and as a stress reliever. But he always went to the gun club. The plant is no place for target practice.

"Well, he can stay there. I am not bailing him out. I am not supporting this behavior. He crossed the line."

"John, you are his partner and his friend. He asked me to ask you. He needs you." Stacy pleaded.

"How is Cindy?" I asked.

"I'm not sure. She is out of the hospital, though. They released her last night."

"What? She was in the hospital?"

"Paul said it was just a precaution. They had to take her, because of the charges and all."

"Stacy, when you talk to Paul, tell him I said 'enjoy jail'. I am not bailing him out."

"What is he supposed to do?" she asked.

"That's his problem. You seem to be his only fan right now, maybe you should bail him out."

I hung up the phone. I leaned back in my chair, bewildered. Of all of the things that went through my mind when I received the urgent message, never did this cross my mind. What a mess. I simply could not condone that behavior. I could care less that he was my partner. Right now, I would be happier if he wasn't my partner. What a jerk.

I went back to work. I had a lot to do and did not want to waste any more energy on this.

The day went by without further incident. The plant did not call once, nor did I call them. I needed to stay away. I was way too hot to be there or to talk to anyone.

The next day, my phone dutifully rang. It was Paul. He was back at work.

"John, it's not what you think."

"How do you know what I think, Paul?"

"Stacy told me. She said you were really hot."

"And why shouldn't I be, Paul? You hit your wife? Are you insane? What could ever cause you to do that?"

"It really isn't what you think."

"Then what is it?"

"Let's meet today, John. I will tell you the whole story. The truth. You need to know what happened and understand that I did not hit her."

I needed time to think. I was still pretty mad, but he was my partner. And right now, I may have been his only friend.

"Alright, Paul," I reluctantly agreed. "I will be there later today. Like 3:30 or 4 o'clock."

The day went by fast. Before I knew it I had to leave to get to the plant. I was not excited about seeing Paul. I wasn't sure how I would react seeing him. My problem is that I respect my wife and my vows of marriage. I don't care how mad I could ever be; I know that I could never raise a hand to my wife. Aside from the love and respect, it's just not fair. I have a huge size and strength advantage. Maybe that is a sexist point of view, but I don't care. That's how I think.

When I walked in, Paul looked awful. He looked tired and humbled. He would not look me in the eye. I looked around his office. There were bullet holes everywhere. Mostly he shot the cement blocks, but he also put a few rounds in the prototype machine in his office. It was a mess. Stacy didn't quite tell the truth about the bullet holes. It looked much different than the target practice that I envisioned.

"Okay, Paul. Let me hear your side of the story."

Paul sheepishly began to tell his side of the story. "I stopped for a couple after work. I met up with a few friends and we had some drinks. Before long, I lost track of time. Next thing I knew it was after 9, so I left. When I got home I was hungry since I did not eat so I asked momma to cook me a steak. She wouldn't do it. She told me dinner was four hours ago and she wasn't cooking again for me. I was pretty mad, so I told her again to cook me a steak. She just laughed and left the kitchen. I followed her into the bedroom. I gabbed her arm and told her again to make me a steak. She looked at me and told me to get out of the house. And she told me that she didn't want me back in the first place, and that if I don't leave she was going to call the police. I was really getting mad, so I pushed past her to get to the closet to get my stuff to leave. She fell onto the bed and started screaming that I hurt her. So she called the cops."

"So that was it, Paul? The cops came and arrested you?"

"Well, not exactly. I stormed out of the house with some of my stuff. Cindy was crying and yelling all at the same time. I got into my truck and took off. I didn't know where to go, so I came to the shop. Meanwhile, it turns out that Cindy did not call the cops. She called her sister. Her sister came over and saw some stuff tossed around and assumed the worst. She convinced Cindy to call the police. Meanwhile, they kept calling my cell phone to find out where I was. Cindy's sister was afraid that I might do something stupid and wanted to find me."

"Well, what happened next?" I asked.

Paul continued "I came to the shop, like I said. I was really mad. I took off my shoes and started going through some paperwork on my desk. I couldn't concentrate because I was so mad. I poured a drink to settle down. Then I just pulled out my gun and started shooting."

"So, that's why the cops came?"

"Not quite. It turns out that when the cops came to my house, Cindy convinced them that I was going to kill myself. She figured I was going to the plant. The county sheriff radioed the city cops. They came here and arrested me."

"And that's it, Paul? Nothing more."

"That's pretty much it."

"So, Cindy is not hurt, you did not hit her."

"No. I did not hit her."

As if on queue, Stacy knocked on the office door and slowly opened it. "John, you have a phone call, it's Cindy."

"I'll take it in the conference room."

I couldn't imagine why she was calling me. I hurried to the conference room phone.

"Hi Cindy."

"John, is he there?"

"Do you mean Paul?"

"Yes"

"Yes, I was just meeting with him. What is going on, Cindy?"

"What did he tell you?" She asked.

"Better yet, Cindy, what happened last night?"

"John, it was out of control. Paul was drunk, I was mad...it was really bad."

"Cindy, did Paul hit you?"

"No" was her quick reply.

"Your not just saying that to protect him?"

"Protect him? Are you nuts? I hate him and want a divorce. But he did not hit me."

I continued my interrogation. "What about the hospital and the police?"

"I did fall on the bed. My sister made it out to be more than it was. The house was torn up. We were throwing things. It was bad. But he did not hit me. Honest. My sister made me go to the hospital because I was shaking. She was afraid for me."

"Cindy, why did you call me?"

"I just wanted you to get the straight story."

"Cindy, did Paul put you up to this call?"

"No! I haven't talked to him and I am filing for a restraining order against him. I hate him. I just wanted you to know what happened."

"Okay, Cindy. Thank you for calling."

I am stuck right in the middle, and I am not happy about it. Our company is failing, money is running out, and the president of the company was in jail over marital issues that are far from being over. What's next?

So I headed back to Paul's office.

"What did *she* want?" Paul asked.

"Just to tell me her side of the story. I'm not sure why, though."

Paul just sat there, looking at me. I was hoping that my comment would invoke a response. It didn't. He just sat there, not even trying to conjure up a response.

So I continued. "So that's it. Cindy's okay, you didn't hit her, you shot holes in your office, and you were in jail. I would say this has been a productive couple of days, Paul."

We were both silent.

I decided to take a walk through the plant. Every time I was there, I made a point to be on the floor. I liked to ask questions and observe the various processes. We were having all types of trouble in assembly, and I was pretty involved in helping with solutions. Being out there, getting first-hand, unfiltered information from the employees was helpful.

As I walked the floor, I kept thinking about Paul's antics. Shooting holes in cement blocks. What a jerk. What would have happened if a bullet ricocheted? Drunken people don't reason. That's the problem.

I walked to the end of the line and propped myself against a box and observed the final assembly process in action. Man, were we slow. Two men were working on the five machines closest to being finished. The machines moved through the plant basically in groups of fifteen. The final assembly area was set up with three rows of five machines. Each of the three rows had a slightly different level of completion. The final row of machines appeared pretty close to being finished. One of the workers was measuring for final "decorative" insulating pieces. After he measured, he put down the plastic strips he had in hand and walked toward his toolbox. He walked back with a hand drill. He then proceeded to drill holes in the frame to re-align the fit for the insulation. For five or six minutes I watched him struggle to attach this 50-cent item to the machine.

I couldn't stand it any longer and had to intervene.

"What's the problem here?"

My approach to the line drew the attention of both the plant manager and assembly supervisor.

The plant manager started to chime, and I quickly quieted him.

"What's your name?" I politely asked the assembly man.

"Joe"

"Joe, what is the problem with the insulation plastic?"

"It doesn't fit right."

"How often does this happen?"

"Not often. Usually they fit pretty easy. In this case, all I needed to do was drill a couple of new holes, and the parts fit right in."

I knew that the plastic part was not the problem. We were still having fit up problems throughout the manufacturing process. The more components that go into a product, the more difficult the process becomes. Each level of assembly has a fit tolerance that must be met.

As the layers build, the tolerances need to increase to allow for subtle irregularities throughout the earlier processes. Either we did not allow for the right tolerances or we did not properly control the quality at the earlier intervals.

"Do you have other parts that won't fit?" I quizzed.

"Sure, but it's not always the same part. Sometimes it's the cover, sometimes the insulation. Sometimes the doors need to be adjusted."

"Okay, sorry to interrupt."

I walked away with the plant manager. I knew that we identified these issues before, and have spent countless hours on defining solutions. I was unhappy because we have not cured the problem. In fact, it looks as if we made zero progress.

After a brief conversation about moving faster to solving the problems, I walked away. I know where the problem in final assembly resides...in Paul's office. He was always defending the processes and blaming the people. I took a different approach; I believed that the process has to be designed to work with any level of employee. The process needed to be controlled by solid engineering, not super-skilled employees.

When I walked back into Paul's office, he seemed refreshed. Color was back in his face, and he was busy working. It was as if he was relieved to tell his story, and consequently he seemed absolved of his sins.

I sat back down and discussed my observations at final assembly. He concurred and commented that we are getting better, but still needed to work on better fit-up solutions. He then vowed he would start working better with Doug and solve the problems.

Our attention soon turned from the plant, and he began to open up a bit more about his night of adventure. Now that the facts had been revealed, he started to tell me the story from his perspective. The untold story.

"John, the other night was unbelievable. When I got to the shop, I was so mad. I lost it and shot the holes in the walls. But get this; about ten minutes later, cops swarmed the building. They had the SWAT units here!"

Paul seemed proud as he continued to tell this part of the story. He leaned back in his chair, with a smile on his face and continued.

"I looked out the window, and the place was surrounded. They even had a guy on a bullhorn, just like the movies! I looked around the office to find my shoes. I could only find one. I could see through the window that more police were arriving, so I figured I better get out and explain what was going on. I walked to the door with my keys in one hand, and my one shoe in the other. I had to unset the perimeter alarm before I left, so I stopped at the door for a moment. Then they shined this blinding light in my eyes, just like in the movies. As I walked out, I was trying to get my shoe on, when they grabbed me. I asked if I could go back in and get my other shoe. They just read me my rights and shoved me in the police car."

He continued "When I got to the police station, I saw one of the machines we donated to the DARE program. I told the cop that was our machine, and that we donate machines every year to their program. I think he felt sorry for me."

As I listened to his continuing story, I felt sorry for him too. He was totally unaware of the severity of his actions. In fact, he almost seemed proud of his actions.

Paul continued with his saga "So they throw me in this cell. The floor was wet and cold and I didn't have any shoes. I lost the one shoe that I had when they grabbed me and stuffed me in the car."

"Is Brookside pressing charges, Paul?"

"No, they let me go. Well, they held me for the county sheriff to come. The county wanted to arrest me for the domestic disturbance. I had to wait all night in the Brookside jail, with no shoes. I was really cold. I tried to sleep, but I couldn't. I just laid there waiting."

"You are lucky that Brookside let you off."

"Yeah, but they remembered me from the DARE program. I think they felt sorry for me. Beside, they knew I was in trouble with the sheriff, so they went easy on me."

"What time did all of this happen?"

"Brookside picked me up at like 3 am. I think I was in jail there until about 7 am. Then the deputies came and took me to the county lockup. It was snowing out and I had to walk out to the car in my socks. I didn't have a coat. I was freezing. When they took me to the county jail, I had to wait until 4:00 p.m. to get bailed. Stacy came. I was freezing. She took me to my apartment and I changed clothes and went to bed."

"Paul, you still have your apartment?"

"Yeah, I kept it just in case we could not make the second try work. I was right. I am glad I kept it."

I was too. I never figured that they would make it. Once a relationship gets past the point of no return, it is almost senseless to try. They were way past that point. And that's probably why this whole incident occurred in the first place. Both sides were stubborn. The stubbornness ultimately led to the breakup, and ultimately to the second try. Neither of them would admit that it wouldn't work. So they tried again. And I was here to witness the result.

Since I am always searching for the lesson, I asked Paul, "So, what, if anything, did you learn from this mess?"

Paul leaned back in his chair deep in thought, took a deep drag from his cigarette, exhaled and responded smiling, "Never go to jail without your shoes."

Chapter 25

The man who is swimming against the stream knows the strength of it.

--Woodrow Wilson

The entire incident with Cindy seemed to humble Paul and bring him back down to earth. Just when I figured he was going off the deep end, Paul began coming to work with his "A" game. And when he was on, he was as good and creative as anyone I have ever met. I was happy he was back.

I was still pretty ticked about what happened. Further, I was worried about him and was wondering what will happen next. But instead of wasting energy on what might happen, I decided to refocus my energy on working with Paul and making amends.

The plant production was improving, which was music to all of our ears. Sid seemed happy with the progress and would report to Smitty every other day about our progress. The word was that Smitty was pleased too.

Our last show was a big success and the orders were beginning to pile up. Because of the growth, our cash position was stretched again. However, Sid called in some favors and was able to negotiate some deposits on several of the large orders that we had coming in from some dairies. The shot of cash was exactly what we needed.

I was beginning to think that maybe we will make it after all and the nightmare is finally over. But, I thought too soon.

It all started with Paul complaining about Doug. The first complaint was that he was not spending enough time on the shop floor. The complaint migrated to all he does is sit in his office and play on the computer. Then it transitioned to he doesn't know what he is doing.

For the most part, I blew off Paul's complaining because I felt it was being brought on by the fact that Doug was having success at fixing production and Paul was simply jealous. Doug's success was essentially a direct shot at Paul's ego. So I ignored Paul.

But just to be sure I was remaining unbiased; I contacted Sid and Brit to get their opinions on Doug's performance. Sid and Brit both expressed their content with the progress and both applauded his commitment.

Sid left for vacation and his parting words to us were, "Gentlemen, it has been a rough road, but we are starting to succeed. Keep up the good work and I will see you in a week."

Sid's vacation was overseas, so I knew that he would not be calling in, nor would we be able to reach him. Sid needed the break, and so did we. For the last months we were all working ourselves to the breaking point. And we all needed a break from each other. While Sid was out, I was planning on staying away from the shop as well, just to get a breather.

It was Monday, the first workday of Sid's vacation and I received a call from Paul. "John, I need to see you right away."

"Why? What's so important?"

"I can't tell you on the phone. You need to come down here." Paul pleaded.

"Well, I can't come over until the afternoon, say 2 o'clock."

"Okay, John, that will work. See you then."

I arrived at the plant about a half hour late. Paul was anxious to see me. He immediately jumped from his chair and walked me out to the shop.

As I walked the plant, I was amazed at the organization and impressed with the changes that Doug implemented. He was following Smitty's recommendations to the letter and the improvement was obvious.

But as we walked, Paul was not seeing what I was seeing.

"John, we need to make a move."

"What?"

"We need to make a move. We need a new production manager. Doug stinks."

"Are you nuts, Paul? This is the most organized we have ever been. Sid is happy, Smitty's happy. Brit said the machines are working. What else do you want from the guy?"

"He's too slow. We should be making twice the machines. Plus everyone hates him. He's mean to the employees. I don't like him."

"Paul, it sounds personal to me. But, if you really have a problem with him, let's meet when Sid gets back into town and solve the problem. If he thinks we need to make a change, I will listen. But for now, we need to wait. Personally, I think the guy is doing a fine job."

"How can you say that? We are only producing four machines a day. We should be making ten a day, at least."

Now, I was not too upset by four machines a day. Granted, it was a far cry from where we needed to be, but it is a long way from where we were. I was optimistic that we were building four good machines a day. And four per day translated to roughly eighty a month, which was the break-even point based on my calculations. If we could improve to five a day, we would be making money. At this point, we were so beat up as a manufacturer that I was pleased at our positive progress. Breaking even felt good.

But Paul would not let it go.

"We need to get rid of him. He's ruining our company. He's going to destroy us."

"What are you going to do, fire him without talking to Sid first? Are you nuts? We are partners you know. He has a voice, and based on my understanding, he gets the swing vote if we are losing money. And, my last calculations indicate that we are still in the red."

"I don't care. He's not here and I'm in charge. I'm firing him."

"Paul, you can't. You don't have the authority. Besides, I'm not even in agreement with you."

We stood quietly for a moment. Then I continued. "Paul, let's calm down and reason this out. If you really think he needs to go, I'm okay with that. But, we need to follow proper governance. Let's go have drink tonight after work and talk it out. Then, put together a list of issues in writing. When Sid gets back we can all go over them. We can solve the problem together."

"Okay. Meet me at 5:45 at Kendal's Bar."

I left to get back to my office for a meeting. What a waste of time driving to and from the plant. Paul knew how to waste my time, and I often thought he did it on purpose. I sucked it up though. I was more concerned with keeping the company operating and successful.

Within minutes of arriving at my office, my cell phone starting ringing. It was Brit.

"Hey FBC, what the heck is wrong with Paul? Is he insane?"

Confused by his greeting, I asked "What are talking about, Brit?"

"You're partner. The idiot. He just fired Doug. Does Sid know about this?"

I was stunned. "What? Are you serious?"

"As serious as a heart attack. Doug just called me and said Paul fired him."

"Brit, I was just at the plant. I told him to discuss his gripes with Sid when he came back."

"Gripes? What gripes? Doug had the plant running well. What was Paul thinking?"

"I don't know" I responded. "He was chiming about this and that today and that we needed to fire Doug. I thought I had him talked down. In fact, I was going to meet him after work to help him draft up his list of complaints for a meeting with Sid. I figured once he wrote it all down, he would realize how foolish he was."

"Yeah, well your plan didn't work. You shouldn't have left."

I was already regretting the fact that I left. But there was nothing I could do about that now.

"Brit, Sid is going to have a cow. Do you think I should call him?"

"He's out of contact, John. It will have to wait until he is back in town. All I have to say is I'd hate to be you."

"What? What did I do? Paul's the moron."

"Yeah? Well who do you think is in charge of that moron? You are. And Sid is going to have a lot to say to you!"

"That's just great, Brit. So the idiot fires the guy and I'll take the heat. It's bad enough that Paul is ruining our revival."

"That's just it, John. Paul can't handle that he's not the 'man' any more. He's too fragile. Sid should can *him*."

Although I didn't say it, I was in agreement. It was time for Paul to go. I thought he was coming around and was buying into the new regime. But he wasn't. I was mistaken.

"Well Brit, I'm not looking forward to telling Sid. But I'll take care of it when he gets home."

"Good luck, John."

I was feeling sick. I cannot believe that Paul would pull this. Firing the plant manager was significant. It certainly fell under the concept of "gross insubordination" which was one of the criteria allowing Sid to can Paul without a buyout of Paul's contract. Paul really did it this time.

The week went by pretty quickly. I tried not to think about telling Sid, but I knew that I would have to soon. He would be home on the weekend.

When Monday morning came, I was driving to my office when my cell phone rang. It was Sid.

"John, do you have any appointments this morning?"

"No, I don't"

"Good, we need to meet. I'm at the plant. Come here first, please."

"Okay. I can do that. What's up, Sid?"

"What do you mean, John? We need to talk about what Paul did with Doug. I want answers."

"Sid, how did you find out already? I was planning on calling you this morning to break the news. How did you know already?"

"John, I told you a long time ago. I know everything that is going on in this industry."

I hung up and drove straight to the plant.

By the time I got there, Sid and Paul were already going at it. Just great, the one time Paul gets in early, Sid is there to confront him.

Paul's path of self-destruction seemed to get worse by the day. His passive resistance and direct defiance with Sid needed to stop. I was in favor of firing Paul and starting over. At this point, I did not care what it was going to cost. Even if we had to buy him out of his contract, it would be worth it just to help the company. It was sad to see Paul behave in this way, but it wasn't up to me. He chose his own behavior.

The argument continued after I arrived. There was little I could add and nothing that I could say that would remedy the situation. Instead, I listened to both of them.

Sid pretty much had it. I could tell he was exasperated with Paul's antics. I then chimed in.

"Irregardless of what happened, we need to hire another plant manager. Do you want me to run an ad?"

Sid stared at me and quipped, "Do you really think that will do any good? This idiot will just fire him the minute I leave town."

I did not have a response. Sid was right. We were now fighting the worst battle in our company life, an enemy among us.

Chapter 26

The important thing is not to stop questioning.
--Albert Einstein

It was start of another day. It was going to be a break from the company problems since I had a full schedule of meetings involving my accounting practice that would last into the evening. I was relieved.

My first appointment was my monthly breakfast meeting with Ned, a friend who was also an accountant. Each month we would get together to discuss our respective accounting practices, client situations, and whatever else was on our minds. It always proved to be a healthy meeting because we could each receive insight into our businesses without any risks.

I learned long ago that having an outside perspective regarding my business was very important. An independent, unbiased perspective can become a catalyst to new ideas and overall company improvement. I always looked forward to my meetings with Ned because he always had a fresh perspective and positive outlook on every situation. I know that my accounting practice is better because of his help and I am eternally grateful.

Our meetings were set a year in advance so that we could schedule everything else around them. I like to schedule all of my monthly recurring meetings this way so that I can always maximize the use of my time. This is especially important when the product you sell is, in fact, time.

I arrived a few minutes early and had a chance to catch the headlines that were playing on the overhead television. I was relieved to learn that not much new was happening in the world while I was wrestling with my personal debacle. It didn't take too long, but I soon started thinking about all of the issues at the plant. It never seemed to leave the back of my mind, but now it was creeping to the front.

Luckily, Ned arrived so I was safe to shake the thoughts loose and turn my attention to accounting.

"John, how are you doing?" was Ned's warm welcome.

"Well, I could be better."

And that's all it took. I knew what the next question would be and that I was not about to escape talk about the plant. I couldn't shake it. It was on my mind and it will soon be obvious to Ned.

"What's wrong?" Ned asked.

I had to answer his dreaded question.

"Well, you know how I have been struggling with my fab deal? Now the whole thing is starting to unravel, and I am in big trouble."

"I thought you had that under control with your new partner?"

"Yeah, well so did I. But it's proving to be a disaster. Paul and Sid do not get along at all. They fight about everything. Well, actually, Paul fights with everything that Sid wants to do. It's terrible and ridiculous all at the same time. I'm at my wits end with all of it. Further, Paul's attitude has become destructive to the company. And to top it all off, his personal life is a disaster. All of this combined is killing our chances of survival. Quite frankly, Ned, I am really at my wits end and I don't know what to do."

"Why don't you just fire him?"

"Well, that's a great idea but we can't. First there are employment agreements for both Paul and me. Like an idiot, I negotiated these so that Sid could not buy into the company and then simply fire us. It made sense at the time, but now it is coming back to haunt us. To fire him, we would have to pay him a severance salary for two years. Plus, we would also have to buy back his shares"

"What is the buyout price for the shares?"

"Another great question. Right now it is pretty low because we are performing so poorly. So, the buyout is not the big deal. Two years of severance is the issue. We don't have the money to do it."

When I stopped talking, I could tell Ned's head was reeling with questions. But I continued to talk.

"And even if we did have the money, it would take a vote of both Sid and me. Sid and I have discussed this at great length, and I have even offered to put up half of the money, which is more than I'm required to do, just to get rid of Paul. But Sid does not want to do it."

"Why not? Based on everything you have told me over the past few years, he deserves to go."

"True, but Sid is worried about a lot of issues. First, he is concerned how our customers would view firing the company president. Will it hurt sales? Will it hurt the distributor relationships? Who knows? It's a big gamble. Plus, Sid is worried that we may not find a replacement for him that understands the mechanics of the vending equipment and the shop. Well, not that we couldn't replace him, but at what cost? Sid is afraid of the cost of the learning curve. It is definitely a big risk."

"Yeah, that may be true John, but you may not have a choice."

"I agree. But trying to convince a guy that has only been involved in this for a few months that we need to can the president is not easy. And, maybe he is right. It may be too big of a risk when you consider the impact that it could have on the customers. We are hanging on by a thread as it is. Any disruption could be the end."

"How in the world did you ever get involved with Paul in the first place?"

"You know, it wasn't always like this. When we first partnered up, we worked so well together. Paul was fantastic in the shop and was a very good businessman. We made money together. We were a good team. His ideas with developing the machine were intuitive and, quite frankly, ingenious. But at some point he changed. It seemed the more successful we became, the more of a playboy he became. Maybe it was his ego. I don't know. I'm not a psychologist."

I paused for a moment to butter my bagel and then continued.

"But he used to listen. If I disagreed with him, he would listen. We would work things out. But, it seemed that the more success we had, the less interested he became in my opinions. But the real turning point was when we started to loose money. This is when his personal life seemed to falter, too. I'm not sure the two are connected, but who knows? Maybe somehow they are."

I stopped to take a deep breath. Ned sensed that I was not done talking, so he said nothing. I then continued.

"The real bummer is that I really liked Paul. Right now I don't, but I did. I was loyal to him as friend. I always figured that at some point we would get this deal turned around and he would snap back and become the guy he once was. Maybe I am loyal to a fault. Maybe I have too much faith in people."

"No, John, you're not wrong in being loyal and you're not wrong in keeping your faith in him. Beside, it's in your makeup. Don't become a cynic. Why don't you try to sell your shares?"

"To who? Who would want to buy into this company now? But even if I could find a buyer, how do I get around the buy-sell agreement? That is another big problem that's out there. I do not have a put option on my shares, so I cannot offer them up for sale at all. Not even to the company or to the other shareholders. The only way I can sell my shares is if Sid offers to buy them. And why would he? I'm the idiot guaranteeing all of the bank loans. There is also that issue to deal with. Even if I could somehow convince Sid to offer to buy my shares, I'm still stuck guaranteeing the loans. I'm better off to stay in and try to make the deal work, then to walk away. If the deal sinks, I'm stuck going down with the ship whether I'm a shareholder or not. I might as well stay in and try to make it work."

"What about buying out Sid?"

"Ned, you're good. And I've thought about this, and I even touched on the subject with Sid one evening over dinner. He would do it if I gave him all of his money back and a 20% premium for control. I could never do it. I couldn't come up with the money. But even if I could, I wouldn't want to. The company's not worth it anymore."

"It seems Sid is dismayed by the deal too. Why don't you just sell the whole company?"

"Now your talking, Ned. That's what I would love to do. But it will take a unanimous vote right now, and I know that will not happen. Here's why: we would not be able to sell it for enough to pay off both banks right now, let alone get any money back to Sid. There is no way he would vote for that. He would be crazy to vote for that."

We both sat quietly for a few moments while we ate our breakfast. After a few bites, I continued.

"The saddest part of all of this is that we had a chance to sell the company three years ago. I would have made a pile of dough –

likely better than one million after tax for my share. Paul's cut would have been three times that. He was convinced that the offer was too low. And based on the projections that we had at the time he wasn't wrong. If we could have gotten to the point of manufacturing 200 machines a month--ten a day, we would make that much in two years and still be able to sell the company. Maybe for double the initial offer. And we always figured we could get to 400 machines a month. But projections are not reality. How stupid were we? We missed them by a long shot. We should have taken the deal and moved on."

I could tell that Ned was getting depressed learning that there really was no way out. I was stuck in a barbed wire net and I had no way out. So I changed the subject to our accounting practices.

Chapter 27

No man will succeed unless he is ready to face and overcome difficulties and is prepared to assume responsibilities.
--William J. H. Boetcker

It didn't take long for the quality problems to occur. Paul was now managing the plant and Sid was in charge of just about everything else. Our production fell to maybe four machines every other day. Brit started calling daily with failures in the field. It doesn't take long for things to fall apart. A lesson I knew all to well already.

It was nearing Christmas time, and Paul and Sid were continuing to be at odds fighting like children. I could tell it was Christmas time by looking around. All the signs were there, the stores, the ads, the lights, and all of the hype. But I couldn't *feel* Christmas. There was no spirit in my life. If it wasn't for the visible signs around me, I probably couldn't even tell what month it was.

When your business starts to fail, you tend to lose all connection with the world. All I could think about was the business. What could I do to fix it? What is going to happen next? How can I raise more money? How could this happen? The questions were never ending. And the answers never seemed to come.

And you start to feel like everyone knows. They see your shame. The feeling of lost confidence begins to affect every aspect of your life. You begin to feel like even the lady making change at the deli when you buy a half-gallon of milk knows what's going on. A scarlet letter of sorts.

The emotional drain was incredible. Nothing else seemed to matter in my life. I lost touch with my friends and my family. I would have conversations with my wife to which I listened, but could not remember. I was like a boxer that took too many punches. I was drained emotionally, physically and spiritually. Nothing really mattered, except the business.

Like most entrepreneurs, up to this point, I was always very lucky, and very successful. Throughout my years in school, I always performed well. I can't remember ever getting a test score lower than a "C" nor can I remember a class grade less than a "B". As an athlete, I was a leader and won championships. I was on the best teams. In college, I was an athlete with both academic and athletic scholarships. I graduated high in my class with awards. I passed the CPA exam in one sitting. I earned advanced certifications for business valuation and forensic accounting. I built a successful accounting practice. I completed a successful turnaround of a transportation company. I was not supposed to fail. I would not fail. I could not fail. I never failed before. What is failure? I didn't even know.

Now the tables were turned. I was facing a situation that I had not personally experienced before. Sure I worked with troubled companies before. In fact the transportation company was a troubled company that my partner and I fixed to become a successful company. I was always the guy that received the call..."we have a problem and need your help" I was always the answer guy, the one with the solution. Now, I was running out of answers.

Dealing with a failed business is no different than dealing with the death of a loved one. The steps are the same, and like dealing with death or a life-threatening situation, the order of the steps can change. But, all of the steps seem to happen at some point. And, each step may take longer or shorter, for no real reason. It just works that way. Denial, anger, bargaining, depression, and finally acceptance are the emotional steps encountered during the demise of a business.

Up to this point of my life, I had already experienced my share of grief. I had lost my daughter on her third birthday, to complications resulting from pneumonia, my mother-in-law to natural causes, and my father to a long battle with cancer. All of this happened within a couple of years. I had learned to live with grief and disappointment. I had paid my dues, and my heart was hardened.

But the stress of the failing business was far worse than death. When dealing with death, whether sudden like my mother-in-law, or lingering like my father, death has finality. And my belief, as taught to me, is that we go to a better place. So be it. In death there is new life for the dead. On earth we grieve and deeply miss the loved ones lost, but there is solace in knowing that the deceased are safe, resting in a place of angels and harps. Not true with a business. The bitter end is not the bitter end. It will linger forever, like a radiation cloud, killing any future opportunity.

When the business first started to suffer, denial was absolutely present. No way can this business go down. In fact, denial is almost necessary. Without denial, most entrepreneurs would fold at the first sign of trouble. Throughout all of the early trouble, I never once thought that we would go out of business. I never imagined that we would fall like a rock. I knew that we had trouble, but all companies experience trouble. Operating a business is never easy. If it were easy, everyone would be doing it. And I was experienced enough to know that business cycles swing, sometimes for the good, sometimes for the bad. The skill came in dealing with the difficulties and solving the problems. Staying alive to play another day. That was the game.

So, even as the company's financial situation worsened, I never once gave up hope. I could always pull it out. I would pull it out. I knew that. It was just a matter of time and energy. If we just keep pushing forward, the cycle will swing and we will have good fortune. Buy more time. Stay in the game. That's what we needed to do.

So, denial existed the entire time.

So, it was Christmas time, and we were once again out of money. Sid spent most of the week at the plant trying to understand what went wrong over the last few months. I spent most of the week trying to figure out what to do and how much money we would need. Paul spent most of the week annoying both Sid and me.

Paul was drinking too much. I could sense he was beginning to hate Sid. The resentment of Sid's control was killing Paul. And Sid was very unhappy with Paul since Paul was not living up to expectations. The creativity was not flowing, his ability to manage the operation was non-existent, and his ability to work with the newest plant manager was miserable. He was checking out fast and acted as if he was giving up.

Weeks prior, as a partial punishment for firing the plant manager, and as an attempt to motivate Paul to get him focusing on developing new ideas, and solving the remaining design problems that we still had, Sid moved Paul's office. No longer was Paul in charge, sitting in the 'presidents' office. Sid now occupied that office. Paul was moved to design. His power was usurped, and everyone in the company knew it. If not by Sid's actions, for sure from the physical office move. Sid was in, and Paul was out.

But it needed to be that way. Sid was much better at running the company. He was smart and in charge. He instilled a fear without a heavy hand. He was leader from behind. He had a way of making people move in the right direction without running out front waving the flag, and without pushing from behind either. He was a subtle leader that got things done. He was a results oriented manager. Paul hated Sid's skill most likely out of jealousy.

Paul's new role in the company was essentially a necessary move for the company. He was no longer effective as a manager. He lost the confidence of his constituents, and it was very apparent. Dissension was everywhere in the shop. No one knew who to follow and who to believe. The stories grew everyday into tales, and the tales grew taller. Paul could no longer control the shop, and the employees began resenting him.

On the other hand, when Paul was on his game in design, there was nobody better. He came up with great ideas and solutions to engineering conundrums, and he made it look easy. The management move should have been good for him and the company. But Paul did not buy into the program. He saw the move as a demotion and a direct shot against his ego. That was a shame. Ego in business is a dangerous thing.

To make matters worse, three weeks had gone by since Sid and I put up more money to keep the operation going. Paul was to invest at least $35,000, the maximum he could raise from refinancing his house. I had knowledge that the loans were approved, but that Paul was stalling putting in his share. My guess is that Paul figured it was pointless since the company was probably going down. It also could have been one last exercise of control, something Paul lost with Sid. Both Sid and I were counting on the money coming in. Paul's resistance gave him some control, even if for just a short moment in time, of both Sid's and my destiny.

It was a battle of wills, with the future of the company at stake. And at this point, essentially everyone had something at stake. There were the banks, Sid's capital investment, my capital and loans, the employee's jobs, the vendor's amounts outstanding as well as the future business, the distributors, the customers, and the families of everyone in the food chain. Everyone was at risk. But Paul didn't seem to care. He was fine with grinding it all to a halt. It was evident by his actions, or should I say, his inaction.

Since it was nearing Christmas, Sid took off early for home. The week was not very productive, except that I outlined a pretty decent cash projection based on the booked orders and projected costs for the next four to six weeks. Based on my estimates, we needed about $200,000 to carry us. It was $200,000 that we did not have. Once we were passed the slow season, however, we likely were okay. On top of this, we knew that Paul's $35,000 would eventually come into the company, so we would make it with a bit to spare.

Sid was unconvinced that $200,000 would be enough capital. But any estimate I provided would have not convinced Sid. And why should it? We burned through money so fast; he didn't believe that anything would work. It was a bad parting. Sid was pretty disgusted with Paul, and was unconvinced of our future. Nothing that I could say would make Sid feel comfortable about our future. I knew that I was losing him, and he was unlikely to make any further investments into this company.

It was more than money, though. I could tell that Sid was unhappy with the Paul's performance. He repeatedly challenged me about Paul, as if I could understand his poor behavior. I offered no answers. I didn't have any. I felt bad because I vouched for Paul's skill at the outset of the deal. Paul let down Sid, there is no doubt, and Paul let me down too. There was no excuse.

I was getting concerned because without Sid, we could not continue to exist. I was pretty much financially tapped. I had maybe one more bite at the apple after this one. My share of the $200,000 shortfall worked out to be $25,000, which I could raise from my accounting practice. Any more dough than this would involve my wife's money. I was not brave enough to even think of going to that well at this point. She was adamantly against loaning any money to the company as long as Paul was even still part of the deal.

Just before the last cash call, Sid and his wife came to town to meet with me and my wife, and Paul and his wife. It was a goodwill meeting of sorts, but I think it was Sid's way of assessing whether he should pony up more dough. Sid and my wife seemed to hit it off very well. Maybe it was their common interests outside of business; maybe it was Sid's charm. I don't know, but they connected well. Over the course of the evening, however, my wife made it clear to Sid that she was very unhappy with Paul's behavior and could not support him. Therefore she would not invest any money into the company as long as Paul was involved. Now, I knew that most of that was because of Paul's extramarital activity. My wife viewed that behavior as the worst character flaw a person could have. It was deceitful and selfish, let alone immoral. I never attempted to change her mind, because I knew she was right. I just ignored it and avoided the subject. It wasn't long after this meeting that Sid exercised control and took over the presidency, relegating Paul to design. Whether my wife had any influence over this, I will never know. It was a strange coincidence, though.

I drove Sid to the airport. He didn't say much on the way. In fact, when I dropped him off, his parting felt like a permanent "goodbye." I was pretty depressed. I left the airport and went to my accounting office. I had plenty to do preparing year-end tax planning and projections for my clients. I got lost in the busy work.

The next day, I went directly to the shop to talk with Paul. I needed to get a feel for where his head was and when he was putting up his money. Also, payroll was due by noon, and I wanted to get the mail. We were expecting a $35,000 check for a deposit on and order from Chicago, and I wanted to be sure that the deposit be made so the payroll would not bounce. That would be an incredible gift for the employees just before Christmas.

Paul was not in when I arrived. I started going through the accounts receivable to see if there were any slow pays that we could call for some cash. Most of the slow pays were due to gripes with the equipment, or they were special deals that we cut. Often, we would ship a machine to unconvinced distributor on deferred payment terms, with the understanding that they could pay for the machine 30 days after it was sold. The problem was if the distributor was not thoroughly convinced that the product was a good idea, they did nothing to promote it. In fact, they often used it to switch an inquiring customer into buying a more expensive competing model. Today, that didn't matter. The prepay would cover the payroll, so we were okay.

Paul rolled in about 10:00. I could tell that he did not want to see me, especially sitting in his office working on his computer. I immediately started to ride him about putting his money in. He seemed annoyed, but unfazed. He stuck to his story that the loan hadn't closed yet. I knew better.

About 30 minutes later, Federal Express came and I rushed to the door to accept the delivery. Before I could sign for the packages, I could tell the delivery was short the most important package.

I went storming back into Paul's office. "Paul, the check from Chicago didn't come. What's going on? We need to call Dale Kohn right away."

"Don't bother" Paul replied smugly.

"Why not?" I asked.

"Dale cancelled the order yesterday."

"What?"

"Yea, the customer backed out of the deal." Paul said coolly.

"You knew this yesterday?"

"Yea."

"Why didn't you say something?"

"I didn't feel like dealing with Sid."

"Are you out of your mind? How are we going to make payroll today?"

After a long silence, Paul shrugged his shoulders and said. "I don't know."

That's it? I don't know? It was unbelievable. This is my partner that swore allegiance to the company and me. They guy that told me that if I get the orders and build the business he could make the machines. The guy that talked me out of selling the company for an amount that would have completely funded my eventual retirement because we could sell the company later for more money. I can't even describe the anger that I felt. I wanted to grab him and just shake him.

"You offer no solutions, Paul?"

"No."

"You don't even care?"

"No. You can figure it out. Call Sid, maybe he has a solution." He smugly replied.

I needed a break. I decided to walk the shop floor.

As I walked through the shop, I began to get depressed. Our cash flow was so bad; we kept most of the lights off to save energy. The plant looked bad. Only a few workers were in the back. A far cry from the days not long ago when we didn't have enough space to even build the bookcase order.

I stood in the back of the shop observing the workers assembling the machines. No one was working that hard. In fact, the pace seemed a bit slow, almost relaxed. It wasn't the pace I would demand if I were the plant manager. Knowing that time is money, I would set the production pace faster.

I paid particular attention to a man sorting out rack assemblies. He was busy arranging the proper pieces on the jig pattern. Once the pieces were properly arranged, he would tighten several nuts and press together various connections, and feed several wire harnesses though a couple of predrilled holes. When he was done, he would carefully place the finished assembly in a gaylord box and begin the process again. I'm sure his mind wandered. He was probably thinking about Christmas, or his bills, or the big game on Sunday. Likely his mind was only half functioning while assembling the racks. He had been building racks for months now, maybe longer. His hands instinctively moved about the table removing thought from the process, allowing his subconscience time to wander.

He had no idea of the magnitude of trouble in the front office. I'm sure the workers knew that the company was in financial trouble. Turning the lights off was indication enough. But they never really knew. Most times, the employees have this belief that the owners left the plant every night with big bags of money under each arm. In most cases, that's not true. But the illusion becomes reality, and no words could ever change the belief of the factory workers.

As I stood there watching, I wished I were he. I wished all that I had to worry about were assembling those racks, collecting my check and moving on. No matter how bad the stress was in his life, it couldn't be as bad as mine right now. The balance of everyone involved was resting on my shoulders and on my decision-making. I was getting more depressed watching him. I needed to move on.

I made my way back to the front office, trying not to make eye contact with any of the workers. I knew that my eyes would give away my fears. I just looked ahead and walked with a deliberate purpose.

When I opened Paul's door, he was sitting at his computer surfing the Internet. Up to this point, he had already had two Internet romances, and was likely on the prowl for a third. I was pleased that he was being so productive.

"So Paul, how is the new rack design coming?"

"Fine"

"Have you even worked on it today?"

"No."

"Why not?"

"We are going out of business. Why should I waste my time?"

"Well, we need to call Sid and let him know that we cannot make payroll. He needs to know."

"Fine"

My hand was almost shaking as I dialed the phone. I knew this call would be difficult. Sid was going to take out all of the problems on me.

"Sid, John and Paul here, how are you?"

"Fine."

"I trust your flight was good yesterday?"

"It was fine. What can I do for you boys today?"

"Well, the check didn't come for the Chicago order today."

There was silence. I tried to wait long enough for Sid to reply, but no reply came. Finally, I continued.

"And it looks as if the order is cancelled, for now."

Still more silence. I was going out of my mind. Between Sid not responding, and Paul just sitting next to me staring out the window and smoking a cigarette, I knew that this was becoming my problem. Neither of my partners was planning on helping.

I broke the silence again.

"We can't make payroll today. What should I do?"

Sid finally responded, "Well Paul, did you put in your money?"

"No" was his quick reply.

"Well, why not Paul?"

Paul rambled out numerous excuses about the loan officer, this that and the other. I knew he was lying. There had to be more to the story. It didn't matter. Sid wasn't buying it. I wasn't buying it. I sat there in amazement listening to the one-sided chatter spewing from Paul's mouth. I was getting sick to my stomach.

Paul finally stopped his excuses and once again the room was controlled by silence.

Again, I broke the silence.

"Well, what should we do?"

"Try calling in some receivables," Sid replied.

"I did that this morning before I called you. We aren't getting anywhere."

"Well, gentlemen, I have no other suggestions," Sid replied.

"What about my plan for the $200,000? Did you get to review that yesterday?"

"John, come on. Do you really think that will work? We have a partner that won't even put up his money. He doesn't believe in any of what we are trying to do. This company is like the Bad News Bears. No matter what we do, it falls apart. This has been a con, as far as I'm concerned. I am out. I am not putting in any more money. I want nothing to do with this company."

Now I expected this to go poorly, but I was not prepared for this at all. I was stunned. How can he be out? He has well over $1 million invested in the company, as well as his time and reputation.

"Sid, you can't give up. We are so close," I begged.

"Forget it, John. I am out."

"What if I tried to raise some additional capital? Would you stay in?"

"Who is going to put money into this mess?"

"Well, the landlord has indicated that he might be interested. Should I call him?"

"Sure, he can have my interest. I will sell it to him today. I want $1.25 million for my share."

"Sid, it's not worth that, and you know it. I could probably get seven or eight hundred thousand for it."

"John, it's $1.25 million or no deal."

I knew that $700,000 was a stretch, but I thought that if Sid realized he could get some of his money back, maybe I could get the dialogue started with the landlord.

I started to bargain with Sid. "You know that you'll lose everything if we shut down. Why won't you at least consider a reduced deal? We can issue options for you so that if we sell the company and come out okay, you can share in the upside...to get the rest of your investment back."

"No deal. It's $1.25 million or nothing."

I could tell I was getting nowhere fast. I needed time to think.

"Sid, let me make a few calls and get back to you."

"I'll be here until noon today. I am then leaving for a trip for four days."

I hung up the phone and sat staring out the window.

"Well Paul, what do you think?"

"We are out of business, that's what I think," was his reply.

"Paul, you have as much skin in the game as anyone. How can you just give up like this?"

"It's easy. I'm going to file personal bankruptcy. I am broke already."

"So you don't care if you leave me holding the bag?"

"It's not my problem."

"Paul, we owe the banks $1.5 million dollars. You are going to stick me with that responsibility? You are joint and several on these with me. Remember how that works? We both individually have 100 percent responsibility for the loan guarantee. So that means if you file bankruptcy, I owe 100 percent of the balance all by myself."

Paul just sat there.

"Well, since you know you are going to file bankruptcy, why don't you just put your money in? It will help us make payroll. It will at least give us a chance."

Paul couldn't answer. I now knew that his motives were more than financial. His delay was a control move to irritate Sid.

I pled with Paul. "Just put up your money, Paul. I think if you do, I think Sid will stay in the business. We need him."

Paul interrupted me, "I can't stand him, John. I knew this would happen. He's a jerk. He's just doing this to ruin the holidays."

At that point, I was reminded that it was December 23, and I was supposed to be getting a list of errands done for my wife. Every year, we hosted Christmas parties for both sides of our family. Time was ticking though, and I needed to call Sid back by noon.

"Paul, if you agree to put your money in next week when the loan closes, I will cover you today. I have enough to cover the payroll. But you must put the money in next week."

"Let me think about it," Paul said.

I left his office and went into the bookkeeper's office. I was hoping that maybe some other smaller checks had arrived in the regular mail. No such luck.

After a few minutes, Paul called me to his office.

"I'll do it. If you cover the payroll today, I will put my dough in next week. My wife is in agreement."

"Your wife? I thought you guys were getting divorced."

"No, we are back together."

I shook my head in bewilderment. No matter. I didn't care about anything but saving the company.

I immediately called Sid, who answered on the first ring.

"Sid, Paul is putting in his money to cover the payroll."

"How is he able to do that? The loan did not go through yet."

"Well, I am fronting the money today. When his money comes in, he will reimburse me."

There was silence on the phone.

"Sid, what do you think?" I asked.

"I think that you will cover the payroll, that's what I think."

"Well, any other thoughts on the forward plan, the $200,000?"

"I gave you my answer. I'm out. I am not putting in any more money."

I had nothing else to ask and Sid obviously had nothing else to say.

"Alright then, Sid, I will work on a new plan while you are gone. Meanwhile, would you at least look at the plan and provide me comments so that maybe I can figure a way out of this for all of us? I'm not giving up...maybe you guys are, but I'm not."

"Okay. I will look at it. We will talk when I get back."

"Thank you, Sid. Good-bye."

And that was it. The deal officially began to unravel.

Paul just sat there with his feet up on his desk, staring off into space, puffing on a cigarette. He seemed unfazed by all of this. He almost seemed happy, as if he wanted this to happen. It wouldn't surprise me, since his behavior seemed so self-destructive of late. The problem, though, was that he was destroying more lives than just his own.

Avoiding any conversation, I leapt to my feet and headed to Rebecca's office. I needed to type up a quick note payable from Paul to me to somehow make our verbal commitment real. I returned a few minutes later with the note. Paul quickly signed it. It wasn't worth the paper it was written on, and I knew that. And so did he.

I needed to leave quickly to get to the bank to make the deposit to cover the payroll, but I needed to get to my office first for my checkbook. The next problem was the amount of money that I committed to deposit. I had $25,000 in my accounting practice account, but I was $10,000 short. I searched around my office and found an old checkbook that was from a line of credit on my house. The problem was that my house was not my house. It was my wife's house. Part of my deal when we bought the house was that it would remain in her name, and that I would never use it as collateral. Further, she would never sign as a guarantor on any debt that involved any of my business deals. So in other words, the house was hers and was off limits.

I grabbed a check and wrote it out for $10,000 to the company. I had no choice; I had to cover the payroll. I hurried to the bank and made the deposit.

When I returned to my office, the events of the morning began to replay in my head. The office was closed for the holiday and I was alone. It wasn't that cold outside, but I was freezing. I just sat at my desk and stared out the window at the cars passing in the street.

How did this deal get so screwed up? Hours seemed to go by as I searched silently for the answer. None came. What was I going to do?

Chapter 28

No passion so effectually robs the mind of all its powers of acting and reasoning as fear.
--Edmund Burke

Things are always darkest before the storm. Those words rang through my head. I couldn't keep my thoughts straight as my mind processed the potential outcomes of this grave situation.

The company could not continue without money, and I did not have enough to keep it going. I was already in too deep, and I was guaranteeing the debt. Paul planned on filing bankruptcy and sticking me with the debt. Maybe I will have to file, too, I thought.

I didn't know what to think.

I couldn't even sell my shares. The deal I signed when Sid bought in was that I would not sell my shares. The only one who could buy them was Sid. And I knew that wasn't going to happen.

And I couldn't buy his shares. $1.25 million was way too much for the ownership position, and I certainly did not have the dough. The company still had potential, but it needed more money. So, to find an investor willing to put up $1.25 million, plus another $100,000 or so into working capital was a pipe dream.

I thought for a while about my plan. Maybe Sid would see the logic in it and stay in. I hoped that was true. Besides, he was the only logical partner since he brought industry experience with him. If anyone understood the potential of the company, he did. Although our future together seemed grave while we were on the phone, part of me kept thinking that he would come through. Maybe I was dreaming.

I tried to make a couple of phone calls just to pass the time. I needed a friend to talk this out. But who? Not many people knew of my involvement with this deal, let alone the predicament I was in. The few people that did know about it probably could offer little advice.

Besides, it was nearing Christmas and I didn't want to saddle my friends with my personal problems. I felt alone.

Bankruptcy. What was that all about? How bad could it be? When do I file? How do I file? Who ends up knowing about it? I needed answers.

I knew that Badger Bob's office was closed, so I started to search the Internet for as much information that I could find about bankruptcy. For the most part, all I found was countless listings for lawyers who provide the service. They tried to make it appear painless. I didn't believe it. It looked pretty painful.

My only real experience with bankruptcy in my accounting practice was mopping up the mess after Chapter 7 filings for businesses. I was involved once in a Chapter 11 filing where I was hired as the accountant responsible for the monthly accounting reports that were required by the court. I was a protected by the court as an administrator, so my fees were protected and collectable. The company messed up their reorganization plan, though, and the creditors had the filing converted to Chapter 7 liquidation. The assets have been frozen now for eight years, and I have still not been paid for my services. Wouldn't that be great, the receiver of my accounting practice could make a claim against the trustee in that case for my fees.

As I tried to stay focused on reading the Ohio Bankruptcy Code that I finally came across, I started to think about my assets. My pension and my accounting practice were my biggest concerns. The house was my wife's, and I was pretty much tapped for cash since I kept feeding the company. Maybe bankruptcy wasn't a bad option. Maybe it was a realistic alternative.

But what about my dignity? I'm an accountant; a financial advisor; a deal guy. My practice would be worthless, maybe even taken over by a receiver. I was getting very depressed. No, I *was* depressed.

Then, I was suddenly reminded of a large case that I was handling. I was actually hired by a bankruptcy trustee to prepare a business valuation report on a business that was allegedly sold for less than fair market value. The general creditors filed a petition for Chapter 7. That led to an investigation and a claim for fraudulent conveyance against the debtor-in-possession of the failing business. My part was specific: I was to opine on the value of the business at the time of the transfer. My professional credibility would be gone in the eyes of a jury if I filed bankruptcy.

There was no way that I could ever conceal this big of an event. A bankruptcy filing would rock my professional career.

I tried to shake the thoughts from my head, but couldn't. I had never felt this low in my life. It was worse than every funeral that I had attended, all rolled into one. I was scared. I put my head down on my desk for a while. I wanted to cry, but I couldn't. I was numb. I couldn't even feel sorry for myself. I didn't know how.

Then it occurred to me. I should just kill myself. I could get a gun and shoot myself. One shot, and it would be over. One irrevocable shot. But I didn't have a gun. I didn't even know how to shoot a gun. Then I thought of other ways to do it. Maybe I could cut my wrist. I had a pretty big knife in my desk that was given to me as a gift. Ad specialties, they will print company logo's on just about anything. But the more I thought about it, the knife idea seemed like a bad idea. That method left way too much time to regret the decision. I needed to use a gun.

My thoughts turned to my wife and my family. My poor wife – for her to have to live the rest of her life knowing that I whacked myself at my desk two days before Christmas. She already lost a daughter and her mom, now her husband and business partner. That was too much for me to bear. Then I thought of my daughter. No daddy to tuck her under the covers.

And what would people say at my funeral? What a jerk! That's what they'd say. And they would be right. Forget the moral issues with suicide; I couldn't take the thought of the people looking at my closed casket wondering why I did it. And the whispering. I just kept thinking of everyone whispering his or her version of a plausible explanation of my motive. And my poor wife having to witness that.

The funeral would be awful, but my wife would get my insurance money and live happily ever after, if she could overcome the grief. Or would she get the money? I started to think about the implications of the buy/sell agreement; the insurance proceeds and my estate plan. Maybe the bank would get all of the money. I wasn't sure, nor could I think straight.

My poor wife, that's all I kept thinking about. The worst part about death was that I never really let on to her just how bad I was feeling. She knew that the company was in trouble and that I was working day and night trying to solve the problems. We spent many long nights at the kitchen table talking out alternatives and plans. She always would listen and add insight when necessary and requested. But I never really let on to her just how nervous and scared I was. I couldn't tell her. That would increase her worry. I knew that she worried about the business enough as it was; adding me to the list of worries wasn't fair. If I whacked myself now, she would probably blame herself, even though it was my stupid idea.

Death was starting to look like a bad alternative. But I wasn't sure I could handle what was next for me in life. I had a life sentence staring at me. There was no way out of this, at least no way that was reasonable. I was going down, hard and fast. I was afraid to live and afraid to die. And there's not much else in between.

It was December 23. I will never forget the day. I just sat thinking about all of the mistakes that we made. How could we get this deep? How could I get so sideways in the deal? Thinking of my mistake getting into this deal made me more angry than sad. I definitely should have seen this coming, but I didn't. All of the education, training and experience could not save me. It couldn't even help prevent this. I was stuck in the deal. Chained to the mast of a sinking boat. There really was no way out.

The worst part of the entire thing was not knowing what was going to happen. I was not in control by any stretch of the imagination. I had partners pulling in opposite directions, I had banks that were likely soon to exercise some of their rights, I had employees that didn't know anything, except the lights were out and we were probably in financial trouble, I had suppliers not shipping us material because we were on credit hold, and I had customers holding orders because of countless reasons. The situation was completely out of my control. I had as much opportunity to control this situation as my thumb has in stopping the flow of water over Niagara Falls.

I was tired and scared, but I was alive. I escaped death. I was too tired to think and too afraid to stay at my office alone. I went home. I was happy to be alive.

Chapter 29

A pessimist sees the difficulty in every opportunity; an optimist sees the opportunity in every difficulty.
                                              --Winston Churchill

It's amazing what a good night's rest can do for dealing with stress. Unfortunately, I didn't sleep. Tossing and turning became normal.

I awoke the next day with a hangover from the events of the prior day. I had a stomachache from the over-indulgence at yesterday's dinner. Everyone deals with stress differently. Some fall victim to alcohol or drug abuse, I over ate, and it showed. I knew that it was not good for my health, but it didn't matter, I needed to cope.

But the next day did bring new ideas. It was Christmas Eve, and we were entertaining my wife's family for brunch and gift exchange. I didn't feel very festive.

As I lay in bed watching the sunlight dance through the cracks in the curtains, I started to think more clearly. Instead of raising enough money to rebuild the company, all we needed was enough money to keep us in the game until we could find a buyer. Suddenly, that didn't seem that difficult. Short term planning had significant advantages. Maintaining a solid core of talented employees becomes unimportant. I could layoff most of my staff and shop employees, and slow down the production. If I could pare down the overhead low enough through deep cost cutting measures to hold out for 120 days, I could likely find a buyer.

Suddenly, I was excited again. I could make this plan happen. And, by removing the stress of long-term planning and long term working capital needs, I could probably sell Sid on the idea. And why not? We could make Sid part of the new deal. He certainly had the contacts and industry acumen to prove his value. Beside, it was becoming obvious that we were not going to make it, so why not hitch his wagon to a stronger horse.

I needed to work out the details. I shot out of bed and went right to my basement office, where I began building the model of a 120-day future. It made total sense, and the numbers were working, for the most part. I still estimated that we would need at least $150,000, and as much as the $200,000 I originally estimated. There was no way around the cash need. But this idea I think I could sell to Paul and Sid.

My plan was interrupted by Christmas Eve and Christmas.

The next week at the plant would be pretty quiet. We had one large order that we were trying to get shipped by December 31. We only had a skeleton staff working, since historically the plant was closed for the week.

I called Paul at home to be sure that he would be in so that I could share my epiphany.

He arrived two hours late. It didn't matter to me, though. I was busy polishing the assumptions in my model. When he did arrive, he was in a bitter mood. Apparently the holiday did not go well for him. The family reconcilement became unglued, and he was out of the house again, living in his apartment. I could tell by the look in his eyes, he would fight my idea.

"Paul, I have the best idea, we need to sell the company."
"What?"
"Yeah, sell the company."
"Are you out of your mind? Who would buy it?"
"I don't know, but I have a plan."

I delivered to him the plan in great detail, explaining the cash flow in detail. Most importantly, I demonstrated to him how we could get out of this deal alive, without either of us filing bankruptcy.

He was not unimpressed, nor did he care. Getting tossed out of the house again was reality enough for him that his life was screwed. I quickly realized that this plan would have to work without him. Further, I needed to be sure that he stayed occupied so that he did not try to torpedo the deal with Sid. I stopped my presentation.

I knew that Sid was out of the country for a few days, so my idea remained with me. It was wasted on Paul, but I wasn't all that surprised. I think that he wanted to fail. Just to give me one big "I told you so" as we burned. I didn't care. I was not giving up.

Feeling energized again, I decided to walk the shop floor. About five people were on the floor building machines. The last order of the year was pretty big, about 30 machines. That translated to close to $135,000, and that was cash flow that we needed to jumpstart my plan. I also needed to have a good month for the bank. We were under serious pressure to perform. Further, I needed the order to ship to help with the bank-borrowing base. We were advanced more money on accounts receivable than inventory, and we were close to a loan curtailment.

The assembly process was going slow, but it still looked optimistic that we could get them out the door. And they needed to be out the door, because the auditors would be on 12/31 reviewing the last shipments for a proper inventory and accounts receivable cut-off. I knew the drill.

After about 15 minutes of wandering, the purchasing manager chased me down in a panic.

"John, we are out of locks."

"So? Order more."

"Well, we can't."

"Why not?" I was afraid that the reason was credit hold. Knowing that we would likely not have any cash flow for a few days, I held my breath waiting for his response.

"It takes six weeks to get the order." He explained.

"And we learned this when?" I asked.

"Just now. I have never ordered these before."

"What about another supplier?"

"I don't know. Do you want me to start calling some?"

"Yes! Get on it. Report your progress to me every 45 minutes."

I couldn't believe it. We were the "Bad News Bears." Even the good orders we can't get out the door.

The locks didn't seem to bother me since they were a stock item. Even if we needed to buy them from a distributor, the cost difference was not a deal breaker. I needed to complete this order. Knowing that Paul had checked out, I stayed on top the progress of the search.

Hours went by, and we still could not find a supplier. It was time for me to take over. So I met with Rod our assembly manager.

"Rod, why is it so hard to find these locks? Every vending machine in the world uses these. Where is the NCV catalogue?"

"Well, it's more complicated than that."

"Why?"

"It turns out that ours are custom made."

"What?"

"Yeah, they are custom made."

I grabbed the catalogue and thumbed through it. There had to be five or six various style locks. Why would we have custom made locks? No one seemed to know the answer.

This was not my first encounter with custom order parts for this machine. Somewhere along the line, Paul and Frank seemed to think that having custom parts made the machine better. All it did was make it more expensive to build and more difficult to plan. More bad decisions coming back to haunt us.

After a detailed meeting with the plant manager, I began to understand why one of the standard stock locks would not work in the machines that we were building. Our current design would not accommodate the standard sizes. It could have, though. Back in the design stages, when it was first determined that the stock locks would not fit; all that was required was two small modifications to the lock location. Instead, Paul and Frank, our prior plant manager, decided to have the locks custom made. This had all kinds of implications. First, the lead times for delivery were ridiculously long, second, the parts were expensive, third, it limited the use of the locks to only our machine, and fourth, it forced us to maintain much higher inventory levels.

I reviewed our inventory reports and noticed that we had at least 300 locks that we used on the small soda machines that we used to make. After we reviewed the configuration of the locks, it didn't appear that they would work either.

So, I started making some calls. It was apparent that our purchasing guy was getting nowhere fast and needed help. Being that this was a holiday week and most plants were closed, getting someone to answer the phone was tough enough, let alone finding the right person at the company to help me. Finally, I found a company that made a standard lock that would come very close to fitting. We needed to make one small modification on the machine door. I begged them to overnight me as many as possible. They could only send 10. Great, we were 20 short.

It was about 4:30 and nearly everyone left. Paul finally came out of his office and started turning the lights off.

"Where are you going, Paul?"

"Home."

"Your not going to stay and help find 20 more locks."

"No. Everyone is closed. It's 4:30."

"Not on the west coast, Paul. We still have plenty of places to call."

Ignoring me, he continued to close up the offices.

"Well, will you at least leave a few lights on for me?"

"Sure. Have a nice night."

I was beginning to see Sid's side. This guy was becoming a real drain on the company. Not only did he not work, his attitude was bad.

I learned long ago that a turn around was more about people than they are about finance or business. It takes the right amount of pure will power and muscle to fix a broken company. In fact, when counseling troubled companies, the first thing that I typically do is assess the owner's and management's willingness to work. If they don't have the right work ethic, then the turn around plan will never work.

Ultimately, it didn't matter at this point. By now a turn around was not going to happen. We didn't have the working capital to sustain any momentum, even if we gained some. My new plan didn't require a turn around, just staying power.

I stayed a couple more hours calling every lock manufacturer and distributor that I could locate. I found five more, but I was still fifteen locks short. As I walked out the door, I grabbed a small box of our old locks and brought them home. I had an idea.

When I got home, I immediately started disassembling a lock set. Parts were all over my kitchen table. It was quite a sight, an accountant rebuilding lock sets. It reminded me of the scene in the movie Apollo 13 when the engineers were trying to build something out of spare parts. The problem was that I was not an engineer and I had no business pretending to be one. But I was desperate and, somehow with some luck my idea worked. I figured a way to retrofit the old locks to work in the new machine. All we needed were fifteen.

The next morning, I pitched my idea and my sample lock to the plant manager. With a few modifications to my crude idea using his real engineering skill, we had a solution. It wasn't great, but it was a solution.

We struggled through the next couple of days, managing to ship the required 30 machines. And it was a struggle. Since Paul was pretty much out of the game and the staff was down to just a couple of people, I was the acting manager. As things would go wrong, or as inventory ran out, I was summonsed to solve the problem or order the parts.

It was interesting for me to be this involved. Actually partaking in the assembly process was important because I could now see first hand just how many mistakes were made through out the process. We were not a good company. We had a great design and a great idea, but we could not build the machines at all.

Throughout the week, I called several of my friends from other plants and manufacturing disciplines to help diagnose many of the problems that I encountered during my short tenure as plant manager. Each visitor revealed more issues that were going to continue to plague us in the assembly process. The basic problem that continued to be revealed was that we did not engineer the machine to be manufactured. Our machine was basically a prototype machine put into production. The bigger problem was how our prototype machine was built.

Our prototype started as a working idea. The idea was manufactured based on the first concept and idea. As the concept changed to accommodate changes and modifications, the prototype was changed. Eventually, the working model was created, and the idea proved to work. This was the critical point. Since we started with a model rather than drawings, the process should have stopped, and the machine should have been reversed to uncover what elements from the original model worked and which elements didn't. The machine then needed to be reengineered to arrive at the final product. Then the machine needed to be engineered again to determine the proper manufacturing and assembly sequences and tolerances.

We were in real trouble. Paul was offering no help and Sid was gone. I was stuck trying to run the company by myself. We needed help and we needed production engineering. Even worse, we were out of money and our bank loan payments were due.

Chapter 30

If you owe the bank $100 that's your problem. If you owe the bank $100 million, that's the bank's problem.

--J. Paul Getty

I had been in constant contact with the bank since the first signs of trouble. And why not? They had been very good to work with. When things got tight in the past, we would share our story and plan, and keep them posted as to the progress. It always worked, and they always worked with us.

We were running out of time, however. Our credit was downgraded based on our recent financial statements. We were watch-listed. This is a bad status to achieve in a bank. Basically, we needed to file financial reports monthly and provide weekly oral updates as to our financial condition.

Initially, our financing required that we provide annual financial statements and copies of our Federal income tax returns. Additionally, we had to provide monthly borrowing base certificates that supported the amount borrowed on our line of credit. This is known as an asset-based loan, whereby the amount you can borrow is dependent on a formula based on specific assets. In our case, we could borrow up to eighty percent of our accounts receivable less than 90 days old, and 50% of our inventory value. Once we were watch-listed, I was required to provide full aged accounts receivable and detailed inventory reports instead of the signed declarative statement.

During my weekly banker updates, I could tell the bank wanted us to leave. And at first they are pretty nice about it. The problem is, however, when a company gets into this mess, there aren't too many other banks that want to provide financing. Maybe a finance company or a factoring company. But making that move would be a disaster since the interest rates are so high, and our margins were already a problem since our sales volume fell off so drastically.

After a while, the questions about refinancing started to become statements. I could see where this was going. An added level of difficulty for the situation was that my banker also handled several very good companies that were my clients. Over the years, as you develop relationships and comfort levels, you tend to favor certain banks and bankers. I liked Hugh Fenner. He was a good banker that understood the deal and the story of the deal before it was told. He was a good performer for the bank, and a great guy to deal with. Unfortunately, since he was so good, eventually he moved up the bank chain via performance promotions. For a while, he still personally managed the portfolio that consisted of my clients and my deals. I think the bank let him do this since there was little to no maintenance since I was always on top of the requirements for annual renewals.

Eventually, Hugh moved out of the local suburban office and was relocated to the downtown headquarters. At that point, his partner Brian took over the entire book of business. He was a good banker and a nice guy. Born from the underwriting department, he was much more conservative than Hugh. Since Brian worked so closely with Hugh, I felt very comfortable with Brian. For me, it is really easy to like the people with which I do business. I have always made it a requirement to only do business with people I like, since life is so short. Brian was no exception to this rule. He was genuinely a nice man.

But the hammer had to fall. The bank was not happy with our lack of progress. Additionally, the economy was on the verge of a recession, and it was time for the bank to batten down the hatches. And I knew that they had to do it. I was a realist and accepted the reality of the situation.

Brian couldn't drop the hammer. I could tell he was trying, but I knew that he was struggling with telling me that the bank wanted me in the work out department. I think he was worried about our relationship and about the sizable book of business that he and I would continue to work on together. It didn't bother me. Blasting me out of the bank for something that I was directly involved with and partially responsible for did not hurt my feelings or change the way I approached my other business with him. Being a professional, I was used to operating at a clinical level. It was just another deal. So, I let him off the hook by suggesting that we work directly with the workout department. I think he was relieved.

Another week went by and eventually I was provided a name of my new loan officer, Joe Rundle. I was instructed that he would call me soon.

Weeks went by, allowing me to numb a bit to the situation that initially did not seem so threatening. The more time I had to contemplate the situation, the more I regretted it. By the time I heard from Joe, the financial situation only seemed to worsen. I was embarrassed and afraid to meet Joe.

The day finally came when I had to face the dragon. We were in workout, or as eloquently phrased by this fine institution: "Special Assets". It is the second biggest fear in an entrepreneur's life, bankruptcy being the first. Unfortunately, however, not every entrepreneur acknowledges these fears, they simply ignore them. Rightfully so, I guess. How could anyone function under that much pressure?

I was living under the fear of what was about to come, mostly because of the events of the prior years. My fears were founded; I knew that this day was coming. One would think that with advanced preparation and forethought it would not be as bad. Wrong. It was worse than I expected.

Many times before I have dealt with this situation, a troubled loan. But when it is for someone else, and someone else's mistakes, it never felt that bad. It was pretty clinical. I knew the situation, dealt with the lending officer in a professional capacity, and relayed the information to the client. I acted as a buffer for all involved, relieving the stress for both parties. In this case, I was emotionally attached, and so was the bank. We were once the poster babies, a rendition of success. Not anymore.

The meeting was scheduled for 10:30 at the "Special Assets" department of the bank's main downtown office. This was an old bank, with a rich regional history. The main downtown branch was at the center of the offices. Rows of columns stretching four stories high lined the oversized teller floor. The oversized limestone columns dwarfed the inhabitants, and acted as guardsmen standing tall over everyone. The floors were made of marble and the ceiling guild with gold. The walls had carvings in the limestone. The teller windows and counters were deep rich mahogany. This was architecture and style, blended together to create an audacious, yet conservative appearance.

Desks neatly dotted the cavernous open floor area. The desk occupants somberly muddled at their tasks with only their faces illuminated from the glare of their computer screens. There was a bit of a muddled hush that could be heard. The sound traveled as if it were a foggy day. Voices were not distinct, but the sound of commerce was in the air. But not the sound of a busy office, but rather a hushed sound, as if working in the reverence of a church, or a funeral parlor. People dashed between the workspaces and phones rang quietly. Everyone was quietly busy at his or her tasks. I imagined a time without computers, and the clangor of tapping typewriters and noisy ringing telephones. This bank was made for those sounds, the high ceilings told me that. Now, it's just wasted vertical space.

The staircase at the end of the hall was reminiscent of a castle, rising up to the authority of the overseer. As I made my way through the bank I tried to keep my head down. But I could not help glancing side to side to see if I noticed anyone noticing me, not one face turned to look as I passed. I was just another shadow passing through the cavern.

I was relieved as I made my way up the stairs, nobody noticed me. As I reached the top, I pulled a crumpled piece of paper out of my pocket. "Go right at the top of the stairs, follow the hallway to room 300. My secretary scrolled, "it's at the end" across the page. I took a deep breath and continued on my journey.

I was now on the balcony that doubled as a hallway overshadowing the cavern. As I made my way, my footsteps called out. Clip, clop, clip, clop. Why did I wear hard sole shoes? I walked briskly, but the room just would not appear. Clip, clop, clip, clop. My steps shouted to the audience below. Now I was noticed. As I walked, one by one, heads slowly turned up to look. They looked at me with sorrow, as if to say they were glad it was me and not them. There was only one office on the third floor in this direction. They all knew. As I walked and the heads turned up I could only think of one thing, "Dead man walking." I was scared.

As the end approached, I took one last glance down. The last curious face looked at me for a moment. We shared a moment's stare that seemed like an eternity before the face turned back to work.

I took a deep breath and turned to the door. "Room 300" in simple block lettering was all that marked the door. A graveled glass window glowed with light. The tired old frame was painted a fitting dark gray. It was an old door with countless stories. I felt sick.

Inside a compassionate lady warmly greeted me. Her outstretched hand waved me to an old steel chair along the wall. "Please have a seat, Mr. Rundle will see you shortly."

The room was cluttered. File folders covered overstuffed gray filing cabinets. Most of the exposed files were dust covered. Wow, could this place use a cleaning. But why should they? This was dead file territory. This room represented the losses of the company. No more energy will be spent on these files than absolutely necessary. It will only increase the cost of an already too costly mistake. In fact, the bank would rather not have this department at all, and likely would love to burn the files. Unfortunately for them, the workout department is a must. It is a fact of banking. Loans will go bad. They will become not collectible. I was now participating in the program. I was not proud.

After a few minutes, I was led to a small office stacked with more files. A man appeared from behind the desk with an outstretched hand. "Hi John, I have been expecting you." He shook my hand firmly. "I am Joe Rundle. I have been assigned to your case."

"It's not my pleasure to meet you, Joe," was my unwitting attempt at humor.

Joe smiled and pointed to the chair across from his desk. We both sat down.

Joe was a tall man with a slight build. The lines on his face told the story of the many that have appeared here before me. He was a hard man, with a soft smile. He had a tough job. The primary duty of a workout officer was to figure out how to get the bank out of a sideways loan. Typically, when a loan gets to workout, the company is still salvageable, or saleable, its just not worthy of financing risk. And there is always a story or should I say, excuse.

This deal, however, has exhausted at least eight of its nine lives. Can someone pull a rabbit out of the hat one more time? That was the key question. I knew that most banks allow one silver bullet. This was my chance to ask to use it. I hadn't a choice.

"Joe, we can't make the loan payment this month, not even the interest." I immediately quipped.

"Can you factor some receivables?" he replied.

"No, in fact, we have been accepting advance deposits on orders."

"What about a cash injection from your new partner?" Joe questioned.

"Joe, I am having a hard time even keeping him in the deal. He wants to shut the place down, take his losses and move on. I am pretty scared he may do it. I don't think it is a bluff." I responded.

"Well, John, what about personal funds? You know you have a personal obligation tied to your guarantee." Joe reminded me, as if I needed reminding.

"Joe, I am broke. I have been feeding this thing since Christmas. But I have a plan, and it can work. I just need more time. Joe, I need your help and cooperation from the bank."

"I'm all ears," replied Joe.

"Well, we have this new idea. We are going to slow down production and reengineer the assembly process to allow for a better workflow and tolerance fit up. We are also experimenting with some new technology that we have been working on that will improve the vend reliability of the machine. The new idea works pretty well and should solve most of the sales objections that we have encountered in the last six months. Our hope is to release the new machine at the trade show in Las Vegas this summer. We all expect a big response." I explained.

"John, what makes you think that this can solve your cash flow problems? How are you going to fill the orders that you think you can get?"

"Who said anything about orders, Joe? I want to sell the company. Our ideas are great, and our concepts are great. Our new idea can be even bigger. We are just a bad company. We've run out of capital, and everyone is pulling in a different direction. I can't lie to you, Joe. The company is a mess right now, but the product line is good. It's the heart of the company. But we have to prove to a potential buyer that the machine could be manufactured. We need a turn-key project to sell."

I continued, "Our competitors are very intrigued with our technology. They may buy us. And I think someone will. Our patents block everyone from using our ideas, and the new one is really good. The patents are already pending. This can work, we just need time."

"How much do you think you can get for the company, John?"

"I'm not sure, but other deals in this industry have gone at high multiples. I can only hope for the best. Anything we can get will help pay you down, maybe completely. I think we at least stand a chance. Without continuing, we will get nothing."

"Alright John, you have my interest. You have been straight with us all along. I will go along with what you need."

I was relieved.

"But, I need to see the latest financial statements. And I want a three month projection." Joe continued, "If everything looks in order, I will grant a forbearance for one month. Interest will continue to accrue at the normal rate. If the plan is working, I will extend you two additional months with interest only payments giving you more breathing room. Any questions?"

"No," I quipped. "Thank you, Joe. I will have the financials faxed to you by Monday." Our handshake sealed the deal.

I left the meeting relieved, but unsure. He seemed to like me, and the plan. But could we actually deliver? I doubted everything that I said. Let's face it, at this point of this deal; all I had left was my word, and nothing else. The problem was that I needed everyone to pull together. That was my biggest challenge.

I was thinking of all of the things that I needed to do today, and over the weekend. Now add to the list cash flow projections based on what? Fiction? They should be renamed predictions. I have no idea how many more machines we can make and sell with out working capital. As I searched for my own answers, I hear my name being called by a familiar voice. Walking in a fog, I didn't even realize I took a wrong turn at the bottom of the stairs, and ended up deeper in the corporate offices, rather out the door, which is where I really wanted to be.

"Hugh Fenner, what are you doing here?"

"This is where I office now. The better question is 'what are you doing here?'"

He hadn't heard yet, or at least he's playing possum.

I replied, "I had a meeting with Rundle today."

"Uh-oh. Someone's in trouble! Is it one of your clients? It's not one of my deals, is it?"

"Hugh, its not one of my clients. It's me. Our fab deal is falling apart. The company is in trouble."

Hugh looked at me in shock. He really did not know what was going on. And why should he? I just assumed he knew. I assumed that everyone knew. What starts to happen when you are failing, is that you think your name is published on a list that everyone reads. You start to think that everyone knows of the failure. I felt ashamed to be standing here explaining it. It would have been better to be posted on a list as just a name without a story. It doesn't work that way.

"It's a long story, Hugh. Someday I'll write a book and you'll get the whole story. But for now, all I have time for is that we blew it. There are a ton of reasons. In the end, I am to blame. I could not keep it together."

"Well, what are you going to do?" he asked.

"I am working on another plan. I need to salvage this as best as I can. I am ultimately going to get screwed in the end. I just feel it. But I can't worry about that now. I have one chance left and that's all I can focus on now. I want to try to get everyone else out whole, especially the banks."

With that, I shook his hand and left. I had a lot to do and did not have time to chat. I had one last shot at saving this thing.

Chapter 31

The first requisite for success is the ability to apply your physical and mental energies to one problem incessantly without growing weary.

--Thomas A. Edison

I received a call after the New Year from Sid. He seemed to be in a very good mood. My first thoughts were that he must have won some money on his last trip. I knew that he was going to visit a casino in Canada and he liked to gamble. He was good at it too.

"John, I really like your plan. I had a chance to read it and I think it has merit."

"Good Sid. I'm glad you are on board."

"Wait a minute, John. I didn't say that. I said I liked the plan."

"Well, Sid, what is it going to take to have you participate?" I asked.

"It's simple. Did Paul pay you back the $35,000 that you put in at Christmas?"

"No, he didn't."

Sid was silent. I went on, "But I really haven't hounded him for it yet."

"Okay, well here is the deal. I'm in under a few conditions. First, Paul has to put in his $35,000. That will get you paid on that loan. Second, you need to hire an engineer to redesign the machine. Third, we will collectively commit to up to $200,000. The money will be put in proportionately to each person's ownership. That's $25,000 for you, $75,000 for Paul and $100,000 for me. If either you or Paul does not put your money in, I will get the proportionate amount of shares based on the amount of shortfall."

"Okay, Sid. I think that is fair and we have a deal. I will tell Paul the terms."

With that, we were on our ninth live, I think. I'm not even sure at this point how many times we staved off disaster. But the plan will work. All we need to do is reengineer the machine to be manufacturing friendly. My plan called for bringing in an engineer to dedicate all of his time to the machine. We would continue producing the orders we had in house, but we would not accept any new orders until the production started up again. Stopping production allowed us to cut our costs to the bone while the engineer worked. Essentially, the only expenses we would have is our rent, which we had not been paying because of our cash flow woes, a little payroll and the loan payments which were now on forbearance. We would restart production once the production processes and the machine were reengineered.

Meanwhile, Sid would begin to market the company for sale. The idea was to sell the concept and production process to another company. The sale would not require upfront funding, but rather it would provide us cash flow from the future sale of units. After one year, we would then retain the option to either begin producing the machines ourselves again, or to continue the contract-to-build relationship. Since we were planning on bringing a reengineered machine to the table, and since we already had a distributor network, we were creating a win-win situation for everyone involved.

Now that the holidays were over, and Paul was officially tossed out again from Cindy, he seemed more interested in working. He was quick to come up with the $35,000 that he owed me, so the first condition of the deal was met. Meanwhile, our cash position had improved based on the order we pushed out the door at the end of the year, coupled with the bank providing the forbearance agreement on the loans.

So, we ran an ad to bring on a new engineer. Just like filling the plant manager position, finding a qualified engineer in our area was a snap. He was able to start within days of being hired.

The plan was coming together. At this point we did not need a cash call, but since production was slowing down, it was only a matter of time.

It had been some time since we had paid our rent and I was getting concerned that the landlord could be the one to foil our new plan. At the end of the prior year, our landlord became part of the process of while trying to turn the company around. And why not? They had a 90,000 square foot factory, on dead factory row. Not many companies were looking for space in a downsizing world spiraling into recession.

I never felt good about reworking our tenancy deal, but we had to get relief. My use of leverage was pretty obvious. We had ten months remaining on our lease and the landlord did not want to lose us. Our deal worked liked this, three months with no payments, three months at 40% rent, and three months at 60% rent. After nine months, we were back to full rent. The discounted rent would be back added to year two and three of a new five-year lease. And, we were required to pay our rent *weekly*.

The deal wasn't great because it forced us to enter into a new lease. But it did buy us time, which was the most important aspect. We needed time. Paul was quick to sign the lease after I provided a cursory review of the document to ensure it met the terms of our oral agreement. My additional personal concern was: Is my name attached to the document? I did not want any more personal guarantees. No sense adding more complication to my future.

Paul signed the lease, as Paul, president of the company, and as Paul, the individual. This would link the liability of the terms of the lease directly to him in the event the company did not keep their end of the bargain.

"Paul, you know when you sign that lease, you are personally guaranteeing the companies performance," I challenged.

"So what? If this thing goes down, I am screwed anyway and I'm filing personal bankruptcy."

"But I thought you were in on the new plan. You came up with the $35,000. I thought you were in?"

"No, I could care less about the money. I figured that Momma would just get it in the divorce. So, I gave it to you instead. A deal is a deal, and I hate her anyway."

"And that's it? You don't care what happens?" I asked.

"Nope."

That statement hit me like a bag of bricks. Paul officially crossed over. His survival instincts were exhausted, and he has become one of the careless. If we lose, he files bankruptcy and starts over. His proclamation made him immune to any of his actions. Now I have a company president that has a devil-can-care attitude and has already accepted the ill consequences of any of his future actions. This is not good.

And what about me? I am jointly and severally personally guaranteeing all of the company bank debt. The calculator in my head quickly began estimating the air ball on the company if we liquidated. Uh-oh. Multiply the difference by 100% and that equals personal bankruptcy for me too.

"Paul, are you out of your mind? You can't file bankruptcy. What about your house? Your family?"

"John, it doesn't matter. I won't be able to recover, and why should I? This company goes down, I am going down."

"Paul, if you file, I will be stuck with all of the debt and I can't file. It will ruin my career, my practice."

Paul stood their indignant, with a stupid smirk on his face. Now I hated him. How can he declare unilateral failure for all of us? I walked out.

As I walked through the plant, my mind analyzed his recent decisions. How have they been tainted? Were there any previous signs that were missed? I couldn't think. So I refocused my energy on the issues at hand.

After a few weeks, the plan was starting to take shape. I was getting into my busiest season at my accounting practice, so my time commitment to the deal was low. But at this point it did not matter. The plan was working.

After about a month, we were getting low on funds, so we needed to have our first cash call. We were ahead of the plan in terms of cash flow, which delighted Sid. He even started to show signals of belief in the new plan.

We agreed that we only needed to come up with $50,000 to cover the next month's activity. Accordingly, Sid wired his $25,000 to the account and I deposited my $6,250. When I called Paul, he indicated that he did not have it and would accept being diluted.

Sid was furious at the news. "I thought we had a deal, John," was his greeting on my voicemail.

When I called him back, I tried to explain Paul's state of mind. Sid could care less about Paul at this point. Instead, he made it my problem to come up with the missing $18,750.

I was out of energy arguing with both Sid and Paul. Seeing the progress of my plan, and knowing that I would be hitting the cash flow season at my accounting practice, I silently deposited another $18,750 to make the deal square. We were good for another month or so.

Over the next month, I spent little time at the shop. On occasion, I would stop by the plant. Things were going as planned. Production was just about stopped, and all of the units on order were being shipped. My conversations with Brit were that the distributors were happy that we were slowing down the process to perfect the machine. They were happy to wait since our machine was still the best solution in the industry for glass front bottle vending. I was optimistic that we were on the right path.

Chapter 32

It is hard to fail, but it is worse never to have tried to succeed.
--Theodore Roosevelt

I arrived at the plant on April 19th. Not one car was in the parking lot and the gate was locked. What was going on? I parked my car in the visitor's parking lot that was not gated and walked toward the front office.

I could see a large red lettered sign on the front door and something attached to the sign flapping in the breeze, like a roll of papers or some type of document. It was wet from an overnight sprinkle.

The sign read:

Notice of Eviction

This premise has been reclaimed by the landlord

Keep Out

The scroll attached was actually the court order. I did not even try my key in the lock. Why should I? I was banished from the building. No sense breaking the law. Where is Paul? What is going on?

I immediately called Paul on his cell phone. After a few rings, I hear a voice but it was not Paul's.

"The number you have dialed is no longer in service."

Now what? Not knowing what to do, I dialed the main number. The phone just rang; a recorded message did not play. Just ring after ring. I stood there in anticipation as if someone would answer, as if anyone *could* answer. There wasn't a soul near the plant.

There I stood in wonderment. As I was finally making my way to leave, a car entered the lot and pulled up behind my car, blocking me in. This was pretty strange since not one other car was in the front lot, and plenty of spaces were available.

I didn't recognize the car, but the driver recognized me and waved as I made my approach. It was Carl, the landlord's son and property manager. He was the person assigned to the collection routine that began months earlier. I met with him several times when we were resigning our lease agreement. I liked Carl.

"Carl, what is going on?"

"Hey John, nice to see you" he replied.

How can he say that to me with that sign on our door? I was pretty confused.

"I am happy to see you, too Carl. Maybe you can tell me what is going on."

"What?" replied Carl.

"Maybe you can tell me why the plant is shut down, Carl."

Carl looked at me quizzically for a moment, scratching his brow. After a few restless moments of silence he finally spoke.

"Are you suggesting that you had no idea that this was coming?"

"Well, actually Carl, I was fearful that this day would come, but I really figured that we would have another discussion with you and your dad. Maybe to have one last chance, or to at least surrender peacefully."

After a short pause, I continued. "Let's face it, Carl, a full eviction is costly with the lawyers and all. Why didn't you call us and at least try to work to some type of reasonable plan for all of us. Some way to..."

Carl cut me off.

"John, we did all of that. You weren't at the meetings. I was here with my dad three weeks ago and again two weeks ago. This was the plan. As a matter of fact, Paul suggested this course of action."

"Why wasn't I invited to the meetings?" I questioned.

"As far as I understood, you were invited. I asked Paul where you were. He and Sid said you wouldn't be here. I just assumed you were tied up with tax season."

"Wait a minute, Sid was here?"

"Yea, he was here for both meetings."

I was astonished. Why wasn't I involved? Only one person could answer what was going on. I needed to get away and make some phone calls.

"Carl, I am sorry I seem so out of it. I am not too sure what is going on, and it's not fair of me to be putting you in the middle. You have been a great help to me."

"John, I am really sorry that it has come down to this..."

I cut him off. "No explanation or apologies from you are necessary. This is justified. You have been more than fair with us. It's all our fault. We were so close, Carl. So close. I am sorry." I continued, "So, what is the next step."

"I'm not sure" he replied. "Our attorney will be in touch with your attorney, I guess."

"We don't have an attorney right now. We can't pay one. Have your lawyer call me. What's his name?"

"Actually, he's a she. Sandra Jenkins. Do you have a card with a number where she can reach you?"

"Yea, its in my car. Give me a minute."

I returned after a minute with a business card.

"John, listen, here's the deal. We are going to need to get the building emptied and the equipment out of here. I know that this is a monumental task. I will work with you as much as I can, and I will get you the access that you need. After Sandra calls you, call me so we can make the arrangements."

"Fine," I replied. "I appreciate your kindness, Carl. I will call you soon."

We shook hands. Carl backed his car out of the way, and I left.

As I made my way back to my office, I needed a break for a few minutes. I turned on the radio and drove off trying not to think about what just happened. That lasted for two minutes. I switched off the radio and began recounting the conversation that I had with Carl. I analyzed every word. I can't believe that they met without me. I wonder if Carl was being straight with me? Would Paul and Sid really sell me out? Would they really commit to closing the plant without my knowledge? Were they trying to protect me, or screw me? With the events of the last two months, I could only think the worst. I needed answers.

The more time you have to speculate on the unknown, the more likely you will lead to thinking the worst. I think it is human nature to fill in the blanks with worst-case outcomes. I don't know why, it just seems that way. This was no different. Not knowing what happened or why was leading me to believe that I had been set up. I needed answers.

I tried calling Paul's cell phone again, and received the recorded message. I know that Paul's cell service was cancelled twice before because of non-payments. It's probably the case again. Or is it? I am getting paranoid. Focus.

Time to call Brit the salesman. He always knows what's going on. Sid typically confided in Brit. He'll know.

Before I can get the number dialed, my cell phone rings. It's Brit.

"Hey John, what's going on over there?"

"I am just leaving the plant, Brit. I was hoping that you had some answers."

"Answers? I can't even get through to the plant. The phone just keeps ringing. What did Rebecca do, not pay the phone bills again? Paul's phone is not working either."

"Brit, I am just as much in the dark as you. What I do know, however, is that we are locked out of the plant."

Brit was silent on the other end of the phone.

"Brit, can you hear me?"

"Yeah, I'm here."

I continued. "We are locked out of the plant. The landlord has locked us out. The doors are shut, there is a court order hanging on the door. Did you know about this, Brit?"

"What? How am I supposed to know? I have been on the road for four days now."

"Well, apparently this has been in the works for some time now, Brit. Paul and Sid had meetings with the landlord a few weeks ago. Apparently they all knew this was coming. All but me."

"John, are you telling me that you did not know?" Brit replied.

"Did you, Brit?"

"No. If I did, I wouldn't have been on the road. Who is going to pay those expenses? I mean the credit cards and all."

"Your guess is as good as mine. Did you sign anything when you got your card?"

"No, it came in the mail from Stacy. Paul signed for it. It's his problem now."

"Brit, I need you to call Sid for me and find out what is going on."

"Why do I have to call him?"

"Come on, Brit. You know he confides in you. He obviously does not want me involved at this point, or he's ticked, or something. Just call him. Be a buddy..."

"All right. I'll call him. I will call you back."

We hang up and I drive on. What am I going to do? What am I going to tell my wife? This is really screwed up and I am really screwed.

I immediately set up an appointment with the bank to inform them what was going on. They needed to know that their collateral was impaired by the landlord's lockout.

Joe Rundle was not happy to see me.

"John, I thought you had the plan in control"

"So did I Joe. I didn't even see this coming. My partners sold me out!"

We discussed at great length all of our options. None of the options were good. Our biggest concern was making sure that the equipment was protected and to get it sold.

I left Joe with my word that I would come up with a solution of either selling the company or liquidating the assets. Either way, I would ensure the collateral was protected.

Meanwhile, I continued to try to reach Paul or Sid. Neither one would return my calls. I could not believe this was happening. After all this time thinking that Sid was working with me to help solve the problem, he and Paul make the decision to shut down the plant. I felt dejected.

Now I was stuck with dealing with the landlord. Initially, the landlord started off acting with some level of compassion towards our situation. And why not? We basically paid for the entire building over the years that the rent rolled in from our lease. It wasn't until the end that we ever missed a payment. Plus, we kept the maintenance up so the building was in very good shape.

Initially, I tried to sell the equipment myself. I sent direct mail and e-mail to as many potential buyers. I had pretty good success. In fact, I had several machine brokers willing to buy a piece here and a piece there. But I did not get one party interested in buying all of the equipment, even at a very low price. Since time was running, it looked as if an auction was inevitable. I had one fish on the hook for all of our press brake equipment and they were willing to pay us about $100,000 for them, sight unseen. I was just about ready to make the deal when a national auction company contacted me. They operated out of California, but had sales associates and appraisers located in Toledo, about a two-hour drive from our plant.

I arranged to have a visual inspection and, of course, I needed access to the plant. Before I set up the meeting, I did some research on the auction company. They had a very good reputation and a significant inventory of equipment. I set a date and time to meet with their appraiser located in Toledo.

The next call was to Carl to arrange access to the plant.

"Carl, John here. I need to get access to the plant next Tuesday so I can let the auctioneer in to inspect the equipment."

"When do you think you will have the auction, John?"

"I am not sure, but the company I am talking to indicated that from the day we sign the deal to final clean up will take six, maybe eight weeks."

Silence.

"No way."

"What?"

"No way, John. We want the equipment out sooner, or we are moving the equipment out of there to a storage facility at your expense."

"Carl, are you out of your mind? If you move that equipment, I can't sell it. And if I can sell it, it won't sell as high from a warehouse. Buyers need to see the equipment set up. Besides, if you break it, its your problem."

"That's too bad, John. We need our rent payments now. We have every right to move the equipment."

I was blown away. I have been in contact with them every week keeping them apprised of our progress. I already discussed the plan with their legal counsel. What was going on?

"Carl, do you have a new tenant? If you do, maybe we can work out a deal with them."

"No. You have had long enough. I have been working there every day for a month cleaning the place. You need to get out."

"Carl, let me call you back."

I hung up the phone and analyzed the conversation and the sudden change of attitude. It had to be a negotiation or positioning of some sort. I pulled out the lease and read it in its entirety. They had the right to recover the space, but a formal eviction had to occur.

I recalled a case that I worked on 10 years earlier. It had to do with a company closing and supposedly defaulting on a business loan. A myriad of tax issues were involved, and I was hired to solve the IRS issues that lingered. The case had twists to it since the company claimed that they did not default on the loan. The real crux of the problem was that the savings and loan that held the note went under. It was one of the first savings and loans to fail. Since the Resolution Trust was not established yet, and the federal regulators had no idea what to do, (or that this would soon become an epidemic), the FBI did most of the investigation. The savings and loan was the real problem. The company, however, was also struggling, but according to the testimony of the owners, the loans were current and all payments were made. To complete the investigation of the S&L, the Fed's requested all of records of my eventual client. After the FBI reviewed all of the documents, they put them in storage at a public storage facility. At the conclusion of the investigation, the FBI exonerated my client. However, as if things could not get worse, the company failed, and subsequently closed. Meanwhile, the FBI pulled out of the investigation. As almost expected, whether by oversight or for some unknown reason, the FBI did not pay the warehouse, so they destroyed the documents. This is where I really came in to the case. Since the records were destroyed, it was necessary to reconstruct the financial statements of the company by piecing together the information so that the final tax issues could be resolved. The thing that I was now recalling about the case was the responsibility of the storage warehouse. According to the contract, if the storage company was not paid timely, they could sell or destroy the property. I could not get the image of over one million dollars of equipment being sold by the storage facility. I could not even dream of the problems this would cause with the bank.

I needed help. It was time to call Badger Bob, my attorney. He always knew what to do. No matter what the situation was, or how grave it looked, Badger Bob had answers. I leaned on him to help me through this. And I needed his help again.

"Bob, I have another issue and I need your help the landlord wants me to move the equipment out right now if I don't they will put it in storage and I am screwed and I have an auction company coming on Tuesday to price out the auction and get pictures of the equipment they won't let me in what am I supposed to do are they allowed to do this how can I stop this..."

"John, slow down."

"What?"

"Settle down, John.

I took a couple of breaths. I felt better. Badger Bob, however, had no idea what I was rambling on about.

Badger Bob was the only person that I could trust. Over the years, Badger Bob and I worked through numerous deals and disputes for not only my businesses, but also for many of my accounting clients. Bob's legal mind was unsurpassed by anyone. In addition to his skill as an attorney he was a talented business advisor. He had a great ability to recognize when it was time to follow the rulebook or time to break out the play book. But most importantly, Bob was my friend...and as much as I needed advice, I really needed a friend.

"Okay, Bob, here is the scoop. I thought I had an agreement with the landlord to let me stay until the equipment was sold. I figured that it would take a couple of months and I told them that. They seemed okay with it. As much as they wanted their money, I think they understood that they were out the dough and nothing could be done about it."

I took another deep breath and continued, "I have been actively trying to sell the equipment. I have had several interested parties on a few pieces, but no real players. I now have a very good auction company that wants to bid the project. I met them through contacting machine brokers in the Midwest. I liked them and they have a very good reputation. They want to meet on Tuesday to review the equipment, photograph and catalog it, and then they will give me a price that they will guarantee for all of the equipment. So I called the landlord to ensure that I had access on Tuesday. Carl went nuts. He told me no, and that the equipment was going to be moved to a storage facility."

Badger Bob was silent. After a moment Bob casually commented, "John, they just want a piece of the auction. It's a negotiation."

"What about them moving the equipment? Can they do that?" I questioned.

"I suppose they can. But there would be implications from the banks. I would need to read the bank documents and the lease." Badger Bob paused for a moment.

He then continued, "But why would they do that? John, they can't get any money from you now. Moving will just cost them more money."

Another pause. I just waited for Bob to continue.

"And if they did move the equipment and damaged any of it, or caused the equipment to become de-valued, both of your banks will have a claim against them. They definitely do not the wrath of two banks on their backs."

I was relieved. "So what do you think I should do, Bob?"

"Can you pay any of the rent, John?"

"Bob, I am tapped. And we owe them like $90,000 or $120,000 of back rent, depending on how you look at it."

"What do you mean?" Bob questioned.

"Well, we had several agreements with the landlord before the lease extension was signed. I think that we probably owe them closer to $120,000, but under the new lease, we probably only owe them $90 or so."

"It doesn't matter" I continued, "I can't raise any of it. I am tapped."

After a minute, Bob chimed "John, offer them a payment from the auction. Give them a guaranteed piece of the collection."

"Bob, that's a great idea. I will call you back."

This makes perfect sense. Money will be coming in from the auction. We can simply have some directed to the landlord. Carl will like this. It's time to call him back.

"Carl, I have an idea. You know that we are going to auction the equipment. And you already knew that this would take a couple of months and basically agreed to let this go forward. So ultimately you knew you were out a couple of months rent. So what if we paid for another month of rent to cover the extra time that we would need."

"And what about all of the utilities, John. Who is going to pay for all of that?"

"Alright Carl, call it $20,000. That should cover the rent, utilities and then some."

Silence.

"Carl, it's a better deal than you have now. I will carve it out of the settlement so you are guaranteed the money."

Carl responded, "So you can't come up with the money now?"

"No, this would be a back ended deal. After the auction, you would get paid out of the proceeds. $20,000 guaranteed."

After a moment of silence, Carl responded, "let me run this by counsel and my partners. If they agree, we will do it."

"How do you feel about it, Carl?" I asked.

"It's fair, but I am not sure what the others will think. I will call you back."

And that was it. I could not even organize an auction without someone patting down my pockets. It was a shakedown at every turn. Everyone wanted a piece of the action, and rightfully so. We owed a lot of people a lot of money. And once they gained any leverage, they used it to their fullest advantage. I would have likely done the same thing if the tables were reversed.

One of the most difficult things to deal with the situation was the loss of control. Everyone else was in control and all I could ever do was react to the situation. This is especially tough for an entrepreneur.

One dominant characteristic of most entrepreneurs that I knew was they liked control. They called the shots and liked it. This was like a walk through the looking glass. I was now in Alice's Wonderland. Everything was distorted and upside down. I was on my heels waiting for everyone else to dictate to me my fate. It was very uncomfortable. I hated it. I hated the waiting.

Meanwhile, time was ticking. It was Thursday, and I made a commitment for next Tuesday, and now I am not sure that I will be able to keep it. I was afraid to call it off yet. Rescheduling busy people always adds another week. So I did nothing and waited.

Friday afternoon the phone finally rang. It was Carl.

"John, I can't reach Sandra Jenkins our attorney. She is on vacation through next week, so I will not be able to talk to her about this. My partners, however, seem to think that this is workable. To keep things moving, have your meeting on Tuesday. I will meet you at the plant. What time are you planning on coming by?"

"They told me they could be here at 10 or 10:30," I said.

"Okay, there will be a few guys there doing some work so the side doors will be open. I may be there as well. If I am not, call my cell and I will be right there. I want to be there."

"Fine. Carl, thank you."

All right, a move in the right direction. Who knows if it will fly, but this has been a game of inches, and I just gained an inch. Now, it's up to the auction company. Can they get the deal done? Can they give a decent guarantee? I had no idea what to expect next.

On Monday I received a call from a guy named Ted. I was out of the office at the time, so all I had was a name, number, and a note from my secretary that he was "some auction guy". I quickly returned the call.

"Ted, John here. I am returning your call regarding our meeting tomorrow, I assume."

"Hi, John. I will be in town tomorrow, but I need to move my trip around. I need to make a stop in Toronto, then Erie, Pa. I will come to you last, probably around four o'clock, if that is okay."

"That's fine, Ted. I will alert the landlord, but it should not be a problem. Where are you now, Ted?"

"At my office in Toledo."

I started to think about Ted's itinerary. He lives in Toledo and is still there at 4 p.m. How is he going to get from Toledo to Toronto, an eight or nine-hour drive, down to Erie, and back to Cleveland in one day? And keep meetings! I had to inquire.

"How are you going to keep all of these meetings, Ted? Even if you left now, you could not make it."

"Oh, I should have told you. I have a plane. Can you pick me up at the IX Air Terminal?"

"Sure. What kind of plane?"

"Oh, it's nothing. It's small. How far are you from the airport?"

"Maybe 15 minutes. The plant is another 15 minutes the other direction."

"That's perfect. I will give you a call when I am in route. Plan for about 4 o'clock tomorrow. I have to run."

I guess I never thought about a plane. What did I get myself into? This must be some company. Corporate planes were only for big Fortune 500 companies, or overly profitable smaller companies. Or mostly, for small companies that spend too much money. In fact, a joke in the consulting business is that the last corporate decision usually made is to buy a corporate plane. This will be interesting.

Carl was fine with the time change and everything was set.

It was 3:30 on Tuesday, and I still had not heard from Ted. Two failed attempts to his cell phone made me even more nervous. Finally, I received a call.

"John, we just left Erie. Why don't you head over to the IX Center? I should be there in 20 minutes."

"I'm on my way."

As I drove to the airport, I had a hard time rationalizing a trip from Erie to Cleveland taking the same time as my commute to the airport. This must be a fast plane.

I arrived at the IX Air Terminal. I never even knew this place was here. It was just two hangers over from the Federal Express terminals that I was all too familiar with. After the Federal Express drop-off points are closed, deliveries can still be made to the airport location until 10 p.m. Since my office was so close to the airport, we took advantage of this late-hour service on numerous occasions when we were not efficient enough to meet the earlier deadlines.

Several pilots were relaxing inside the terminal. It was quite a setup. There was a recreation room fully equipped with a pool table, several pinball games and a juice bar. There were numerous comfortable looking couches and reclining chairs, and a big screen TV broadcasting *Headline News*.

I walked over to the window to watch a jet approach the terminal. The door opened and a man quickly hopped down the gangway and trotted into the terminal. He had a briefcase in one hand, and a camera bag tossed over his shoulder. He barged through the door with his arm outstretched for a hearty handshake.

"Hi, John. Ted. Nice to meet you."

"Hi, Ted. Some plane. I was expecting a small prop plane."

"Na, they are too slow. I have a vigorous schedule to keep."

Ted spent the 15-minute ride on his cell phone, setting appointments for the next two days. I tried not to eavesdrop, but it is difficult when inside a car. I could not believe how many companies were going to auction.

We arrived at the plant, and Ted popped through the side door and went right to work. While he surveyed the equipment, I searched for Carl. He had already left, so I called his cell phone and left him a voicemail message.

I still can recall just how empty the plant looked when I arrived. The landlord had been there for more than a month cleaning. What happened to the raw material inventory? That's what I wanted to know.

Before long, Carl walked through the doorway.

He immediately introduced himself to Ted. They talked for a few minutes.

I followed the two men, and said nothing. Now was not the time to question Carl about anything. I was a guest at this point, and did not want to wear out my welcome.

Ted worked quickly. He would scurry around the machine, moving objects from the area that would clutter his picture. Where the floors were messy, he would hastily broom them. He was efficient. All told, he spent maybe 20 minutes cataloging and photographing the equipment. And just like that, we were done.

"Okay, John. Off to the boozer. I need one beer before I fly home."

Once we got in the car, Ted slowed down. He seemed relieved that his workday was over. We made some small talk on the way to the bar. Once there, we spent most of the time discussing the various auction options.

Ted liked our equipment. It was clean and well maintained. His recommendation was a percentage-based auction whereby the auctioneer receives a flat guaranteed fee for administration, advertising and overhead, and a percentage override. This would yield the highest amount of cash to the company if the auction went well. But there was no guarantee on the amount that the auction would yield. He felt that the equipment condition could increase the value by at least 10%.

Ultimately, it would not be my decision, since I needed to confer with the bank and my shareholders, if I could find them.

I dropped Ted off at the airport, where his plane was ready and waiting. He quickly hopped on the plane and off they went. He will be home in time for dinner.

I headed back to my office. I had several hours of accounting work to do.

Chapter 33

It's always too early to quit.
--Norman Vincent Peale

At this point of the deal, I was willing to try anything. I could not reach my partners and I was completely alone. The bank was calling me every day for updates, for which I did not have news.

Eventually, I got in touch with the XYZ Company that looked at possibly buying the company before Sid became involved. They were moderately interested, and sensing blood, they were ready to move in for the kill.

Since they had already visited our plant, and since we were already comfortable in working with each other, the deal discussions started right away. I was not in any position to negotiate, so I basically listened to what they had to offer.

The deal was simple; they would buy the product line, patents, product name, marketing materials, and all fixtures, jigs and drawings for making any and all of the vending machines we built. Additionally, they would consider buying the three turret presses with the robotic loaders and the computer numeric controlled press brakes. The equipment roster represented about one half of the equipment that we owned. The price was coming out to be about $600,000 if they bought everything. They would pay us up to $300,000 for the manufacturing equipment, depending on the appraisal. The equipment would be paid at 50% down and 50% over two years. They would pay a royalty up to $300,000 for the product line. Based on their projections, the royalty amount would be paid out in about three years. In addition, I would be able to sell the remaining equipment for some level of value, but I was uncertain as to how much I could get.

I was not thrilled with the offer. In fact, I was pretty disappointed. At this point, we owed about $1,500,000 to the two banks, so we were coming up very short. But I was not in a position to negotiate.

Meanwhile, Ted from the action company contacted me to go over their proposal. I thought the XYZ deal was low. The auction company provided an offer of $350,000 for all of our plant equipment and inventory. Any amount collected over the guarantee would be split 60/40, with the auction company getting 60%.

Since the bank was ultimately in control, I needed to share with them the two offers. Joe Rundle was also not happy with the XYZ deal; especially since it involved a term buyout, rather than an easy cash up-front arrangement. Further, he was not familiar with the auction company to which I spoke, so he was hesitant to agree to their terms.

Another big issue that was surfacing was the eviction. At this point, the landlord was willing to let me stay for $20,000. But that changed quickly when the bank called to get a release for access to inspect the equipment. Immediately my deal was off the table and the landlord now demanded $50,000 from the bank.

I couldn't believe it. Just when I thought it was not possible, this whole thing continued to turn into a bigger mess. The bank, being lousy negotiators, agreed to cough up $40,000, which was twice the arrangement that I had made.

The other big issue that I faced at this point was executive authority. I was not the controlling interest in the business, yet I was making all of the executive decisions. Based on my conversations with Badger Bob, I was able to do so in the absence of my partners. To be extra cautious, I sent out corporate resolutions to Sid, Paul and Cindy's last known addresses. Not one was returned, so I was on my own.

It was taking the bank a while to decide exactly what they wanted to do. Since two banks were involved, they were likely consumed with legal meetings to ensure that nothing could be claimed against them by Lake Bank. I was getting tired of waiting for their reply, but I certainly understood because of the circumstances.

While all of this was taking place, I received an order of eviction hearing that would take place the next day. Since there was absolutely nothing I could do to stop the legal proceedings, I decided it would be pointless to attend.

But the next day when I awoke, I changed my mind and decided to go to the court. I wasn't sure exactly what would transpire since I had never been involved in this type of proceeding before through my consulting practice.

I arrived at the courthouse at the specified time, checked in and took my seat in the gallery. When I scanned the room, I noticed a gentleman that looked familiar. It was Badger Bob's law partner. Not wanting to explain why I was there, I ducked my head and hoped he would not notice me. Lucky for me he continued on with his business and never spotted me. If he did spot me, he spared me the embarrassment of a greeting.

Soon after my arrival, the attorney for the bank arrived. They were there to ensure that the court knew of the agreed-upon terms that protected the bank's interest in the equipment.

"John, what are you doing here?" the attorney asked.

"I figured someone from the company should be present. Since I'm the only one left, I decided to come."

"Well, you really don't need to be here. You know, the judge will ask if anyone from the company is present and would like to address the court. You can choose to address the court, or keep silent. It will not matter either way."

"I guess I can make that decision when the time comes. Thanks." And that was all I said.

While I sat waiting for our case to be called, several other eviction matters were handled. In each of them, the landlord was the only party present, and each verdict was in favor of eviction.

I tried to think of what I would say to the judge if I made my presence known, but nothing came to mind. It was justified that we should be evicted.

When our case was finally called, the judge asked, "Is anyone present from the company?"

I sat with my head down, starring at the floor. The judge asked three times, and each time, I remained quiet. It was over in a manner of minutes. We were officially evicted.

The next day, I finally heard back from the bank.

"John, Joe Rundle here. I need you to sign some papers surrendering the company assets to the bank."

"Am I allowed to sign them? I don't have voting power."

"It doesn't matter, really. It's just a formality. We can claim the assets in foreclosure if you would prefer. But an asset surrender is easier and does not involve a court filing."

"No, I'll sign the documents. Send them over."

"You will have them tomorrow," he replied.

"By the way." I asked, "Have you come to a conclusion as to which deal you would like to pursue?"

"Yes we have. In fact that is why we need the asset surrender. We have decided to contract our own auction company and liquidate the assets of the company. We think it is in the best interest of the bank."

"What about the sale to XYZ?" I asked.

"We are not interested in that deal. It's over, John. This is what we decided to do."

And that was it. The asset surrender papers arrived at my office the next day. I read them, signed them, and put them back in the mail. It was over. There was nothing else I could do. I had lost. Now, I only had myself to worry about. What was going to happen to me?

Chapter 34

None of us can be free of conflict and woe. Even the greatest men have had to accept disappointments as their daily bread.
--Bernard M. Baruch

The auction was over. The total earned was more than the minimum guarantee, but by the time all of the costs were subtracted, the remaining amount to split between the auctioneer and the bank was minimal. My guess is that the extra proceeds did not even cover the legal fees associated with reviewing the initial proposal from the auction company.

I was disappointed in the outcome. That disappointment was added to my disappointment in the entire process with the bank, my disappointment with the deal, and my disappointment with my partners. I was dejected. The sense of failure loomed over me and I could not shake it. The auction was the final exclamation point on what was appearing to be one very intense, and very long nightmare.

Well, at least it was over. I tried to feel relieved, but I was not. Although the company was gone and my corporate responsibilities were completed, I still had to deal with my unconditional personal guarantee.

The way most guarantees work is that they are joint and several. What this means is that all of the parties guaranteeing the loan are each 100% responsible for paying the balance. It does not matter to the bank which party pays; they just want their money. For the guarantors, it is up to them to determine how to share the responsibility. In this case, I was the only shareholder standing and essentially at this point, the only shareholder that they knew. So guess what? The entire remaining balance was now my entire problem.

Since Sid was never signed as a guarantor, he was home free. He lost his investment, which by no uncertain terms was a sizable loss. But that was it. He was in for the investment amount and nothing more.

Paul and Cindy had both signed the guarantees with me. So they needed to know what was going on. At this point, I made one last effort to reach Paul to involve him in the settlement process. I tried all of the phone numbers that I had for him to no avail. I sent letters to his last known addresses. Two were returned and one disappeared. I even tried to reach out to our ex-office manager Stacy to see if she knew of his whereabouts. She did not call me back.

So, as I expected, I was on my own. At this point, having more people involved probably would make it more difficult to effectuate any type of deal.

But as the advent of my personal demise approached, I could not stop thinking about what was still left in the company. I also could not stop thinking about how to rekindle the value of the patents. The machine concept that we had was still viable. It was the company that ultimately failed, not the idea. I still believed in the idea. I also believed that our ideas in a viable company would still lead to success. Maybe it wouldn't be the level of success that I once dreamed of having, but at least it wouldn't be a disaster

Like a true entrepreneur, I still was not ready to wave the white flag. I wanted to take one last stab at buying the smoldering embers to see if I could fan the flame. I wanted to buy the patents.

It did not take long to find interested parties to work with me. I was already in the process of rebuilding the plastics company with another partner. I originally bought the company to manufacture all of the plastic parts for the new machine. Paul had been in agreement, but did not want any part of another deal. But he was game to giving my company all of the work. But when it came time to transfer the relationship from the current injection molder, Paul got cold feet and went back on his word. Eventually, he reconsidered and gave us some tidbits, mostly because we lost credit terms with our existing molder.

So we were still feeling the double sting of not getting any of the promised work from Paul, and then dealing with the write-off the uncollectible balance once we finally did get some work from Paul. I guess that goes into the category of "be careful what you wish for." But we were gaining our foothold, and were well connected with other manufacturing companies that could build the machines for us on a contract basis. My plastics partner was in.

The rejuvenated plan involved buying the patents and designs from the bank. My plan was to re-engineer the machines to work correctly. Then, we would contract another manufacturer to build the machines for us. We would use as much "stock" equipment as possible, such as standard circuit boards and standard refrigeration systems. The hope was to rebuild confidence in the machine and ideally find a suitor in the industry to finally buy the concept and build on it.

The plan had charm. It was a long shot, no doubt. But I still believed it could work. My new partners in the concept believed in it too. Since we were all in based on sweat equity, and since there was not a great need for cash to make this start up possible, we were all pretty excited about the prospects.

At this point, the bank was short at least $1,000,000 on the loans. And Lake Bank also was owed another $500,000 or so.

But I was pretty miffed at the $1,000,000 remaining balance. Based on my review of the file, the balance should have been lower. Additionally, I reviewed the activity of bank blunders and I became more steamed. The bank turned down a potential sale of $600,000 out of hand because the deal required a three-year payout. Then they turned down the guaranteed auction fee of $350,000 that I negotiated. Instead, they handed the auction off to their approved "preferred" company and negotiated a whopping $185,000 guarantee. In my opinion, they botched at least $165,000 with the auction, and possibly as much as $415,000 based on the potential sale.

But before I pitched my new idea to the bank, I needed to discuss the possibilities with Lake Bank, our second lender. They still were owed a ton, and they had a judgment lien filed against me based on the personal guarantee that I signed with them.

Because of the total amount of financial pressure put on me personally, I think that both banks were at the point of realization that I did not have enough assets to liquidate to satisfy either of their claims, let alone both. Beside, most of the liquid assets I did own were in my pension and IRA accounts, which were off limits for collection enforcement in my state.

A long time prior to ever buying any companies, I was very careful on how my assets were owned and titled. First of all, from an estate planning perspective, it is always best to keep assets allocated equally, or at least in a manner to take advantage of certain estate tax credits that exist at death. Since my wife was also a CPA, we were bound to structure our assets wisely. So we were both careful to keep our assets split.

But it is not enough just to split the assets 50-50. Knowing that I was a risk taker, I had the presence of mind to structure my assets so that the risk-based assets were mine and the non-risk assets were hers. From the outset, she owned our properties. I, on the other hand, owned the operating businesses. Her paychecks were then used to support the real estate and savings accounts (non consumables). My paychecks were used to fund the family expenses (consumables). None of this was fancy, and it was all legitimate. And most importantly, we were very consistent month to month on how we operated. Furthermore, I disclosed only my assets on any of my financing statements that I completed for any of the banks. Since my wife was not a guarantor, I did not want to ever mislead any of the underwriters as to what I owned and when I owned it. Still, to this day, I have difficulty getting a credit card because I do not own a home.

But none of this mattered to me at this point because I wanted to try again.

After building my initial business plan, I structured a settlement for both banks that I thought would be fair and equitable. The plan called for Lake Bank to have an option to buy into the company for a nominal amount at their election. The price of the option was low, like $1,000, and the funds would be used in the company. Additionally, there was no time limit on exercising their option, so they could wait to see if we were successful and chose to share in the upside. Once they exercised the option, they would get 10% of the company, and in addition they would get $150 per machine that we sold. In exchange for the deal, I would be released from my personal guarantee.

For the purchase of the patents and designs, our primary bank would get a promise of payment for $250,000 that I would personally guarantee. And it would get another $50,000 that would not be personally guaranteed. The terms of the agreement would be interest deferred for six months; interest accrued for three months, and then interest only for nine months after that. This basically gave us a year and half to get the project up and running. After that period, we would begin paying principal and interest for five years. Similar to the Lake Bank deal, I was requesting to be released from the personal guarantee. Essentially, my guarantee would be limited to the new loan for $250,000.

Lake Bank immediately jumped on the deal. But Joe Rundle was not too receptive.

For months I have been working with him attempting to find a solution for the company. For the most part they were receptive to working toward a common goal, but never once did they think outside the lines. They only thought about recovering as much money as possible immediately, period. I suppose I was being silly even thinking that they would buy in to the idea. But I could not stop thinking about the possibilities. So I called for a Joe for a face-to-face meeting.

When I arrived, Joe seemed to be preoccupied by the next failing deal and showed little interest in my presence. I think since I had built a rapport with him over time he granted me the meeting. Throughout the work out period through liquidation, which lasted for better than nine months or so, I met with him at least weekly. Normally I would arrive at his office at 9 a.m. Friday to provide him with a complete update, whether good or bad. But now, he was onto the next deal. The issue of the guarantee was the legal department's issue now and not his.

"Joe, I am happy that you are taking the time to hear me out on this." My welcome was coupled with a firm handshake.

"John, have a seat." Joe smiled and pointed to the chair across from his overly cluttered desk. He continued, "I read over your proposal again and I have some questions."

I was immediately encouraged that he was not dismissing the idea outright. I had a chance.

Joe continued, "What are you going to do for working capital to make this deal work?"

"It's simple, Joe, we are all putting up $20,000 apiece. We have four partners. Based on our plan, we should only need about one-third of that. We are all pretty much doing this based on effort. The only money we really need is to have a new prototype built. That's it."

"Then why didn't you do this with Paul and Sid?" Joe asked.

"I tried, and essentially, this is similar to what we were trying to do earlier this year. But, you see, once the deal fell apart both Paul and Sid spent all of their time blaming each other and fighting. They did not want anything to do with this. I thought it would work then, and I think it will work now."

Joe responded grimly, "I'm not convinced it will work, John. In fact, I think you are wasting your time. This deal is dead. The company is dead."

I said nothing. Instead, I sat quietly looking out the dirty window at the pigeons sitting on the ledge. Joe sensed my disappointment. Minutes passed. Joe pretended to read my financial projections included in my business plan. Finally the silence was broken.

"Did you show this to Lake Bank yet?" he asked.

"Yes I did. They are on board. In fact, they seemed to embrace the deal."

"And they are accepting all of the terms? Even the guarantee release?"

"Yes they are."

"I find that odd, John. I figured that they would be first to enforce since they were so quick to file for the judgment lien. What's your read on that?"

"Well, Joe, I think they realize that I am pretty much toast right now. My assets have been depleted through trying to salvage the company. What are they going to gain by me filing bankruptcy? For that matter, what do you think you gain?"

Joe was silent. I could tell he was thinking for a response but one would not come. He went back to looking at the projections, but I could tell he was not reading them. His eyes never moved. He just stared at the paper.

Again, Joe finally broke the silence. "When is the last time you updated your financial statements for us?"

"Maybe three months ago. Probably right before the auction." I replied.

Again silence and I just stared at the pigeons.

After a few minutes, Joe stood up and addressed me as if he were the principal of a school. "Okay John, here is what we will do. I will have my legal department look at this offer and look at the patents. I will also have my computer department look at the computers that contain the drawings and codes. Meanwhile, get me your updated personal financial statements. Give me a week and I will give you an answer."

"Thank you, Joe." I stood up and we shook hands.

As I turned to the door to leave, Joe muttered, "I still think you are wasting your time."

With that, I left. I was encouraged and called my new adventurous partners to let them in on the progress. I also called Lake Bank to give them the news. Everyone was satisfied with the progress.

Only a couple of days passed and I received a call from Joe Rundle. He was very anxious to speak with me and wanted me to come to his office. I set the appointment for the next day.

When I arrived, Joe did not ask me to sit down. Instead, he walked to the door and led me down a hallway. He said nothing and I was getting worried as to what was going on.

After a couple minutes of walking, we came upon a very small office that had computers piled up everywhere. We walked up to a man that was working hunched over a computer that was in pieces on his desk. Without saying a word to me, Joe tapped the man's shoulder to get his attention.

Startled, the man turned and looked at both of us. Without any introduction, Joe quickly and quietly said, "Tell him what you told me yesterday."

The man looked down at his shoes, winced, and then addressed me. "The computers that I reviewed are blank. The hard drives are empty. There is nothing on them."

"What?" I replied.

"All of them. Not one has anything recognizable on the hard drive. One doesn't even boot."

I stood their perplexed. These were the computers with the drawings and designs. These were the computers that were the lifeblood of any hope to resuscitate the patient. I was stunned.

"I know that one was not working properly, and it had trouble booting. But the rest should work. What about the tape back up or the CD's?"

"I don't have anything but these three computers."

"What happened to the backups?"

"I have no idea," he responded. "All I was given were these three computers."

"Do you mind if I try booting these?" I asked.

Both men stepped back and motioned for me to try. After a few minutes, the computers booted. The operating system started to load, and then I would get the blue screen of death indicating a major failure. I sat there stymied.

"What happened to these?" I asked.

"We were hoping you could tell us," Joe responded. "These guys have been working on these for hours trying to figure out what's wrong, and they have no ideas."

Neither did I.

"Joe, all I can tell you is that they worked in our plant. These were the computers I worried about when we had the auction. They contain all of the important information for the patents. These are the lifeblood. They needed to be protected."

Joe did not respond.

We thanked the computer guy and walked back to Joe's office in silence.

We stopped along the way and each grabbed a cup of coffee. We then sat down in Joe's office. Neither of us said a word.

I think that Joe was nervous thinking that the bank screwed this up, which they may have. However, I was thinking to myself as to what Paul did to those computers. Ultimately, it could be anyone's fault. When everything came tumbling down, there was no chain of custody. There was no accountability. Any angry employee could have sabotaged the computers for spite for all I know.

"Well John, what do you want to do now?" Joe asked.

"Joe, this does change the plan, no doubt. Without drawings we are stuck with reverse engineering this thing. I bought two machines at the auction, so it could be done."

Joe cut me off. "That's not all, John."

Before he could continue, my mind raced. Now what else could possibly go wrong? Haven't I run out of bad luck yet?

"Legal did not like the deal, either. They are nervous about transferring the patents. To sum it up, there is not going to be a deal. I'm sorry."

Just like that it was over. I was finally out of options.

Knowing that I had nowhere to go with this negotiation, I stood up, shook Joe's hand and started to walk out.

As I was leaving, Joe asked, "Did you bring your financial statements with you?"

I stopped and opened my briefcase. I handed him a copy and walked out without saying a word.

At this point, I realized that the only logical next step was to contact a bankruptcy attorney. I had nothing else left to try.

Chapter 35

Sooner or later, those who win are those who think they can.
--Paul Tournier

About three weeks went by, giving me enough time to contact several attorneys to find one that I felt comfortable handling my affairs. Badger Bob set up the meetings as a favor to me.

The asset I was most concerned about was my accounting and consulting practice. Essentially, the value of the businesses was transferable, but conditioned upon me not competing with next owner. But in liquidation, there wasn't much value beyond accounts receivable and office equipment. The thought of starting over scared me though. Further the stain that a bankruptcy could leave on my professional life may never be removed.

I finally decided on which lawyer to retain, wrote him a check and listened to his advice. To sum it up, he suggested that I try one last time to settle without filing bankruptcy. I thought it was a good idea so I called Joe Rundle for one last try. He agreed to meet.

When I arrived, I got right down to business.

"Joe, I'm not sure how much more I can talk to you about any of this because I have retained counsel."

"Who did you retain?" Joe asked.

"Paul Steinman."

At that statement, Joe tossed his pen in the air, rolled his eyes and leaned back in his chair. Based on his reaction, Joe had previous dealings with Steinman. He was not happy.

After a few moments of silence, Joe asked, "Have you thought about making a settlement proposal to the bank?"

"What do you mean?" I asked.

"A proposal. Make me a proposal of what you would pay to buy out your guarantee. Put it in writing to me and I will take it upstairs to legal. Maybe we can work this out."

I knew that Joe was not happy with the idea of me filing bankruptcy. In the end, they knew that they would never get the balance owed to them. They also knew that bankruptcy could take a very long time. Additionally, whatever funds I did have would ultimately be soaked up by the bankruptcy court administration. In the end, the bank was not going to come out well in the deal. That was a reality determined long before this day.

But I knew that I needed a universal settlement. I could not settle with one bank, and still be liable to the second bank. Essentially there were two 800-pound gorillas in the room, and I needed to wrestle both of them.

I went back to my office to try to come up with the right settlement. I first called Paul Steinman who suggested that I make a very small offer and let them negotiate the amount up. I thought about it, but I never liked that strategy. I was always a "this is my best offer" kind of guy. I decided to sleep on it.

Overnight it hit me. I would make an offer that is equal to the amount that they would get in the event that I filed for bankruptcy. To me this was fair. The bank would get the highest amount of which they would be entitled, and I would be spared the stigma. I decided to tie my offer to an acceptance by both banks. Both would need to agree, or it was no deal.

That morning, I called Joe.

"I am faxing to you this morning my offer. Please let me know by Friday if you will accept it. If I don't have acceptance by then, I will file."

"Okay, John. Fax it to my personal fax."

It did not take long for Joe to call me after he received the fax.

"John, we are not agreeing to anything that allows Lake Bank to collect anything."

"Well then Joe, there will be no deal. They agreed to release me if they receive 15 percent of the settlement. I think it's fair."

Joe was miffed, although he was not challenging the amount but the terms. I was feeling that we were close to getting a deal.

"Okay, I will take it to legal. I will let you know by Friday." Joe then hung up.

It seemed like eternity waiting for Friday to roll around. I began to sweat every time the phone rang. But before long, it was 4:40, well past closing time at the bank. They did not call.

Soon Monday, Tuesday and Wednesday went past – and still no call. I was getting nervous and was ready to call them for an update, but I knew that the next person to call would lose the negotiation. So, as hard as it was, I waited.

Before long, another week went by. At this point, Lake Bank was calling to see if we were close to a deal. I could only give them the information that I had. We were still waiting.

Finally, by Tuesday of the next week, I heard from Joe.

"John, we are going to accept your offer. Legal will be in touch with you. Meanwhile, I will sign the offer and return it to you. Congratulations."

I was relieved. What a ride this had been. I then called Lake Bank to get their legal department moving.

A few days passed and I had not yet received my signed acceptance from Joe. I was starting to worry so I put in a call.

"Joe Rundle, please."

The voice on the phone sounded nervous. She quietly responded, "I'm sorry sir, but Joe no longer works at this bank."

"Excuse me. I'm sorry, but did you say Joe no longer works at the bank?"

The voice replied softly, "Yes, that is correct."

"Well, what about my deal?" I asked.

"Sir, I can take your name and number and have someone call you."

"What happened?" I asked.

"Sir, I cannot answer that question. All I can do is take your name and number and have someone call you."

"Okay."

And that was it. Joe was gone. What about my deal? I started calling people I knew that were in the know in the banking world. I eventually got in touch with a friend that told me that the entire workout department was canned, including the support staff. He wasn't sure why, he just knew they were all gone.

I was feeling pretty sick about this. I didn't know what was going to happen or who or if anyone would ever call. I waited about a week and started calling again. After several attempts, I was finally connected with someone in Columbus. His name was Terry. After several minutes of explaining my plight, he interrupted me.

"John, I have no record of Joe accepting any deal from you."

"What? There is no record?"

"No. And based on my review of the case file, I'm not interested in any deal."

What was I supposed to do now? I thought this whole ordeal was finished, and now I am essentially starting over. All of the goodwill that I tried to build up with Joe was now lost. My goose was cooked, again.

"Terry, with all due respect, we had a deal. If I can prove that to you, will you reconsider."

"Maybe. Send me your files and your reasons why we should reconsider and I will reevaluate your case."

"Fine, you will have it in a week."

In response to the request, I sent a copy of every piece of correspondence that I ever had with the bank from the inception of the deal. I also documented conversations and then wrote a 25-page summary of all of the activities that ensued from the point of entering "Special Assets". For some reason, I believed that Terry already had all of this information, but I was going to demonstrate to him that I was well prepared and that my offer was worthy of acceptance.

The entire file filled two bankers boxes. I had them sent to him by common carrier.

At least three weeks went by after I received confirmation of delivery before I heard from Terry. I was sweating when I picked up the phone. I tried to sound calm.

"Hi Terry, did you receive my files?"

"Yes I did, John. Your records were very complete. I reviewed your file with my supervisor and we both agree that you acted in the best interest of the bank at all times and we feel that your offer is fair. We will need you to complete an affidavit regarding your finances, and we will need a disclosure statement. We will also need a copy of the release from Lake Bank. We should have all of this wrapped up inside of two weeks. Our legal department will call you to set up a time to sign all of the releases."

I orally agreed to all of the terms.

Within a couple of weeks, I met with the legal department of both banks. The first meeting was at 10 a.m.; the second at 2 p.m. In the short time between meetings, I was able to buy Badger Bob a nice lunch, which he more than deserved for being so supportive through my ordeal.

In the end, my supporting cast of friends and advisors helped me through the aftermath of the deal. I was thankful for all of them. I was relieved. I escaped bankruptcy.

I always figured that if, or should I say when, this was done that I would celebrate. But now that the time had come, I did not feel at all like celebrating. It was a very long road from the beginning to the end. I learned a lot about others and how each person deals with this level of stress differently. More importantly, I learned a great deal about myself.

Paul chose to run from the deal. Sid, well Sid was indifferent. I chose to deal with the problem head on and try to help solve the problem. When everything was over, it was this approach and attitude that helped me settle all of my affairs. Ultimately, it was a very bad ending. But, it could have been a lot worse.

So instead of celebrating I went back to my office with a copy of my affidavit and my releases from the personal guarantees. And as if to seal the deal forever, I locked them in the fireproof safe.

Chapter 36

That is what learning is. You suddenly understand something you've understood all your life, but in a new way.
--Doris Lessing

Ultimately, the biggest failure of this deal would be walking away without seeing the lessons within this debacle. I find it interesting to compare what I was taught to what I actually learned.

I was taught that a minority position is worth less than a majority position. In business valuation, it is well understood that there is a premium for control. This is well documented by studying the stock market. Shares traded on the public exchanges are minority positions simply because of the scale. Think about the last trade that you made. The 100 shares, or even 1,000 shares that you bought represent a very tiny sliver of ownership. Sure, you get to vote your shares, but with what level of influence? Basically you do not have any influence and are at the mercy of management.

The control premium is most visible when a corporate take over occurs. Typically, a tendered offer is made that is in excess of the stock-trading price. This is measured in relation to the stock's price to earnings ratio. For example, if a stock was trading in the market at a price to earnings (P/E) ratio of 10 times, and an offer was made to purchase a controlling block of stock at a price to earnings ratio of 13.3, that would translate to a control premium of 33%. In simple terms, the cost of control was 33% higher than the minority-trading price in the market.

It is simple to understand why this occurs. Control provides the ability to influence corporate policy, fiscal policy, management, direction, marketing, and operations, basically everything.

Conversely, the inverse of a control premium is a lack of control discount, also known as a minority discount.

The inverse of a 33% premium translates to about a 25% discount. The discount is calculated like this: P/E of 13.3 minus P/E of 10.0 over the P/E of 13.3.

All of this is fantastic theory. It is true, measurable, logical and predictable. In most cases, minority discounts are calculated in a range of 20 to 30% based on various studies and resources. In my experience as a business valuator most minority discounts seem to be calculated in the middle of the range at about 25%.

So, at a point where this business could have been worth say $1 million on a controlling basis, my interest, at least theoretically (and ignoring the voting trust) would be worth $187,500 rather than the pure calculated equity division amount of $250,000.

What I learned in this situation is that the minority discount can be deep enough to make the shares worthless. Being a minority shareholder is like being a flea on a dog. You go where the dog goes. And if the dog decides to goes for a swim, you can drown.

The amount of the minority discount is inversely related to the ability of the controlling management. The better the controlling management, the lower the discount. The worse the controlling management, the higher the discount.

Going into this deal, I was well aware of the importance of control. Using the voting trust, I was able to even out my vote with Paul, even though I did not have the same ownership percentage. It was a very useful tool that I still do not see utilized enough.

In the beginning of the deal we were working together and making decisions together. This was partly because of the voting trust, and partly because we recognized the value of each other's input. We had very different perspectives and very different problem solving skills because of our different backgrounds. Together we made a complete manager and very skilled management team.

When Paul started forcing decisions, things started to unravel. Further, when Sid became involved the balance was upset to the point that we could not function as a team. Instead, Paul looked out for his own interests. I tried my best to keep it working, but the disdain Paul had for Sid, and Sid's eventual disgust for Paul's actions led to a disaster. I could not provide enough influence to outweigh the pressure they both felt because of each other.

When the voting trust collapsed because of Sid taking control, I was truly relegated to a bystander. That is when my shares became worthless. Even if the company had any value left, my value was gone. There was no one that would pay a penny to be in this situation. Our leadership was poor and the situation was on a collision course.

I was tied to the deal with barbed wire. There was nothing I could do and nowhere I could go. I had to swim with the dog. The only thing I could do was to try and stay as high up as I could so I did not drown.

In the end, I would have paid someone to take my shares. How do you calculate that discount?

I was taught that turning a business' performance around could be accomplished by increasing capital and market share.

I learned that turning a business' performance around is almost entirely about the people involved. This doesn't reduce the need for capital, but I am convinced that business performance is more influenced by the behavior of management than capital. Leadership comes in many forms and strong leadership can create an environment where everyone operates at a higher level.

However, there is a breaking point that exists that eventually erodes management's ability to continue managing effectively. Paul seemed to eventually reach his breaking point. The intense, continued stress of trying to operate a failing business weighs heavy on a person. It affects sleep, diet, and emotions -- basically everything. I think eventually it consumed him modifying his behavior. It brought out the worst in him. I don't think that I hit that point with this deal, but that was probably because I was making my living from my accounting practice. If I were facing losing that, maybe the weight would have been insurmountable for me too.

Forevermore, when I am asked to consult on a business turn-around, the first thing I do is try to determine where management is in the cycle and how much more pressure I think they can withstand.

I was taught that a business needs a solid business plan. This makes total sense because a company absolutely needs a business plan irrespective of its financial condition. However, it is way to often that companies do not follow this advice until trouble starts.

When a company is in financial trouble it is even more critical to have a solid business plan. The plan should include financial projections that can be quickly adapted to changes in performance or expectations. By modeling the future outcome based on expectations, the company is in a better position to invoke changes before it is too late.

I learned that a company does need a business plan, but if management does not buy into the plan, the best business plan in the world will be useless.

I was taught that the value of the business stock couldn't go below zero. This statement is theoretically true.

The capital stock of a company represents the money that was invested into the company. Because corporations are separately existing entities from the shareholders, and because of state corporate statutes, the shareholder is at risk for the amount of money invested in the company, but generally that is all.

A corporation can become insolvent. The broadest measure of insolvency is that a company does not have enough assets to pay all of its liabilities. Essentially, this means that the company has a negative equity.

Because a shareholder in a company with negative equity is not required to put up any more money to restore that equity, the value of the capital stock is reduced to zero, but not any further.

I learned that the loss of value could far exceed zero once the shareholder personally guarantees the liabilities of the corporation.

There are several levels of liabilities that a company may have. The most senior level of liabilities is federal taxes. These debts reign supreme. The next level is known as secured liabilities. These are debts that are secured by specific liens on assets, or secured by a blanket lien on all assets. The next level would be subordinated secured debts, or sub debts. These liabilities are also secured by liens on the assets, but are second in position to the senior lender. The final level is unsecured debt, which is generally the trade accounts payable, and any shareholder debt.

When small business borrows money from a bank or financing company, the shareholders are almost always required to personally guarantee that the loans will be paid back. When more than one shareholder is involved, the guarantee is normally "joint and several" which means all of the parties are 100% responsible for the guarantee. So, essentially, even though each shareholder owns a fraction of the business, each one can be held 100% responsible for repaying the debt in the event that the company does not make the payments.

In the end, the company did not have enough assets to satisfy the loans made by its senior lender and subordinated lender. So the responsibility was shifted to the shareholders.

In our case, only Paul and I guaranteed the loans since Sid was not involved at the time that we borrowed the money. By the time this ended, Paul was broke, Sid was not responsible, and so I was left standing. It was not a good feeling. In my case, in the end I owned only 12% of the company, yet I was held responsible for 100% of the shortfall in the loan payments.

My ownership caused me to have a value less than zero by virtue of the guarantee. So, essentially, I had to pay to get out of the deal.

I was taught that the equity risk of a company is constant over long periods of time. This is most often seen expressed in terms of a capitalization rate, and it is evident in the use of the capitalized earnings approach to business valuation.

There are numerous methods used to value the cash flow of a business. One common method is to capitalize the earnings using an expected risk rate of return. The principle is really simple. The expected normalized cash flow of the business is divided by the capitalization rate. The capitalization rate represents the rate of return that an investor would expect to receive for the risk associated with the business.

Here is a very simple example:

Expected cash flow / Risk Rate of return = Investment Value

$100,000 / 20% = $500,000

The inherent assumption is the risk within the business is constant over the perpetual life of the business.

Even when alternate valuation methods are considered, such as the discounted earnings method, at some point in time, it is assumed that the risk will stabilize over time.

From a theoretical perspective it makes sense because the stability of a business is expected to improve over the life of the business. It is easy to understand and expect a business in a start up phase to indeed be riskier than a mature business. So it is a logical conclusion that the function of time has something to do with the risk associated with the company. Absent any foreseeable changes to the business, the longer the business is established, the more stable it becomes. More stability means less volatility, which translates to less risk. Over a very, very long period of time, the risk ultimately stabilizes.

Ultimately proof exists when the rate of risk is analyzed in publicly traded securities. The longer the period of time that is studied, the more stable the expected rates of return become.

But, I learned that the equity risk is extremely volatile and over time, and the risk can actually increase over time. This is especially true when considering medium length holding periods. In our case, the risk increased due to a culmination of all the events that occurred. But did any one action increase the risk? Or was the risk always present, but not always evident?

In the initial stages of my involvement of the business, the risk was pretty low. We had positive cash flow, we were profitable, and the company had assets well in excess of the liabilities. From all perspectives, the company was low risk. However, our growth actually caused the first risk modification. Adding new equipment thus increasing our debt was a major change in the business. By increasing our fixed costs, the company was much more susceptible to losses based on changes in sales volume. So the risk increased because we became more dependent on stable or increasing sales, which is not always easy to predict or maintain.

As our capital wore thin, the risk again increased. The ability to sustain the business gets weaker as the ability to pay bills declines. But what caused the erosion of working capital? In our case it was two things. First, our profitability declined to an amount that was less than our debt service. What this means is that we were profitable, but we did not make as much as our loan principal payments, so we needed to get cash from somewhere else. Ultimately, what we were forced into was using our short-term working capital line of credit to make the loan payments. All this did is trade one debt for another.

The second cause of our working capital strain was the constant reinvestment into research and development. Over just a few years, we spent better than $1,000,000 developing the new machines. The most interesting part of this was that we pursued the development to reduce risk by attempting to position the company in a more stable, higher margin market place. Ironically, the high cost of development helped increase the risk in the company.

By the end of the deal, the company was pretty much toxic, and I'm not sure it was even possible to calculate the rate of return required to entice any investor to make the investment in the company.

Chapter 37

Forget the times of your distress, but never forget what they taught you.

--Gesser

In the end, after all of the analysis, I cannot stop thinking about what may have been.

What if we did not buy the robotic loaders? The high fixed costs that we incurred to spare operating a third shift became one of the biggest hurdles as our sales volume fell off. When sales slowed, we could have simply laid off the third shift cutting the costs. But, we could not lay off the loan payment. The financing costs were a substitute for the costs of the third shift. And initially, when we were operating at full capacity, the fixed costs were low in comparison to the cost of the third shift. This allowed us to be wildly profitable when sales volumes were very high. But when the sales volume declined, our fixed cost became a higher percentage of sales forcing us into a very volatile state. In the end, the high debt service costs could have been the key ingredient to failure. We had to keep selling to keep covering the payments. There was no exception.

What if the custom job shipped as planned? Losing $300,000 of cash flow may have been too big of a hurdle to ever overcome. We were not capitalized well enough to sustain that type of hit. We never would have needed the mezzanine capital. Well, at least at that point in time. Or maybe we could have still used the mezzanine capital to slow down the development of the turret machine just a bit to be sure we had our new product working. Essentially, all of the decisions that were made after that point of losing that job were biased by the need for cash flow.

What if we did not give up the book case job? This decision was in our control, and proved to be a huge mistake. Like it or not, not every piece of business a company has is a perfect fit. Every company has a "worst" job and every company has a "worst" customer. But the definition of "worst" needs to be examined. The book case job truly did not fit in to our product and manufacturing mix, so maybe by that definition it was our "worst" job. But on the flip side, it was a short duration, high margin job for a customer that paid quickly. I knew that job was vital to our success as a company from a financial perspective, and it made sense to focus a couple of months on it. Paul did not see it that way. He only saw the inconvenience of the job. It got in the way. We really blew it on this one. Once it got away, we could never get it back even when we tried.

What if we did not stop making the small machines? The small vending machines were our bread and butter. We made so many of them, most of the employees could make them in their sleep. The small-line machines were simple, unsophisticated and required very little shop management time. The gross profit was not especially high on this product line, but the contribution margin was critical. The small vending machines covered more than half of our overhead. Essentially, this allowed us to focus our management time on developing the newer technologies used in the full line machines. Further, it took pressure off of the new lines because we did not need to have huge initial success, which provided us time to launch the new equipment slowly into the market. But once we stopped manufacturing these machines, all of the weight of the overhead was placed on the new turret line. There was never enough sales volume for the turret to ever replace the loss of the small line vendors, regardless of the higher margins obtained on the turret machines.

What if we would not have invented the turret machine? The turret machine was the best idea that we ever had. Conceptually, the machine answered all of the objections in the field. But the implications of the turret machine cut deep into the company. The amount of capital that was required to complete the development was more than we could withstand. And it was more than just money. It was the management resources required to develop the product. We spent the remaining resources building the prototype machines, rather than working toward perfecting the machine that we were already selling. If we had kept improving the machine we were selling, we likely would have succeeded. Since we needed to sell only about 100 machines a month to cover our costs, we could have easily managed the business and the working capital. If we would have stopped here and combined with Sid, we may very well be in business to this day.

What if we would have waited to introduce the turret machine? The cost of developing the machine was such a strain on the company; we were forced into launching the machine before it was ready. Well, at least that was the attitude of Paul, and this attitude caused rifts between us that probably never mended. But, more important was the impact it had on the current sales of the existing equipment. Paul grossly miscalculated the time it would take from prototype to production. This miscalculation forced us into releasing a machine that was not completely field-tested. The concept was completely overshadowed by the failures.

What if we could have worked together? The fighting that occurred in the company in the end was miserable. In the end, we could not agree on anything. Paul and Sid fought non-stop. They could not even agree on where to go for dinner. When a company is in trouble, the team needs to pull together. We did not. I tried the best I could to keep things together, but one against two does not work. In fact, it may have made things worse for all I know. In the end, we really needed Paul to step up like in days gone by. But he didn't. I could not coax him, nor could Sid. Without production we were nothing.

What if we would have put up more money? I think about this all the time. Even through all of the problems and issues, if we could have lasted three more months we very well could have made it all work. How much did we need? In the end, I calculated that we were probably only $250,000 short from making the whole company work. But in the end, with everything that happened between Paul and Sid, no amount of money was going to be enough to fix the divide that was created. Ultimately, we would have needed to can Paul and start over in the shop. This was too much risk for Sid to think about, and he was out enough money at this point. He cut his losses and moved on. There was nothing else I could do at this point. I did not have the dough to do it on my own. And if I did, I don't think that I would have made the bet considering all of the facts.

For months I could not shake the stigma of the deal. No matter where I went, no matter who I saw, I always felt like there was a sign above me with an arrow pointed at my head that read "Business Failure." I couldn't even face the grocery clerk without thinking to myself that somehow they knew that I could not save our company. But as time went on, it started to occur to me that no one knew, and more importantly, no one cared. It was my problem and I was fine with keeping it quiet.

I will probably never stop asking questions about this deal. So many things went wrong. Even after so much time has gone by, it gets difficult to determine what really caused the meltdown. Did the business fail because we failed as individuals? Or did the business failure cause us to fail as individuals?

Was Paul's betrayal caused by the business failure? Or did his betrayal contribute to the business failure. And whom did he really betray? Did he betray his wife, the business, his partners, or himself? Or maybe because he betrayed himself we were all victims of the collateral damage he caused.

I guess I will never really know the answer. All I can do now is move on and use the lessons learned to improve my other businesses, my clients, and myself. There is no shortfall of lessons in this experience. And every time I need to dig into that locker and dredge up the lesson, I feel another twinge of pain. It seems like it will never really go away.

I am thankful for the notes I took during the ordeal. I am also thankful that I have told the story so many times, because, in many respects, I never want the lessons to fade. They are too valuable. And to think that I could repeat this again in my life would be the greatest failure.

It is an unfortunate fact that this will happen again to someone. Businesses fail, period. Sometimes they fail with a story like this. Sometimes they break and fall. Sometimes they just fade away. For whatever reason, no matter how large or how small, the failure will hurt. The business owner will be scarred and bruised. Their lives will be forever changed. But rest assured that new life would come. The scars will heal over and skin will thicken a bit, but rest assured, new life will come.

I have since moved on and continue to invest in new deals and new ideas. I will never stop. I am an entrepreneur. Even in ashes of this disaster, new life continues, and I will always stand back up and face the new life.

Every so often I cut down the street where the plant once was. It's a nice shortcut. The building is still vacant. They had a tenant for a short period of time, but that company closed too. Maybe the neighboring ghosts actually did haunt the building, but I suspect not. The "available" sign was beginning to fade, just like the other remaining businesses on that street. It was a sign of the times. It was a signal that new growth was not in the immediate future.

I never heard from Paul again. I know that he skipped town, but I am not sure to where. Rumor has it that he went to either Chicago or Las Vegas. Although it is disappointing that I never did hear from him again, I'm not sure that I care. He left me stranded holding the bag as he fled. I will never forget that. The saddest part of all of this is that we were once very good friends. We were partners. But it doesn't matter now. I'm not sure what I would say to him, or how I would react if I saw him. Maybe it is best for both of us that it ended the way it did between us.

The last I heard, Brit moved on and was selling something. Brit was always selling and always telling a story. Guy's like Brit always end up on their feet. I know it took him a while to get secure in new place, but he did it. He's a survivor.

I ran into Sid one last time a few months after the business closed. At the time I was still knee deep in headaches trying to get the company liquidated. I attended an industry trade show to see if there was any opportunity left to sell the scattered remains of the business. We didn't have too much to say to each other. I was pretty guarded about what I said because of trying to save my hide with the bank. Likewise, he was pretty guarded because he did not want to get sucked into the vortex in which I struggled. I do know that he thought I was nuts to even try to rekindle any deals. But I needed to try. Maybe it was a closure thing, but I needed to do it.

I never thought that when I saw Sid at that show that it would be the last time. Even at that point in time, I still believed that somehow I could rise from the ashes and reintroduce the machine with a new company, a new look and a new future. After which time, it was always my intention to involve Sid to allow him to earn some, or all of his investment back. Well, none of that ever happened.

I really liked Sid. He was always a perfect gentleman and was an extremely intelligent businessman. But even his skills and experience were not enough to save the company. He put up a lot of money to make the deal work, and lost all of it. For that I will always feel bad. However, we all lost a lot. Not one of us was spared.

As for the rest of the players, well they have all faded into oblivion. I have not seen or heard from anyone of them.

And much like the players, the deal has faded too. It is now a ghost.

Just a couple of weeks ago I was walking down Ontario Street, hurrying to the courthouse to testify at a hearing. It was bitterly cold and snowing. The snow was melting on my glasses and making it hard to see, so I ducked my head as I walked looking over the top of my glasses to find my way. Out of the snowy fog approached a familiar shadow making his way in the opposite direction.

"Hey John!" he shouted. "Is that you?"

I stopped dead in my tracks. It was Greg Foster, a banker from my past. I had not seen him for at least nine years. He was once one of my "go to" guys for banking deals. But he moved out of the commercial banking division and went to either the trust side or the personal side of the bank, I wasn't sure which. Because of his move, we lost touch since our business paths no longer crossed.

Smiling, I replied, "Greg, it's nice to see you."

"What have you been up to, old man? Is life treating you well?" He asked.

"Sure Greg, things have been good. My accounting practice is growing, my plastics deal is doing well, my family is healthy...I have no complaints. How about you?"

"Well, John, I'm out of banking. I retired not long ago. Now I'm working as a consultant structuring deals. In fact, your name came up not long ago regarding the value of a business. The deal fell apart, so I didn't get a chance to call you. I've been meaning to though, just to catch up."

"Greg, let's have breakfast one of these days. Here's my card. Call me and we can catch up. I want to learn more about what you're doing. You know, Greg, we booked a lot of deals together."

"That we did, John. That we did." After a pause, Greg continued "Hey, whatever happened to that metal fab business you had? I heard some rumors about that deal, but I can't recall. What happened?"

"Well, we did the deal, grew the sales, made a ton of money. Then we ran into some trouble and sold part of it. Then, we ran out of money and we closed."

"No kidding? That's it?"

"Yea, that's pretty much it."

With that we shook hands and promised to meet the next week.

As I walked away, I thought about the deal. I thought about Paul. I thought about the days before Christmas just a few years ago. My stomach started to hurt. I shook my head to regain my focus on the hearing. This is not the time to be thinking about the past. There's no sense wasting time telling the rest of the story. That deal has faded.

Now, it's just another tale of a business failure.

In Mememorium

~

Robert H. Stotter
Aka "Badger Bob"

Bob, my dear friend, thank you for all that you have done for the world.
May you rest in peace.

About the Author

John D. Davis, CPA/ABV, CVA, CFE is a Certified Public Accountant, Accredited in Business Valuation by the American Institute of CPA's, a Certified Valuation Analyst by the National Association of Certified Valuation Analysts, and a Certified Fraud Examiner by the Association of Certified Fraud Examiners. He founded Davis & Company, CPAs in 1988, where business valuation and consulting is his primary focus.

Mr. Davis has extensive experience in pricing, negotiating and structuring business transactions relating to purchases, sales and mergers. Because of his diverse background, he also provides consulting services regarding capitalization, profit improvement, and general business planning.

In addition to his professional accounting experience, Mr. Davis is an active shareholder in several businesses in addition to his accounting practice. He has purchased five companies, one of which was sold, and three of which he continues to successfully operate.